THE HTML SOURCEBOOK

Ian S. Graham

John Wiley & Sons, Inc.

New York • Chichester • Brisbane • Toronto • Singapore

Publisher: Katherine Schowalter
Editor: Paul Farrell
Assistant Editor: Allison Roarty
Managing Editor: Frank Grazioli
Interior Design & Composition: Benchmark Productions, Inc.

Designations used by companies to distinguish their products are often claimed as trademarks. In all instances where John Wiley & Sons, Inc. is aware of a claim, the product names appear in Initial Capital or all CAPITAL letters. Readers, however, should contact the appropriate companies for more complete information regarding trademarks and registration.

This text is printed on acid-free paper.

Library of Congress Cataloging-in-Publication Data:
ISBN 0 471-11849-4

Printed in the United States of America

10 9 8 7 6 5 4

CONTENTS ▬

INTRODUCTION ▬

It is fair to say that the World Wide Web project has taken the Internet by storm, confounding Internet skeptics and supporters alike. In hindsight, however, the reasons are obvious. The World Wide Web (WWW) model makes accessing the Internet easy, both to consumers of Internet-based information and to information providers. It's downright easy to distribute information via the Web, and just plain fun to go out and look for it. It is no surprise that World Wide Web utilities have grown, in less than three years, to be the most popular tools on the Internet.

A tool may be easy to use but often requires skill and training to be used well. This is certainly true of the tools involved in preparing and distributing information via hypertext documents and Internet hypertext servers. Preparing well-designed, useful, and reliable resources requires an in-depth understanding of how the tools that deliver these resources work and how to use them *well*. The intention of this book is to provide this understanding. Assuming that you are familiar with traditional Internet resources, such as FTP, telnet, electronic mail, and Gopher, there are essentially three new components to consider:

1. *Uniform Resource Locators*, or *URLs*, which are the scheme by which Internet resources are addressed in the WWW.

2. The *HyperText Transfer Protocol (HTTP)* and HTTP *client-server* interactions. HTTP servers are designed specifically to distribute hypertext documents, and you must know how they work to take advantage of their powerful features.

3. The *HyperText Markup Language*, or *HTML*. This is the markup language with which World Wide Web hypertext documents are written, and is what allows you to create hypertext links, fill-in forms, and clickable images. Writing good HTML documents involves both technical issues (proper construction of the HTML document) and design issues (ensuring that the information content is clearly presented to the user).

The goal of this book is to explain all three of these issues and to give you the tools to develop your own high-quality World Wide Web products. The remainder of this introduction looks briefly at these three components and explains their basic features. This is followed by an outline of the book and some suggestions as to how to best approach the text and examples.

UNIFORM RESOURCE LOCATORS

Uniform Resource Locators, or URLs, are a naming scheme for specifying how and where to find any Internet server resource, such as from Gopher, FTP or WAIS servers. For example, the URL that references the file *macweb.zip* in the directory */pub/web/browsers* on the anonymous FTP server *ftp.bozo.net* is simply:

```
ftp://ftp.bozo.net/pub/web/browsers/macweb.zip
```

WWW hypertext documents use URLs to reference other hypertext resources.

THE HYPERTEXT TRANSFER PROTOCOL

The *HyperText Transfer Protocol*, or HTTP, is a new Internet protocol designed expressly for the rapid distribution of hypertext documents. Like other Internet tools, such as FTP, WAIS, or Gopher, HTTP is a *client-server* protocol. In the client-server model, a *client* program running on the user's machine sends a message requesting service to a *server* program running on another machine on the Internet. The server responds to the request by sending a message back to the client. In exchanging these messages, the client and server use a well-understood *protocol*. FTP, WAIS, and Gopher are other examples of Internet client-server protocols, all of which are accessible to a World Wide Web browser. However, the HTTP protocol is designed expressly for hypertext document delivery, so most of your communication will be with HTTP servers.

At the simplest level, HTTP servers act much like anonymous FTP servers, delivering files when clients request them. However, HTTP servers support additional important features:

- The ability to return to the client not just files, but also information generated by programs running on the server

- The ability to take data sent from the client and pass this information on to other programs on the server for further processing

These special server-side programs are called *gateway* programs, because they usually act as a gateway between the HTTP server and other local resources, such as databases. Just as an FTP server can access many files, an HTTP server can access many different gateway programs; in both cases, you can specify which resource (file or program) you want through a URL.

The interaction between the server and these gateway programs is governed by the *Common Gateway Interface (CGI)* specifications. Using the CGI specifications, a programmer can easily write simple programs or scripts to process user queries, interrogate databases, make images that respond to mouse clicks, and so on.

THE HYPERTEXT MARKUP LANGUAGE

The *HyperText Markup Language*, or *HTML*, is the language used to prepare hypertext documents. These are the documents you distribute on the World Wide Web and are what your human clients actually see. HTML contains commands, called *tags*, to mark text as headings, paragraphs, lists, quotations, emphasized, and so on. It also has tags for including images within the documents, for including fill-in forms that accept user input, and, most importantly, for including hypertext links connecting the document being read to other documents or Internet resources, such as WAIS databases and anonymous FTP sites. It is this last feature that allows you to click on a string of highlighted text and access a new document, an image, or a movie file from a computer thousands of miles away. And how does the HTML document specify where this document is? Through a URL, which is included in the HTML markup instructions and which is used by your browser to find the designated resource.

What resources can URLs point to? They can be other HTML documents, pictures, sound files, movie files, or even database search engines. They can be on your computer or anywhere on the Internet. They can be accessed from HTTP servers or from FTP, Gopher, WAIS, or other servers. The URL is an immensely flexible scheme and, in combination with HTML, yields an incredibly powerful package for preparing a web of hypertext documents linked to each other and to Internet resources around the world. This image of interlinked resources is, in fact, the vision that gave rise to the name World Wide Web.

OVERVIEW OF THE BOOK

This book is an introduction to HTML, URLs, HTTP, the CGI interface, and the design and preparation of resources for delivery via the World Wide Web. It begins with the HTML language. Almost every resource that you prepare will be presented through an HTML document so that your HTML presentation is your *face* to the world. It is crucial that you know how to write proper HTML, and that you understand the design issues involved in creating good documents, if you are to make a lasting impression on your audience and present your information clearly and concisely. It won't matter if the Internet resources you make available are the best in the world if your presentation of them is badly designed, frustratingly slow, or difficult to follow.

HTML is also an obvious place to start. You can write simple HTML documents and view them with a WWW browser, such as **Mosaic, MacWeb, lynx, Cello,** or **Netscape** without having to worry about CGI programs, HTTP servers, and other advanced features. You can also easily add to your documents URLs pointing to server resources around the world, and get used to how the system works: Browsers understand HTML *hypertext anchors* and the URLs they contain, and they have built-in software to talk to Internet servers using the proper protocols. You can accomplish a lot just by creating a few pages of HTML.

Chapter 1 is an introduction to HTML and to the design issues involved in preparing HTML documents. This nontechnical chapter combines a brief overview of HTML with important aspects of the document design process. The details of the HTML language and more sophisticated client-server issues are left to Chapters 2 and 3.

Design issues are very important in developing good World Wide Web presentations. HTML documents are not like text documents or traditional hypertext presentations, since they are limited by the varied capabilities of browsers and by the speed with which documents can be transported across the Internet. Chapter 1 discusses what this means in practice and gives guidelines for avoiding major HTML authoring mistakes. In most cases, this is done using examples with the important issues being presented in point form so that you can easily extract the main points on first reading.

One point that is emphasized in Chapter 1 and everywhere in the book is the importance of using correct HTML markup constructions when you create your HTML documents. Although HTML is a relatively straightforward language, there are many important rules specifying where tags can be placed. Ensuring that your documents obey these rules is the only way you can guarantee that they will be properly displayed on the many different browsers your clients may use. All too often, writers prepare documents that look wonderful on one browser, but end up looking horrible or even unviewable on others.

Although some general rules for constructing valid HTML are included in Chapter 1, Chapter 2 and the references therein should be used as detailed guides to correct HTML. In particular, Chapter 2 presents a detailed exposition of the HTML language and of the allowed nesting of the different HTML markup instructions. It also explains the syntax and rules for constructing URLs.

Chapter 3 explains the structure and syntax of Uniform Resource Locators (URLs). This is the addressing scheme used in HTML documents to indicate the target of hypertext links.

Of course, HTML is only a beginning. To truly take advantage of the system, you must understand the interaction between WWW client browsers and HTTP servers, and be able to write server-side gateway programs that take advantage of this interaction. Chapter 4 delves into the details of the interaction between WWW clients and HTTP servers and explains the Common Gateway Interface (CGI) specification for writing server-side programs that interface with the HTTP server. Chapter 4 includes simple examples to demonstrate the HTTP protocol and the CGI interface, as well as useful references to sites on the Internet that contain instructional interactive documents. Chapters 2, 3 and 4 are the technical core of this book and should be of use as reference material when writing HTML documents or server CGI programs.

Needless to say, there already are many useful CGI programs available on the Internet, ranging from the **imagemap** program for handling clickable images to sophisticated front-end packages for databases. These and other useful CGI tools are discussed in Chapter 5, which also looks at auxiliary tools useful in developing and organizing HTML documents. For example, there are tools for converting collections of e-mail letters into hypertext archives, or for creating a hypertext "Table of Contents" for large collections of related HTML files. The second half of Chapter 5 discusses these tools and indicates sites where they can be obtained. Almost all of them are available over the Internet, either from anonymous FTP sites or from HTTP servers. URLs are used to indicate the locations of these programs and of additional documentation when available.

Preparing HTML documents can be tedious, since HTML markup tags are complicated text strings that must be included in your text document. HTML codes are not only time consuming to type, but also a common source of error: It is easy to make a mistake typing all those tags! You will not be the first to notice this fact, and many individuals, groups, and companies are actively developing HTML editors to help in the document creation process. Chapter 6 summarizes and briefly describes the various HTML editors available on PC, Macintosh, and UNIX platforms, and explains how to obtain them.

In some cases, you may not want an editor, but would rather be able to convert documents from another format, such as Microsoft's Rich Text Format, FrameMaker's MIF format, LaTeX, and so on into HTML. Chapter 6 includes a summary of several of these packages, including instructions on how they can be obtained. Finally, there are a number or useful tools for *validating* the HTML document for conformity with the language specification and for checking the validity of hypertext links within a document. These tools are listed at the end of Chapter 6.

Chapter 7 is a brief review of the different browsers available for exploring the WWW and for viewing HTML documents. You *should* be interested in how the documents you design will look on browsers other than the one you regularly use. Designing for a single browser is dangerous, since there is a tendency to tailor the HTML for the peculiarities of that particular program. This can lead to HTML documents that look fine on your browser, but horrible on others. It is wise to pick up another browser or two, just to avoid these problems.

Chapter 8 discusses the issues involved in setting up an HTTP server and briefly reviews the commonly available server packages. Again there are many URL references to additional documentation and to locations where server software can be obtained.

Chapter 9, the final chapter in the book, gives some examples of WWW sites containing interesting and well-designed presentations. These sites range from business and entertainment to those devoted to scientific research and education. I asked the creators of these sites to describe the creation process so that you can get a feel for what was involved. I encourage you to visit these sites and see how they work. I can guarantee you will be impressed.

Finally, you should just go out and browse! Writing a book and spouting off one's own ideas of good and bad design is all well and good, but you, as a writer of HTML documents, will appreciate how things look and feel only by going out there and looking and feeling. This book is merely a framework for appreciating what tens of thousands of creative individuals are already doing. So, go and see for yourself!

ACKNOWLEDGMENTS

I would first like to thank my coworkers in the Instructional and Research Computing Group at the University of Toronto: Without their support and encouragement this book would not have been possible. In particular I want to thank John Bradley and Anna Pezacki for giving me the time off to write, probably against their better judgement! I also must especially thank Allen Forsyth and Norman Wilson for critically reading several sections of the manuscript and for removing the "lumpiness" from my early drafts (thank you, Norman, for that elegant image). I also greatly benefitted from the technical expertise of Rudy Ziegler and Terry Jones, who helped me through several problems with image file conversion and computer networking.

Most importantly, I would like to thank my wife, Ann Dean, both for her editing skills and for her unwavering support and patience during the past few months. Without her, this book would not have been possible.

DEDICATION

To Ann

INTRODUCTION

TO THE HYPERTEXT

MARKUP LANGUAGE

The *HyperText Markup Language*, or HTML, is designed to specify the logical organization of a text document, with important extensions for hypertext links and user interaction. HTML was *not* designed to be the language of a What You See Is What You Get (WYSIWYG) word processor, such as Word or WordPerfect. Instead, HTML requires that you construct documents with sections of text marked as *logical* units, such as titles, paragraphs, or lists, and leave the interpretation of these marked elements up to the browser displaying the document. This model builds enormous flexibility into the system and allows browsers of different abilities to view the same HTML documents. In fact, there are browsers for everything from fancy UNIX graphics computers to plain-text terminals, such as VT-100s or old 8086-based DOS computers. As an example, in viewing the same document, a graphical UNIX browser may present major headings with a large, perhaps slanted and bold-faced font (since elegant typesetting is possible with graphics displays), while a VT-100 browser may just center the title, using the single available font. Both presentations will look different, but both will reproduce the logical organization that you built in with the HTML tags.

So, what does an HTML document look like? A simple example is shown in Figure 1.1. As you can see, this looks just like a plain text document. In fact, that is exactly what it is. Thus, an HTML document can be prepared with a simple text editor, such as the **NotePad** editor on a Windows PC, **TeachText** on the Macintosh, or **vi** on a UNIX workstation. You don't need a special word processor or fancy HTML editor to create HTML documents.

The difference between an HTML document and a simple text document lies in the HTML markup *tags*. These are the portions of text surrounded by the less than and greater than signs (< . . .>) and are the *instructions* that tell the browser what each part of the document means. For example, the tag <H1> indicates the *start* of a heading of level 1, while the </H1> tag marks the *end* of a heading of level 1. Thus, the text string

```
<h1> This is the Heading </H1>
```

marks the string "This is the Heading" as a level one heading (there are six possible headings levels, from **H1** to **H6**). Note how a forward slash inside the tag indicates an end tag. The names inside the tags are case-insensitive so that <h1> is equivalent to <H1>, and <STRONG> is equivalent to <StROng>. Capitalization is recommended to make the tags stand out.

An HTML document is described as being composed of *elements*. The string

```
<h1> This is the Heading </H1>
```

is then an **H1** element, consisting of an **H1** start tag, the enclosed text, and an **H1** end tag. You will also often see an **H1** element referred to as the *container* of a heading.

Some elements are called *empty* elements, which simply means they do not affect a block of text and do not require an end tag. An example is the **BR** element in Figure 1.1. The tag `<BR>` forces a line break at the location of the tag. This does not affect any enclosed text, since a line break does not *contain* anything.

Sometimes, elements take *attributes*, which are much like variables and are usually assigned *values* that define special characteristics of the element. An example is the **IMG** element, which is used to include an image within an HTML document. An **IMG** element might appear via the tag:

```
<IMG SRC="filename.gif">
```

Here, **SRC** is an attribute of the **IMG** element and is used to specify the name of the image file (actually, a Uniform Resource Locator (URL) *pointing* to the image file) to be included in the document. The attribute name, like the element name itself, is case-insensitive. Thus, the above line could equally well be written as `<iMg src="filename.gif">` or `<iMg SrC="filename.gif">`. However, the value *assigned* to the attribute **SRC** is *case-sensitive*; case-sensitivity is preserved by enclosing the string in quotation marks. As you may have noticed, the **IMG** element, like the **BR** element, is empty, since it merely inserts an image and does not affect a block of text.

Finally, we emphasize that HTML is a *structured* language, which means that there are rules for where element tags can and cannot go. These rules are there to enforce an overall *logical structure* upon the document. Thus, a heading element, such as `<H1>..... </H1>`, can contain text, text marked for emphasis, and a few other text-like elements—but it cannot contain elements that mark other headings or lists. This means that such constructions as

```
<H1><H2>...text ... </H2></H1>
```

are invalid. Obviously, it does not make sense for a heading to *contain* a list or another heading, and the HTML language rules reflect this. In addition, elements cannot overlap—this means that such things as

```
<EM> <H2> ....... text .... </EM> </H2>
```

are illegal and lead to unpredictable behavior when the document is rendered for display. There are many such structural rules; they are given in detail in Chapter 2. This chapter illustrates the most obvious cases.

BASIC OUTLINE OF THE HYPERTEXT MARKUP LANGUAGE

1. HTML documents are divided into *elements*, which are marked by *tags* of the form `<NAME>..... some text ...</NAME>`, where the enclosed text is the content of the element. Some elements do not affect a block of text and are hence called *empty* elements, which do not require end tags.

2. Element names and attributes are case-insensitive. Thus, `<NAME ATTRIBUTE="string">`, `<NamE ATtRiButE="string">`, and `<name attribute="string">` are equivalent. However, the attribute value (here the string "`string`"), when enclosed in quotation marks, is case-sensitive.

3. The placement of elements in a document must obey the HTML rules of nesting, which simply means that there are rules about where elements can and cannot appear. For example, a Heading element, such as **H1**, cannot contain a list or another heading, but can contain a hypertext anchor. In addition, elements cannot *overlap*. Details of the nesting rules for each HTML element are given in Chapter 2.

EXAMPLE 1: A
SIMPLE HTML DOCUMENT

We could go on explaining the language, but it is easier to get a feel for it by looking at some examples; the details of the HTML language are found in Chapter 2 if you are already burning to find out. Figure 1.1 shows a simple but complete HTML document, illustrating the overall structure of a document and some of the simpler markup elements. This document was created using the UNIX **vi** editor and was saved in a file named *ex1.html*. The *.html* filename extension is important, as WWW browsers and HTTP servers understand files with this suffix to be HTML documents as opposed to a *plain* text document, such as e-mail letters or program listings. On PCs, this extension is *.htm*, since four-letter extensions are not possible. More will be said later about extension names and what they mean.

The rendering of Figure 1.1 by two different browsers is shown in Figures 1.2 and 1.3. All browsers allow you to load and view locally created HTML documents simply by giving the browser the name of the local file. To view the example using the **lynx** browser you type

```
lynx ex1.html
```

at the DOS or UNIX command prompt. With the Macintosh **MacWeb** browser, you just start the program and select the Open... menu from the File pull-down menu at the top of the window, then select the file you wish to open. Similar procedures are possible with all of the graphical browsers.

```
<HTML>
<HEAD>
<TITLE> This is the Title of the Document </TITLE>
</HEAD>
<BODY>
<H1> This is a Heading</H1>

      Hello.  This is not a very exciting document.
I
    bet you were expecting <EM> poetry</EM>, or

some kind of <STRONG> exciting <BR> fact</STRONG> about the Internet and
the World Wide Web.


<P> Sorry.  No such luck.        This document
does
contain examples of HTML markup, for example, here is an "unordered list":
<UL>
   <LI> One item of the list,
   <LI> A second list item  <LI> A third list item that goes on and on and
   on to indicate that the lists can wrap right around the page and still
   be nicely formatted by the browsers.
   <LI> The final item.
</UL>
<p> Lists are exciting. You can also have ordered lists (the items are numbered)
and description lists.
<HR>
<p> And you can draw horizontal lines, which are useful for dividing
sections.
</BODY>
</HTML>
```

Figure 1.1 Contents of the example HTML document ex1.html. The rendering of this document by different browsers is shown in Figures 1.2 and 1.3.

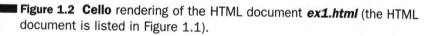

Figure 1.2 Cello rendering of the HTML document *ex1.html* (the HTML document is listed in Figure 1.1).

Figures 1.2 and 1.3 show this document as rendered by two different WWW browsers. Figure 1.2 shows what the document looks like, using the graphical **Cello** (for Windows 3.1) browser, while Figure 1.3 shows what you get from the character-based browser **lynx**.

HTML ELEMENT

What do these markup tags and elements mean? Since HTML is a hierarchical language, this is best analyzed by starting from the outside and working in. The outermost element, which encompasses the entire document, is named **HTML**. This element indicates that the enclosed text is an HTML document. This element allows the browser to distinguish between differing versions of the HTML language.

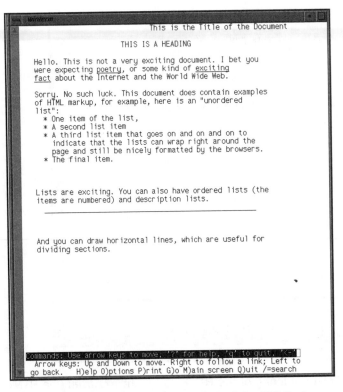

This is the Title of the Document

THIS IS A HEADING

Hello. This is not a very exciting document. I bet you
were expecting poetry, or some kind of exciting
fact about the Internet and the World Wide Web.

Sorry. No such luck. This document does contain examples
of HTML markup, for example, here is an "unordered
list":
  * One item of the list,
  * A second list item
  * A third list item that goes on and on and on to
    indicate that the lists can wrap right around the
    page and still be nicely formatted by the browsers.
  * The final item.

Lists are exciting. You can also have ordered lists (the
items are numbered) and description lists.

And you can draw horizontal lines, which are useful for
dividing sections.

Commands: Use arrow keys to move, '?' for help, 'q' to quit. '<-'
 Arrow keys: Up and Down to move. Right to follow a link; Left to
go back.   H)elp O)ptions P)rint G)o M)ain screen Q)uit /=search

■■■■■■■ **Figure 1.3** **Lynx** rendering of the HTML document ***ex1.html*** (the HTML document is listed in Figure 1.1).

HEAD AND TITLE ELEMENTS

The next element below the **HTML** element is named **HEAD**. The **HEAD** element is a container for information *about* the document, such as the **TITLE** element. This information is not displayed as part of the document. Looking at Figures 1.2 and 1.3, you will see that the contents of the **TITLE** element are displayed apart from the text. With **Cello**, the title is displayed in the frame of the window, while with **lynx**, the name is displayed at the top of the screen and to the right.

Because of the way it is used, you want the **TITLE** to be both descriptive and short. The **TITLE** is displayed separately from the text and usually in a restricted space, such as a window title bar, a small fixed-size text box, or as a single line at the top of a text screen. If a **TITLE** is too long, it simply will not fit. The **TITLE** should also be descriptive of the document, as it is often used as a reference to visited sites—you should be able to guess the content of a document from the **TITLE** alone.

BODY ELEMENT

Parallel with the **HEAD**, lies the **BODY**. This element contains *all* the text and other material that is to be displayed. Notice in Figure 1.1 that all the displayed material lies between the `<BODY>` and `</BODY>` tags. Everything that does not go in the **HEAD** goes here.

Why bother with this **HEAD/BODY** separation? Recall that HTML is designed to organize your document in a logical way. It then makes sense to separate the document itself (the **BODY**) from information *about* the document (the **HEAD**). Currently, there is not much to put in the head, other than the **TITLE**. However, there are several other **HEAD** elements (discussed in Chapter 2) that describe the relationships between a document and other documents. These will be extremely useful for indexing, cataloging, and organizational purposes once they are more commonly used. Indexing programs will be able to quickly read the document **HEAD** (which is always much smaller than the **BODY**) and obtain useful indexing material without having to read the document **BODY**.

The first element in the **BODY** is an **H1** element. **H1** stands for a level-one *heading* element; in HTML, headings come in six levels—**H1** through **H6**—of decreasing rank. The **H1** element means that the enclosed text is a heading and should be rendered to reflect this fact. The **Cello** browser (Figure 1.2) shows the heading

```
<H1> This is a Heading</H1>
```

as a large, bold-faced string of characters, left justified and separated by a wide space from the following text. **Lynx**, on the other hand (Figure 1.3), shows this as a capitalized text string centered on the page. This example should remind you of the point made at the beginning of this section: that different browsers may render the same elements in very different ways. HTML markup instructions are designed to specify the logical structure of the document far more than the physical layout. Thus, the browser is free to find the best way to display items, such as headings, consistent with its own limitations.

Referring back to Figure 1.1, review the next few lines of text:

```
    Hello.  This is not a very exciting document.
I
    bet you were expecting <EM> poetry</EM>, or


some kind of <STRONG> exciting <BR> fact</STRONG> about the Internet and
the World Wide Web.
```

You will see in Figures 1.2 and 1.3 that these lines have been rendered as a continuous paragraph of text, ignoring the blank lines, extra spaces, and tabs that are actually present. The rendering of an HTML document *ignores* extra spaces, tabs, and blank lines, and effectively treats any combination of them as a single space character. This means that you can use spaces, line breaks, and indentations to organize the logical layout of an HTML document. This will be familiar if you write computer programs or have used typesetting languages, such as TeX, and is equivalent to using spaces and tabs to make a program easier to read.

HIGHLIGHTING ELEMENTS

This sentence contains two new elements: **EM** for *emphasis* and **STRONG** for *strong emphasis.* These are *logical* descriptions of the enclosed text. The recommendation in the HTML specification is that text marked with **EM** be italicized if possible, while text marked with **STRONG** should be rendered as bold. This is exactly what is done by **Cello**, as shown in Figure 1.2. **Lynx**, on the other hand, renders both **EM** and

STRONG as underlined text (Figure 1.3). Character-based programs, such as **lynx**, can really do only four things to text: Underline it, bold-face it, force it to capital letters, or display it in reverse video. Given these limitations, **lynx** cannot render as distinct all the different elements in HTML. It therefore renders **EM** and **STRONG** in the same way.

Highlighting elements, such as **EM** and **STRONG**, can be placed almost anywhere you find regular text. The only exception is the **TITLE** element in the **HEAD**. The text inside a **TITLE** element can be text only; there can be no HTML elements inside a **TITLE**. Recall that the text inside a **TITLE** is not part of the document, but simply a text string providing information *about* the document.

HTML has several other logical highlighting elements, such as **CODE** for computer code, **KBD** for keyboard input, **VAR** for a variable, and so on. HTML also has physical highlighting elements, such as **B** for bold-faced, **I** for italics, and **TT** for a typewriter font. It is recommended that you specify logical meaning for text strings rather than specific physical styles, since this assigns more meaning to the associated text and also gives the browser more flexibility in determining the best presentation.

PARAGRAPHS

Look at the next line, beginning with the string `<P> Sorry....`:

```
<P> Sorry.  No such luck.      This document
does
contain examples of HTML markup, for example, here is an "unordered
list":
<UL>
```

The `<P>` tag marks the beginning of a paragraph and can best be thought of as marking the start of a paragraph *container*. Most browsers interpret a `<P>` paragraph mark as a skipped line, as shown in Figures 1.2 and 1.3.

Note, also, that a paragraph mark can be anywhere in a line and need not be the first piece of text on a line. For example, the three lines:

```
the World Wide Web.

<P> Sorry.  No such luck.      This document
```

could be written:

```
the World Wide Web.  <P> Sorry.  No such luck.  This document
```

and both would be rendered the same. Recall that the rendering of an HTML document depends only on where the markup tags are located relative to the text they are marking. Of course, putting `<P>` at the beginning of a line makes it easier to read the *raw* HTML and is strongly recommended.

You will notice that there is no ending tag `</P>` in Figure 1.1 to mark the end of the paragraphs. In HTML, the ending paragraph tag is optional. The rule is that a paragraph is *ended* by the next `<P>` tag starting another paragraph, or by any other tag that starts another *block* of text, such as a heading tag (`<Hn>`), a quotation tag (`<BLOCKQUOTE>`) , list tags, and so on. Thus, the paragraph ending with the words "unordered list" is actually ended by the following `<UL>` tag that marks the beginning of an *unordered list*.

You may have noticed that the first paragraph in Figure 1.1 had no paragraph tags. This is because an initial break is caused by the first heading element. A correct HTML document should have a `<P>` tag at the beginning of this first paragraph. This does not change the spacing between this paragraph and the previous heading.

The HTML definition states that if two adjacent elements describing the logical structure of the document require some special vertical spacing, then only one of them (the largest spacing value) should be used and the other should be ignored. This implies that silly and invalid constructs, such as:

```
<p><p><p><p>  This is a paragraph
```

should yield, at most, a single paragraph break and nothing more. You should avoid doing such things, since, by definition, paragraphs should not be empty.

UNORDERED LISTS

Having beaten paragraphs into the ground, we now move on to the next part of this example, namely the unordered list. HTML supports various types of lists; the example given here is an unordered list. An unordered list begins with the tag <UL>, such as:

```
<UL>
    <LI> One item of the list,
    <LI> A second list item  <LI> A third list item that goes on and on and
    on to indicate that the lists can wrap right around the page and still
    be nicely formatted by the browsers.
    <LI> The final item.
</UL>
<p> Lists are exciting. You can also have ordered lists (the items are numbered)
```

Lists are definitely not empty, and every list must be terminated with an end tag, here </UL>, to define the end of a list. Other similar list elements are: the *ordered* list element **OL**, the *menu* list element **MENU**, and the *directory* list element **DIR**.

A **UL** , **MENU, OL,** or **DIR** list can contain only **LI** list elements. A *list element* has the start tag <LI> and cannot be empty, as every list item must consist of some text. Nevertheless, an ending </LI> tag is not required, as the ending of a list element is implied by the next <LI> or by the </UL> tag that finally terminates the list.

In general, unordered lists are just that—unordered lists of items, with each element marked by an indentation of some type and a star or bullet. It is up to the browser to format them nicely, and, as you can see, both **lynx** and **Cello** do very similar things. However, you will also note that **lynx** and **Cello** do different things to the spacing that surrounds the list; such browser to browser variations are common.

As mentioned, the only thing that can go inside a UL element is an LI element. Thus, you cannot write such things as:

```
<UL>

     here is some non-list text inside a list

     <LI>  Here is list item 1.

</UL>
```

A list item (**LI**) element, however, can contain lots of things. For example, an **LI** element can contain text, the **IMG** element (for inline images), text emphasis (such as the **STRONG** element), another list, and even a fill-in HTML form. However, it cannot contain a heading element. Heading elements can be only directly inside the **BODY**, or inside a **FORM** (for fill-in forms) or a **BLOCKQUOTE** (for quoted text) element.

HORIZONTAL RULE ELEMENT

The final element in Figure 1.1 is the **HR**, or horizontal rule, element. This element simply draws a horizontal dividing line across the page, which is useful for dividing sections. This is also an empty element, since it does not act on a body of text.

LESSONS FROM EXAMPLE 1

1. Titles should be short and descriptive of the document content.

2. HTML is a hierarchical set of markup instructions. The outer layer of this organization, showing the basic document outline, is:

```
<HTML>

        <HEAD>

        .. document head ..

        </HEAD>

        <BODY>

        .. document body ..

        </BODY>

<HTML>
```

The **TITLE** goes inside the **HEAD**, while the text to be displayed goes inside the **BODY**.

3. White spaces, tabs, and blank lines are irrelevant in the formatting of a document; the only thing that matters is the placement of the HTML markup *tags*.

4. Heading elements (**H1** through **H6**) can go only inside the **BODY**, **FORM**, or **BLOCKQUOTE** elements.

5. **UL**, **OL**, **MENU**, and **DIR** lists can contain only **LI** list item elements. The **LI** elements can contain text, images, and other lists, but cannot contain headings.

EXAMPLE 2: IMAGES AND HYPERTEXT LINKS

Figure 1.1 served to illustrate some of the basic features of HTML. This second example consists of two distinct documents, *ex2a.html* and *ex2b.html*, with a hypertext link from one to the other. The documents are shown in Figures 1.4 and 1.5. *Ex2a.html* also includes inline images to illustrate a few things to think about when using images in your documents. Notice how space characters are used to make the HTML documents easier to follow.

```
<HTML>
<HEAD>
<TITLE> Example 2A, Showing IMG and Hypertext Links </TITLE>
</HEAD>
<BODY>
```

```
<H1> Example 2A: Image Inclusion and Hypertext Links </H1>

<P> Greetings from the exciting world of HTML Example documents. OK, so text
    is not so exciting.  But how about some pictures!

<P> There are many ways to fit in the image.  For example,
    you could fit it in this way:
    <IMG SRC="home.gif" ALIGN="top">, this way
    <IMG SRC="home.gif" ALIGN="middle"> or this way
    <IMG SRC="home.gif" ALIGN="bottom">.

<P> Another important thing: you can make
    <a href="ex2b.html"> hypertext links </a> to other files.
    You can even make hypertext links using images,  for example
    <a href="ex2b.html"> <IMG SRC="sright.xbm" ALIGN="middle"> </a>.

<P> Lastly, here is a row of images:
    <IMG src="home.gif" alt="[Home Icon]">
    <IMG src="home.gif" alt="[Home Icon]">
    <IMG src="home.gif" alt="[Home Icon]">
    <IMG src="home.gif" alt="[Home Icon]">
    <IMG src="home.gif" alt="[Home Icon]">
    <IMG src="home.gif" alt="[Home Icon]">
    <IMG src="home.gif" alt="[Home Icon]">
    <IMG src="home.gif" alt="[Home Icon]">

</body>
</html>
```

Figure 1.4 Contents of the example HTML document *ex2a.html*. The rendering of this document by the **Mosaic for X-Windows**, **MacWeb**, and **lynx** browsers is shown in Figures 1.6 through 1.8.

```
<HTML>
<HEAD>
<TITLE> Example 2B: Target of example Hypertext Link</TITLE>
</HEAD>
<BODY>


<h2> Target of Hypertext Link </h2>


<p> OK, so now that you are here, how do you get back?  This document
    doesn't have any hypertext links, so you have to use a "back" button (or the
    'u' key if using lynx) to move back to the previously viewed document.


</BODY>
</HTML>
```

■■■■■■■ **Figure 1.5** Contents of the example HTML document ***ex2b.html***. This document is the target of a hypertext link from the file ***ex2a.html*** shown in Figure 1.4.

THE EXAMPLE DOCUMENT

Figure 1.4 and the contents of the file *ex2a.html* will be examined first. The first paragraph is a simple text paragraph. The second paragraph is similar, except that it contains three images included using the IMG element: `<IMG SRC="home.gif">`. ***Home.gif*** is a GIF format image file; I know this by the *.gif* filename extension (and, of course, because I created it). GIF files are one of the three image formats that can be included within HTML documents.

EXAMPLE DOCUMENT RENDERED

The rendering of the document *ex2a.html* (listed in Figure 1.4) is shown in Figures 1.6 through 1.8. Figure 1.6 shows the document as presented by the **Mosaic for X-Windows** browser (Version 2.4). Figure 1.7 shows the same document viewed using the Macintosh **MacWeb** browser, and Figure 1.8 shows the document as seen by the **lynx** browser. Many of the differences amongst them are simply due to the different window sizes and fonts. Still, there are differences that warrant mention.

Note the appearance of the images in Figures 1.6 and 1.7. Images are included as if they were large letters or words appearing in line with the surrounding text and deforming the line spacing to ensure that no text overlaps the image. By default, the included image is inserted to align the bottom of the image with the bottom of the text. Note that there is no special wrapping or flowing of the text around the image and, since you have no way of guaranteeing how the document will be presented, no guarantee that an image embedded in the middle of a sentence will appear in a particular place on the screen. The only way you can guarantee image placement is to put it as the first item following a paragraph (or other) break; then, it will always be the first item on a line.

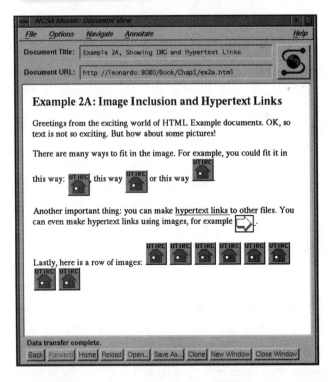

Figure 1.6 Mosaic For X-Windows rendering of the HTML document *ex2a.html* (the HTML document source is shown in Figure 1.4).

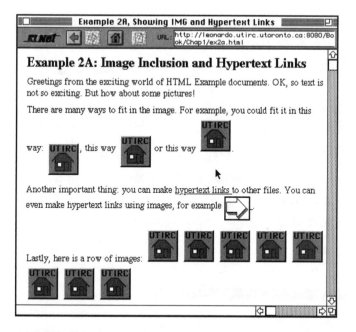

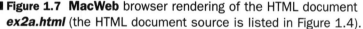

■■■■■■■■ **Figure 1.7** **MacWeb** browser rendering of the HTML document
ex2a.html (the HTML document source is listed in Figure 1.4).

ALIGNMENT OPTIONS

There are three alignment options for the image. These are specified by the
ALIGN attribute, which can take on the three possible values: ALIGN=top,
ALIGN=bottom, and ALIGN=middle (the argument is case-insensitive),
with align=bottom being the default. The three options are illustrated
with the three Home Icons (I am afraid I am not a great graphic artist).
The first, ALIGN=top, aligns the top of the image with the text, while the
ALIGN=middle value aligns the middle of the image with the bottom of
the text and ALIGN=bottom aligns the bottom of the image with the bottom of the text.

LYNX INTERPRETATION

Figure 1.8 shows the **lynx** interpretation: **lynx** is a text-only browser and
cannot display images. **Lynx** simply replaces each occurrence of an image

with the text string [IMAGE]. This is not very descriptive, but it tells you at least what you are missing. If the string [IMAGE] is insufficient, you can replace it with something more useful by using the ALT="string" attribute to the **IMG** element. You use the **ALT** attribute to specify a text alternative for an image, which is particularly useful when a browser is unable to display images. The usage is simply:

```
<IMG SRC="image.file" ALT="[A text alternative to the Image]">
```

The string specified for **ALT** is case-sensitive, and it is common (but not necessary) to surround the string with square brackets. An example of this use is shown at the bottom of *ex2a.html*, where the attribute alt="[Home Icon]" is used with all the inline images. The resulting text rendering is shown in Figure 1.8.

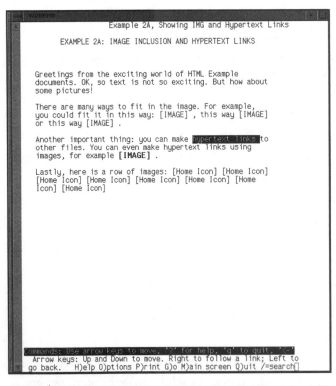

■■■■■■ ■ **Figure 1.8** **Lynx** browser rendering of the HTML document *ex2a.html* (the HTML document source is listed in Figure 1.4).

How does the browser actually obtain the images and complete the document? The browser first obtains the HTML document and then looks for **IMG** elements. If it finds **IMG** elements, the browser makes additional connections to the server to obtain the required images. Thus, a single document containing ten images requires 11 distinct connections to complete the document. Needless to say, this can be slow, particularly if you have a slow network connection. Most graphical browsers, such as **Mosaic** or **MacWeb,** have a Delay Image Loading button or pull-down menu selection that disables the automatic loading of inline images. This can save time when viewing a document, but is useful only if the author has written the document to be understandable without the pictures.

ANCHORS

The third paragraph in *ex2a.html* shows a hypertext link. The form is straightforward:

```
<A HREF="ex2a.html"> hypertext links </A>
```

The element marking a hypertext link is called an **A,** or *anchor,* element, and the marked text is referred to as a *hypertext anchor.* The area between the beginning <A> and ending </A> tags becomes a *hot* part of the text. With **Mosaic** or **MacWeb,** this section of text is displayed with an underline and usually in a different color (often blue), while with **lynx,** this region of text is displayed in bold characters. Placing the mouse over this region and clicking the mouse button, or, with **lynx,** using the tab key to move the reverse-video region to lie over the hot part and pressing return, causes the client to access the indicated document or other Internet resource.

You can also use images as hypertext anchors. At the end of the second paragraph in *ex2a.html* (Figure 1.4), I have marked the image *sright.xbm* as the anchor (the *.xbm* means this is an X-Bitmap image). The relevant piece of HTML is:

```
<a href="ex2a.html"> <IMG SRC="sright.xbm" ALIGN="middle"> </a>
```

The graphical browsers indicate this by *boxing* the image with a colored or highlighted box, while **lynx** simply bolds the `[Image]` text string it puts in place of the image. With this mechanism, you can use small images as *button* icons, as is commonly done in multimedia applications. This doesn't do much good with **lynx**, of course, so, if you do employ *navigation icons* such as these, you had better add an **ALT** attribute to let your **lynx** guests know what is going on.

This second image is in the X-Bitmap format, as indicated by the extension *.xbm*. Only three image formats can be included inline within HTML documents. These are:

.gif	GIF image files (color, grayscale, or black and white)
.xbm	X-Bitmaps (black and white)
.xpm	X-Pixelmaps (color)

Thus, if you want to display images within your document, you must ensure they are in one of these three format options.

PARTIAL URLs

The *target* of the hypertext link is indicated by the anchor attribute **HREF**, which takes as its value the URL of the target document or resource. As mentioned in the Introduction, a URL is a text string that indicates the server protocol (HTTP, FTP, WAIS, etc.) to use in accessing the resource, the Internet Domain Name of the server, and the location and name of the resource on that particular server. Obviously, the **HREF** attributes in Figure 1.4 do not contain all this information! These URLs are examples of *partial* URLs, which are a shorthand way of referring to files or other resources *relative* to the URL of the document being currently viewed. For

Figure 1.4, this means: Use the same protocol, Internet Domain Name, and directory path of the present document (*ex2a.html*), and retrieve the indicated file *ex2b.html* from the same directory.

If you click the mouse button over the hypertext anchor, the browser downloads and displays the linked document, as shown in Figure 1.9. To return to the previously viewed document, press the Back button on the browser control panel (with **lynx**, you press the letter "u"), which takes you back to the previously displayed document, namely *ex2a.html*. Figure 1.10 shows what this document looks like the second time around, using **Mosaic for X-Windows**. The document is now subtly different: The portion of text that served as the launching point for the hypertext link, previously underlined by a solid line, is now underlined by a dashed line. On a color display, you also see the anchored text rendered with a changed text color. Programs such as **Mosaic** and **MacWeb** use this change in highlighting to let you know that you have already visited this link. This helps to keep you oriented by letting you know where you have already been. Unfortunately, this is not possible with **lynx**, as there are an insufficient number of highlighting modes to allow for this level of subtlety. With **lynx**, you have to pay a bit more attention to what you have been doing.

As mentioned, the anchor

```
<A HREF="ex2b.html"> hypertext links </A>
```

uses a partial URL, which refers to locations relative to the URL of the document itself. This partial URL idea is great news, because it means that you need not specify entire URLs for simple relative links between files on the same computer. Instead, you need only specify their position on the file system relative to each other, as was done in Figure 1.4.

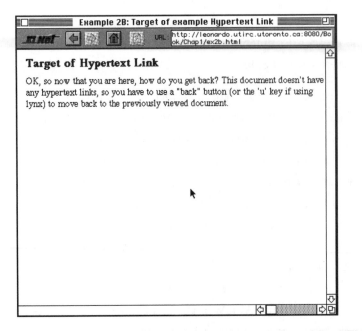

■■■■■■■ Figure 1.9 MacWeb browser rendering of the HTML document ***ex2b.html***
(the HTML document source is listed in Figure 1.5).

Partial URLs can also point to directories other than the one containing the
current document. Specification of these relative directories is done using a
UNIX-like path structure. Suppose that our example documents ***ex2a.html***
and ***ex2b.html*** lay in the directory structure shown in Figure 1.11. That is,
our files ***ex2a.html*** and ***ex2b.html*** are in the directory ***Project1/Examples***,
while the file ***e2c.html*** is in ***Project1/Examples/SubDir*** and ***ex2d.html*** is
located in ***Project1/Other***.

How do you reference the files ***ex2c.html*** and ***ex2d.html*** from the file
ex2a.html? To reference ***ex2c.html***, you simply create a hypertext link that
accesses the partial URL ***SubDir/ex2c.html***:

```
<A HREF="SubDir/ex2c.html"> hypertext links </A>
```

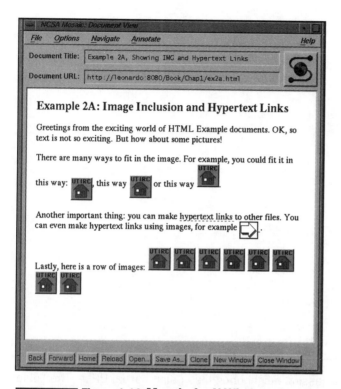

Figure 1.10 Mosaic for X-Windows browser rendering of the HTML document *ex2a.html*, after returning from a hypertext jump to the document *ex2b.html*. Note how the line under the anchor is now dashed instead of solid.

Notice the UNIX-like directory pathnames in which the forward slash character indicates a new directory. The specification of the URL syntax uses the forward slash to denote directories or any other hierarchical relationship (formally, URLs can reference not just files, but also programs and other resources). Note that you *cannot* use backslashes as you do with DOS and Windows, or colons as you do on Macintoshes.

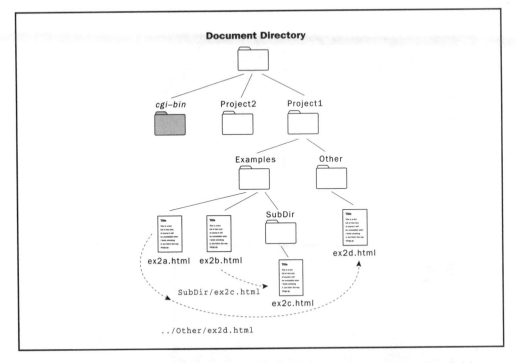

Figure 1.11 Accessing neighboring files using partial URLs. The Folders and files show the organization of files lying in the *Document Directory*—the directory that contains resources available to clients accessing an HTTP server. The dotted lines and the corresponding text strings show partial URLs relating the file ***ex2a.html*** to the files ***ex2c.html*** and ***ex2d.html***. The grayed directory, ***cgi-bin***, is a special directory used to store programs that can be executed by the HTTP server. This directory is kept physically distinct from the true document directories, since programs present a security risk to the server and must be guarded more carefully than documents (see Chapter 4 for more details).

CREATING LINKS

If you want to create a link from *ex2a.html* to *ex2d.html* in *Project/Other,* write the URL as:

```
<A HREF="../Other/ex2d.html"> hypertext links </A>
```

since the file is one directory level up (the symbol ".." meaning one directory up) and one level down into the directory *Other*. Also, a single dot (.)

implies the current directory, so `HREF="./Subdir/ex2c.html"` and `HREF="Subdir/ex2c.html"` are equivalent.

Of course, this is going to be a problem if you actually have the slash character in a filename, since the URL convention will try to interpret it as a directory change. You therefore should avoid directory or filenames containing this character if at all possible. The URL specification does have a way of allowing this and other *special* characters to be in a URL without having them interpreted specially. This *encoding* mechanism is discussed in Chapter 2.

There are a lot of other partial URL forms, and of course, the format for full URLs has yet to be discussed. More examples of URLs appear later in this chapter, while a detailed description of the URL syntax is given in Chapter 2.

Finally, we refer to the last line of *ex2a.html* (Figure 1.4), which is simply a row of inline images. Note that these wrap to best fit the width of the screen, just as if they were a sequence of words (Figures 1.5 and 1.6). Consequently, if the user changes the size of the browser window, these icons will be repositioned. This once again points out the wide variation possible between different renderings of the same document.

HYPERTEXT LINKS: THE GOOD, THE BAD, AND THE UGLY

As you can see, hypertext links are easy and can be very useful. However, you should not get carried away, as they can quickly become a source of irritation. For example, it is usually best that hypertext links flow naturally out of the text. Thus, it is better to write:

```
<p> The issue of hormone-controlled ostrich-feather growth has recently been a
topic of intense <A HREF="ostrich-paper.html"> interest </A>
```

than:

```
<p> For information about current hormone-controlled ostrich-feather growth press
<A HREF="ostrich-paper.html"> here </A>
```

```
<HTML>
<HEAD>
<TITLE> Examples of Bad Hypertext Links </TITLE>
</HEAD>
<BODY>
<H1> Examples of Good/Bad Hypertext Link Design</H1>

<p> <B> 1) Don't distort the Written Text  </B>
<P> <B> Good: </B>
<BR>The issue of hormone-controlled ostrich-feather growth has recently
    been a topic of intense <A HREF="ostrich-paper.html"> interest</A>.

<P> <B> Not So Good: </B>
<BR> For information about current hormone-controlled ostrich-feather
     growth press  <A HREF="ostrich-paper.html"> here </A>.
<p> <B> 2) Keep the linked text section short. </B>
<p> <B> Good: </B>
<br> The life cycle of the  <A HREF="animal.html"> atlantic polar-bear
     ocelot </A> is a complex and .......

<p> <B> Not So Good: </B>
<br> <A HREF="animal.html"> The life cycle of the atlantic polar-bear
     ocelot is a complex </A> and .......

<p> <B> 3) Link Icon and Text Together </B>
<p> <B> Good: </B>
<br> <A HREF="file.html"> <IMG SRC="home.gif"> The latest </A> home
     security systems breakdown show......
<p> <B> Not so Good: </B>
<br> <A HREF="file.html"> <IMG SRC="home.gif"></A> The latest home
     security systems breakdown show......

</BODY>
</HTML>
```

Figure 1.12 Listing for the document *badlinks.html*. This document illustrates good and bad examples of hypertext links. A **Mosaic for X-Windows** rendering is shown in Figure 1.13.

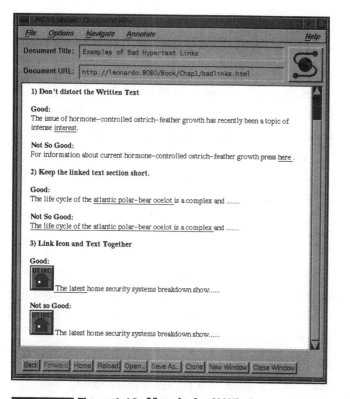

Figure 1.13 Mosaic for X-Windows rendering of the file *badlinks.html* (shown in Figure 1.12).

You also don't want the link to be gratuitously long. It is much more effective to link to a single word or selection of words than to a whole sentence. Thus such links as:

```
<p> <A HREF="animal.html"> The life cycle of the atlantic polar-bear ocelot </A>
is a complex and interesting example of .....
```

are probably better when written:

```
<p> The life cycle of the  <A HREF="animal.html"> atlantic polar-bear ocelot </A>
is a complex and interesting example of .....
```

These (and other) examples of bad hypertext links are included in the HTML document shown in Figure 1.12 and displayed in Figure 1.13. There is no hard and fast rule for creating bad and good link presentations.

In general, if you are adding links within a text document that is intended to be easy to read, it is best to make the links as unobtrusive as possible.

Sometimes, it is useful to include the URL of a document you are referencing as part of the text—you don't always have to hide the URL in the HTML markup. This is particularly useful if your document is likely to be printed by a browser, since the HTML markup tags are lost on paper. For example, the WWW FAQ document, a wonderful repository of useful information about the World Wide Web, contains such lines as:

```
<p> ....Read the Wusage home page, which is found at
<A HREF="http://siva.cshl.org/wusage.html">
    http://siva.cshl.org/wusage.html
</A>
```

If you are reading the HTML document containing this markup, just click on the anchored text to view the referenced document. If you are reading the printed version, you still have all the information you need to access the site when you next have access to the Internet.

If you are putting together a collection of links, you want to think carefully about their organization. Should they be in a paragraph? Probably not. More likely, they should go in a list or as a menu bar. You will also want to organize them in some logical manner, particularly if you have a lot of hypertext links to present—a page full of random links is exceedingly frustrating to use. Link-mania pages like this can occur quite innocently, often when you have been slowly assembling lists of interesting URLs. This may be fine for you, but can be confusing to someone else.

Figure 1.15 shows a *home* page constructed using some of the above thoughts on "bad" anchor design (the source for this document is in Figure 1.14), while Figure 1.17 shows an improved and better organized home page using the suggestions given in the preceding paragraph (the source is in Figure 1.16). We will talk more about home pages in the next example, but, by simple comparison, you will see that Figure 1.17 is much easier to understand than Figure 1.15, even though Figure 1.17 contains less textual information.

Finally, and most important of all: Make sure all your hypertext links work and go to the right place! There is nothing worse than clicking on a hypertext link only to get "ERROR. Requested document not available" in response. Actually, that's not quite true. It is even worse to click on an anchor that indicates a particular destination and find that you have actually accessed something completely different and obviously incorrect. These types of errors tell the user that the document developer did not bother with even the simplest checks of his or her work and immediately brings into question the contents of the documents themselves. It is easy to check your links: Just do it.

LESSONS FROM EXAMPLE 2

1. Images are included via the IMG element, such as:

```
<IMG src="prism-small.gif" ALT="[Text stuff]">
```

SRC specifies the URL of the image file to be included. This image file can be in one of three formats (the format is specified by the filename extension):

.gif	GIF format image file
.xbm	X-Bitmap (black and white)
.xpm	X-Pixelmap (color)

The **ALT** attribute gives a text string to be displayed by browsers that cannot display images.

Images are treated as if they were big text letters; the surrounding text does not flow around the image.

2. Hypertext links to another document are included using the **A** (anchor) element, such as:

```
<a href="SubDir/example1.2B.html"> hypertext links </a>
```

where HREF is used to specify the URL of the target of the link. The examples here are of partial URLs: Partial URLs assume the same

Internet site and protocol as for the document currently being viewed, and look for the file (or resource) relative to it. In this regard, the slash (/) and double dot (..) characters are special, representing relative positions in the directory (or other) hierarchy.

Images can also be hypertext anchors via constructs, such as:

```
<a href="someplace.html"> <img src="image.gif"> </a>
```

3. Don't use hypertext links gratuitously. If they are embedded in the text, try to make them flow with the text. If a paragraph has many links, try thinking of another way to present the material: Maybe it should be a list or a menu, or perhaps the hypertext anchors could be combined into a less intrusive form. Above all, make sure the links work; links going nowhere or to the wrong place are cardinal sins of HTML authoring.

EXAMPLE 3: HOME PAGES

This time, we will explore an example that is a bit more meaningful. This is an example of a *home* page and is based on a page constructed for the Instructional and Research Computing Group at the University of Toronto. A home page is designed to be the first page seen by explorers from the outside world and is your introduction to new Web visitors to your site. It is used to direct people to other interesting resources that you have and perhaps to other resources in your Internet neighborhood. This example comes from an academic institution, but the organizational model will be largely the same for business, entertainment, or other applications, although the details will certainly be different. Chapter 9 gives some examples from these other environments.

There are several issues to think about when designing a home page. A home page should be:

1. Small—A home page should be a small HTML document with a minimum of extraneous graphics or text. Large images and the details of the resources at your site should be elsewhere, with hypertext links from your home page to these locations.

2. Concise—A home page is like an introductory map of your site, explaining what the site is and where to find the local resources. Thus, it should briefly outline the content of your server and provide hypertext pointers to those resources. It should also briefly outline the organization of your site, such as the meanings of icons or menus, so that visitors will know how to navigate their way around.

3. Not Dependent on Graphics—You can include graphics in this page, but they should be small. Many people have slow Internet connections and don't want to spend many minutes waiting for thousands of kilobytes of gratuitous imagery. Icons or images on a home page should be small image files, totaling less than ten kilobytes if possible. Also, you must ensure that a user can navigate from your home page without a graphical browser, since many users will be accessing your site with text-only browsers. Thus, if you use icons for navigation buttons you should also provide a text-only option.

In addition your home page should provide:

4. Contact Information—Someone will want to contact you at some point, perhaps to point out a problem or even compliment you on your work. The home page should include contact information for the administrator of the resources. A common, generic e-mail address for the site administrator is *webmaster@www.domain.name*. This information should be included somewhere on the home page, usually at the bottom.

```
<HTML> <HEAD>
<TITLE> Instructional and Research Computing </TITLE>
</HEAD> <BODY>
<hr>

<h1> Instructional and Research Computing </H1>

This is the home page of the Instructional and Research Computing
Group <STRONG>(IRC)</STRONG>, one of seven departments of the Division
of Computing and Communications.
The IRC group provides support for
<A HREF="MulVis/intro.html"> multimedia and visualization techniques</A>,
access to and support for
<A HREF="HPC/intro.html"> high performance computing</A>,
and support for <A HREF="AdTech/intro.html"> adaptive technology
</A>.  (aids for the physically challenged)  We also have some interesting
links to <A HREF="Lists/Lists.html"> WWW Starting Points </A>,
a big list of <A HREF="Lists/Lists.html"> WWW Search Tools</A>,
another list of hypertext pointers to
<A HREF="Lists/Libraries.html"> Libraries </A> resources, and a
link to the  <A HREF="http://www.utoronto.ca/uoft.html"> Main University
Home Page </A>.

<p>
If you become lost in our documents use the navigation icons.
The <EM> home </EM> icon brings you back here, while the <EM> up </EM>
icon takes up up one level in the document hierarchy.  <EM> Info </EM>
and <EM> help </EM> are also useful, while the <EM> letter</EM> icon let
you send us a message, and the <EM> search </EM> icon allows you to do
a textual search of our pages.
<hr>
  <A HREF="home.html"><IMG SRC="home.gif"    ALIGN=TOP ALT="[Home]"  ></A>
  <A HREF="help.html"><IMG SRC="ic_help.gif" ALIGN=TOP ALT="[Help]"  ></A>
  <A HREF="info.html"><IMG SRC="ic_info.gif" ALIGN=TOP ALT="[Info]"  ></A>
  <A HREF="/cgi-bin/mail.pl"> <IMG SRC="ic_mail.gif" ALIGN=TOP ALT="[Mail]"  ></A>
  <A HREF="home.html"><IMG SRC="ic_up.gif"    ALIGN=TOP ALT="[Up]"     ></A>..
   <A HREF="cgi-bin/doc-search.pl"> <IMG SRC="ic_find.gif" ALIGN=TOP ALT="[Search]"></A>
<hr>
<ADDRESS>
<A HREF="Staff/web_admin.html"> webmaster@site.address.edu </A>
</ADDRESS>

</BODY>
</HTML>
```

■■■■■■■ **Figure 1.14** HTML document listing for the file ***home_bad.html***, which contains a poorly designed home page. Figure 1.15 shows the rendering of this document on a PC browser (**Air Mosaic**).

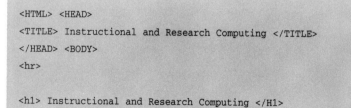

■■■■■ **Figure 1.15 Air Mosaic** rendering of the HTML document
home_bad.html.

Figure 1.16 shows a typical HTML home page document, while Figures
1.17 and 1.18 show how this page looks using the Windows **Air Mosaic**
and UNIX **lynx** browsers. Let's first look at the document structure shown
in Figure 1.16 and review how the home page was constructed.

```
<HTML> <HEAD>
<TITLE> Instructional and Research Computing </TITLE>
</HEAD> <BODY>
<hr>


<h1> Instructional and Research Computing </H1>
```

```
<HTML> <HEAD>
<TITLE> Instructional and Research Computing </TITLE>
</HEAD> <BODY>
[<A HREF="home.html">              Home        </A>]
[<A HREF="help.html">              Help        </A>]
[<A HREF="info.html">              Info        </A>]
[<A HREF="/cgi-bin/mail.pl">        Mail        </A>]
[<A HREF="home.html">              Up          </A>]
[<A HREF="cgi-bin/doc-search.pl"> Search       </A>]
<hr>

<h1> Instructional and Research Computing </H1>

This is the home page of the Instructional and Research Computing
Group <STRONG>(IRC)</STRONG>, one of seven departments of the Division
of Computing and Communications. We provide:

<UL>
<LI> support for <A HREF="MulVis/intro.html"> multimedia and visualization
     techniques</A>
<LI> access to and support for <A HREF="HPC/intro.html"> high performance
     computing</A>
<LI> support for <A HREF="AdTech/intro.html"> adaptive technology </A>
     (aids for the physically challenged).
</UL>
Some other useful University resources are:
<p>
  <A HREF="Lists/Lists.html"> WWW Starting Points </A> |
  <A HREF="Lists/Lists.html"> WWW Search Tools</A> |
  <A HREF="Lists/Libraries.html"> Libraries </A> |
  <A HREF="http://www.utoronto.ca/uoft.html"> Main University Home Page </A>
<p>
If you become lost in our documents use the navigation icons.
The <EM> home </EM> icon brings you back here, while the <EM> up </EM>
icon takes up up one level in the document hierarchy.  <EM> Info </EM>
and <EM> help </EM> are also useful, while the <EM> letter</EM> icon let
you send us a message, and the <EM> search </EM> icon allows you to do
a textual search of our pages.
<hr>
  <A HREF="home.html"><IMG SRC="home.gif"      ALIGN=TOP ALT="[Home]"  ></A>
  <A HREF="help.html"><IMG SRC="ic_help.gif"   ALIGN=TOP ALT="[Help]"  ></A>
  <A HREF="info.html"><IMG SRC="ic_info.gif"   ALIGN=TOP ALT="[Info]"  ></A>
  <A HREF="/cgi-bin/mail.pl">
     <IMG SRC="ic_mail.gif"  ALIGN=TOP ALT="[Mail]"  ></A>
  <A HREF="home.html">
     <IMG SRC="ic_up.gif"    ALIGN=TOP ALT="[Up]"       ></A>..
  <A HREF="cgi-bin/doc-search.pl">
     <IMG SRC="ic_find.gif"  ALIGN=TOP ALT="[Search]">
  </A>
<hr>
<ADDRESS>
<A HREF="Staff/web_admin.html"> webmaster@site.address.edu </A>
</ADDRESS>

</BODY>
</HTML>
```

Figure 1.16 Listing of the example home page document *home.html*.

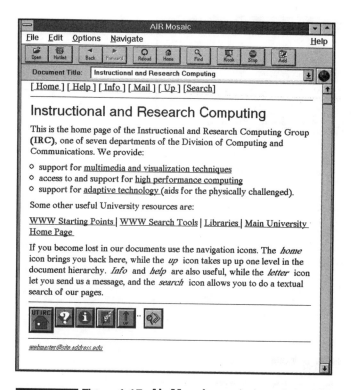

Figure 1.17 Air Mosaic rendering of the HTML document ***home.html*** (the HTML document is shown in Figure 1.16).

TITLE AND HEADING

Figure 1.16 begins with a **TITLE** and a **H1** heading. These are both clearly descriptive of the contents and origin of this document. As mentioned earlier, headings can range from **H1** down to **H6**, in decreasing order of importance. Documents should use heading elements that retain this sense of relative importance, as it helps to build organizational structure within and between documents. There are, for example, useful programs that can build a Table of Contents for large collections of HTML documents based on the contents of the heading elements. This, of course, will work only if the heading elements were used correctly.

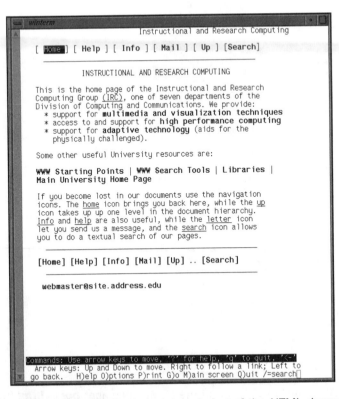

■■■■■■■■■ **Figure 1.18 Lynx** rendering of the HTML document ***home.html*** (the HTML document is shown in Figure 1.16).

Some sites place a GIF image containing the company or organizational logo at the top of the document. This can look very nice and add much to the character of the page. You must be careful, however, that the image not be too big or contain too many colors. Most computer graphics boards are capable of displaying only 256 colors simultaneously and many World Wide Web browsers limit each image within a document to less than 50 colors so that they can display more than one image at the same time (with 50 colors per image, the browser can display up to five images before *running out* of colors). Thus, attempting to display an image containing 256 colors can present problems—in fact, the image can look downright ridiculous. Most graphics editing programs allow you to process images and reduce the number of colors they contain, often with very little loss of image quality. This is very useful for the reason just mentioned and has the added bonus of making the image files smaller.

TEXT PORTION

The text portion of the home page document (Figure 1.16) should provide clear and concise descriptions of the site and the material it contains, with a minimum of extraneous detail. This should match the type of introduction you prefer: polite and well mannered, or eclectic and off the wall. In the example in Figure 1.16, the first paragraph explains what the site is and provides links to the major areas of interest. Each of these areas may, in turn, have their own home page, specific to the subject at hand. This hierarchical structure lets people quickly find what they are looking for and makes it easy to organize your documents. For example, your HTTP server can have independent subdirectories for each distinct project, with your server's main home page having hypertext links to each project's home page. Other hypertext links will provide alternative relationships between documents, but within this overall hierarchical arrangement.

ORGANIZATION

This home page (Figure 1.16) also contains a second, less detailed list that provides a brief selection of alternative services. These items link to documents or services that are perhaps peripheral to the main purpose of the server, but that may be useful in directing the visitor to his or her destination. In our case, this is a collection of hypertext pointers to other resources that our group commonly uses.

Referring to Figures 1.17 and 1.18, you can see how clean the organization appears. Since the document is written in correct HTML, both browsers display it clearly, subject to their own limitations. Comparing this with the less thought-out version (Figure 1.15) shows the importance of good organizational design: A little thought about how the hypertext links should be organized makes an enormous difference in the clarity and readability of the presentation.

It is useful to think how this home page model might apply to other applications; for example, to an electronic magazine, or *e-zine*. E-zine home pages often have a magazine title bar (a graphic), followed by the magazine title (an **H1** heading) and a brief introduction to the e-zine. This is usually followed by a collection of pointers to "this month's articles," followed by a hypertext link to a reference document that, in turn, contains a list of links to the home pages of previous e-zine issues. This is very similar to the model just presented. Some examples of different successful home page designs are shown in Chapter 9.

ICONS

Let us return to our example and to the bottom of the HTML document shown in Figure 1.16 and displayed in Figures 1.17 and 1.18. The noticeable feature is a collection of small *icons*, preceded by a short explanation of their meaning. These icons appear on every HTML document at our site and provide universal cues to navigating through the local document collection. For example, the *home* icon always links back to this home page, while the *up* icon links up to the top of whatever set of documents you are looking at. Thus if you had selected to visit the High Performance Computing section, then the *up* icon would bring you back to the High Performance Computing home page. At our site, the *Info* icon refers to a page giving a brief description of IRC and its mandate, while the *Help* icon connects to a page that briefly describes the meanings of all the icons. Finally, the *Mail* icon links to a program on the HTTP server that allows the user to send mail to the server administrator, while the *Search* icon links to a server program that allows the user to do keyword searches on the collection of HTML documents. Note that all these icons are equipped with an ALT="string" text alternative. If you are going to navigate with icons, be sure that people using a text-only browser, such as **lynx**, know what the icons mean!

Having navigation icons is extremely important, particularly when you have a large number of related hypertext documents. It is very easy to get lost when you are browsing through such large collections. Hypertext is not like a *linear* book, where you can always tell where you are by the page number or the thickness of the remaining pages. Navigation icons replace these tactile methods of navigation with symbols that link you to reference points within the collection. In addition, icons can direct the user to general services that may be useful wherever they are in a collection, such as a search tool for searching a database or a mail tool for sending an electronic message to the site administrator.

The very top of this home page shows a text-only variant of the navigation icons (see Figures 1.16 to 1.18). This was added for contrast with the iconic approach. Text or icons both add the same functionality, and choosing between one or the other is largely a matter of taste. Text-based navigation aids can take up less space on a page and do not require that you access the server several times to obtain icon images. The latter problem is mitigated by using the same icons in all your pages. Most clients keep local copies of images once they have been accessed, and don't bother to retrieve them from the server when they are required on subsequent occasions.

Image downloading problems can also be alleviated by using small icons and a reduced number of colors per image. The icons included in the document shown in Figure 1.16 and displayed in Figure 1.17 are only 36 pixels square and contain only 16 colors each (4 bits/pixel). As a result, each icon takes only around 280 bytes so that downloading them to the browser is fast and does not place large demands on the network.

UNIFORM RESOURCE LOCATORS

Looking at Figure 1.16, you will see that most of the URL references are partial references. There is one, however, that is not. This is the URL pointing to the *main* University Home Page. This is a complete URL that specifies the complete information needed to access the main University HTTP server. This URL is:

```
http://www.utoronto.ca/uoft.html
```

The URL has three main parts:

1. `http:`—The protocol specifier. The string `http:` means that the HTTP protocol is to be used. Other possible protocols are `ftp:` (FTP protocol), `gopher:` (Gopher protocol), `wais:` (WAIS protocol), and `news:` (NNTP protocol). These and other schemes are discussed in Chapter 3.

2. `//www.utoronto.ca`—The Internet domain name of the server. This gives the Internet name that the client should contact. Sometimes, you will see this with a number after the name; for example:

   ```
   www.somewhere.edu:8080
   ```

   This number is a *port number* and specifies the port number that the server is actually talking on. Most HTTP servers "talk" at Port 80. You can leave out the port number if you are contacting the server at the default port.

3. `/uoft.html`—The path and filename to the desired file (or other resource). The part after the last slash specifies the path to a file (or another resource, such as a program), and the file or program name itself. Here, the URL is to the file *uoft.html* that lies right at the top of the server's *document directory*: This is the directory under which the HTTP server keeps the documents. This directory can contain subdirectories so that such paths as */Project1/Examples/ex2a.html* are possible (as in Figure 1.11).

Programs are often placed in a special virtual subdirectory of the document directory, often named *cgi-bin* or *htbin*. Thus, if you see a URL that looks like:

```
http://some.where.edu/cgi-bin/stuff
```

or

```
http://some.where.edu/htbin/stuff
```

then stuff is a program, not a regular file.

The URL scheme allows for all sorts of protocols: `ftp` for the FTP protocol; `gopher` for the Gopher protocol; `wais` for the WAIS protocol, and so on. Thus, using URLs, you can create hypertext links to anonymous FTP servers, Gopher sites, WAIS databases, and many other Internet resources. Clients, such as **Mosaic** and **MacWeb**, are designed to understand these protocols. When they encounter a hypertext reference in an HTML element, such as `HREF="url"`, where `"url"` points to an anonymous FTP or Gopher site, they are able to contact the site, using the appropriate protocol, and interpret the returned results.

The final important point regarding Figure 1.16 concerns the **ADDRESS** element and the *signature* e-mail address located at the bottom of the document. It is always a good idea to sign your HTML documents, particularly the home page or other major pages. The HTML **ADDRESS** element is specifically designed for this purpose. This document places the e-mail address relevant to this page inside the **ADDRESS** element, and also has a hypertext link from the e-mail address to another page containing additional information. This page, here named *web_admin.html*, often contains additional information about the server and server administrator. For more personal projects, this might be an HTML document containing a brief biography of the document author.

LESSONS FROM EXAMPLE 3

1. A home page should be small and should not contain many large images.

2. Home pages should clearly and concisely describe the contents of a World Wide Web site and should contain hypertext links to these resources.

3. A home page can explain and introduce navigation icons if they are used.

4. Home pages should contain contact information for the administrator of the documents managed at the site.

EXAMPLE 4: COLLECTIONS OF HYPERTEXT DOCUMENTS

This example looks at a hypertext collection of text-based documents. One common use of HTML is to prepare online documentation or online collections of reference materials. These can be large collections of documents, often with some overall hierarchical structure (such as sections and subsections), but also with many hypertext links crosslinking these documents and linking them to other resources, such as programs that can search the documents for keywords, or to other Internet sites containing related information.

There are several design issues to consider when developing large document collections:

1. Each document should be small, usually no more than two or three screens full of data. The advantage of the hypertext model lies in the linking of various components of the documentation package. This advantage is largely lost if you are viewing a single, huge document containing hundreds or thousands of lines of displayed text. Although you can build hypertext links within a document to other points inside the same document, this is generally more difficult to navigate than a collection of smaller files.

2. Each document should have navigation tools in the form of hypertext links that connect the document to other documents in the hierarchy and to general navigation points within the collection. Thus, each page

should have links to *next* and *previous* documents (if there is an obvious order to the pages) and to a Table of Contents or the section heading. If the document is big, say more than two or three screens full of text, then it might be a good idea to place the navigation icons both at the top and bottom of the document. This makes them easier to find.

3. Documents should show a consistent presentation style. Each document should be consistently designed, with the same heading structure, the same navigation icons, and similar contents outlines. This makes it easy to get the *feel* for the collection, and also makes it possible to index or catalog the collection using programs that take advantage of this structure.

Artistic license is, of course, allowed! But these are general guidelines, based on experience, that help to make your work more pleasing and easier to use.

```
<html><head>
<title> HR element in HTML </title>
</head><body>
[<a href="htmlindex.html">Index</a>]
[<a href="body.html">Up</a>]
[<a href="lists_reg.html">Back</a>]
[<a href="entities.html">Next</a>]

<H1> 4.7 Horizontal Ruled Line </H1>

The HR element is used to draw a horizontal dividing line
completely across the screen. This can be to logicallyseparate
blocks of text, or to separateicon lists from the body of the text.

<p> The HR element is empty (you don't need a
<code>&lt;/HR></code>).
```

```
<h2> Example </h2>

The following shows an example of the use of &lt;HR> and the
resulting rendering (on your browser).

<blockquote>

<pre>

The following document is scanned from the back of

a cereal box. To see the scanned image, press the

icon at the bottom of the text ....

&lt;HR>

&lt;H1> MIGHTY CHOKEE-OS! &lt;/H1>

The cereal of chocolate deprived kiddies everywhere!

&lt;p> Aren't you lucky your parents love you enough

to buy you CHOCKEE-OS!

&lt;p> Remember to ask Mom and Dad for NEW SUPER

CHOCKEE-OS, now with Nicotine!!

</pre>

</blockquote>

<p> <b> This is rendered as:</b>

The following document is scanned from the back of a

cereal box. To see the scanned image, press the icon at

the bottom of the text ....

<HR>

<H1> MIGHTY CHOKEE-OS! </H1>

The cereal of chocolate deprived kiddies everywhere!

<p> Aren't you lucky your parents love you enough

to buy you CHOCKEE-OS!

<p> Remember to ask Mom and Dad for NEW SUPER CHOCKEE-OS,

now with Nicotine!!

<hr>

<p> [<a href="htmlindex.html">Index</a>]

[<a href="body.html">Up</a>]

[<a href="lists_reg.html">Back</a>]

[<a href="entities.html">Next</a>]

</body> </html>
```

Figure 1.19 HTML listing for the document *hrule.html*, a typical text-only HTML document.

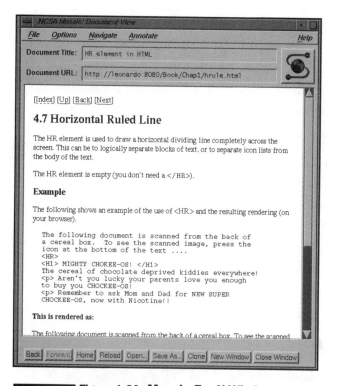

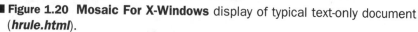

Figure 1.20 Mosaic For X-Windows display of typical text-only document (*hrule.html*).

Figures 1.19 and 1.20 show an example HTML document from a large collection of related files. This particular example is one of approximately 70 documents that discuss various aspects of the HTML language (although, in significantly less detail than in this book!). This collection of documents can be accessed at the URL:

```
http://www.utirc.utoronto.ca/HTMLdocs/NewHTML/htmlindex.html
```

This is a *flat* collection of documents, in that all the files lie in the same directory and are linked together in a serial fashion. However, there are many hypertext links relating the documents together (for example, one document discussing the **IMG** element has a sentence mentioning URLs, which, in turn, contains a hypertext link to a document giving a more detailed discussion of URLs). The documents are also ordered hierarchically. Thus, this example document discussing the **HR** element is "under" the **BODY** document which is, in turn, "under" the Table of Contents. The Table of Contents page contains hypertext links to all the documents in this collection and is an easy tool for quickly finding and accessing a particular section.

Note the navigation text icons at the top of the page. There are four navigation buttons: *Index*, *Up*, *Back*, and *Next*. The *Index* button takes you directly to a Table of Contents page, while the Up button takes you one level up in the hierarchy; in this case, to the BODY page. The *Back* button takes you backwards to the preceding document in the hierarchy, while the *Next* button takes you forwards to the next document. The *Back* and *Next* buttons are the ones to use if you want to read the document straight through.

PRE ELEMENT

As an HTML aside, you should note the HTML **PRE** element in Figure 1.19. The **PRE** element is used to enclose preformatted text for presentation as is, preserving the space characters and carriage returns typed into the HTML document and displaying the characters using a fixed-width typewriter font. Thus, you should use the **PRE** element to display computer codes, text examples, or verbatim text sequences. This is also the only way that you can currently create tables for display in an HTML document, since this is the only element that preserves the horizontal spacing needed to align columns.

The usefulness of the **PRE** element is well illustrated in Figure 2.18 (Chapter 2), where it is used to display both program code and a small table. You can include character emphasis elements within a PRE element so that you can use the **STRONG** and **EM** elements to emphasize certain text strings. You can also include hypertext anchors. However, most other elements, such as headings, list elements, or the **ADDRESS** element, are prohibited.

▬▬▬▬▬

```
html>
<head>
<title> HTML Documentation Table of Contents</title>
</head>

<body>

<h1> HTML Documentation Table of Contents </h1>

<dl>
<dt> <a href="htmlindex.html"> Table of Contents (this page)</a>
<dt> <a href="about_the_author.html"> About the Author</a>
</dl>
<ol>
<li> <a href="intro.html"> Introduction to this Document</a>
<li> <a href="html_intro.html"> Introduction to HTML </a>
<ol>
    <li> <a href="elements.html"> HTML Elements </a>
    <li> <a href="doc_struct.html"> HTML Document Structure</a>
    <li> <a href="naming.html"> HTML Document Naming Scheme </a>
</ol>
<li> <a href="head.html">HEAD</a> of an HTML Document
    <ol>
    <li> <a href="title.html"> TITLE</a>
    <li> <a href="isindex.html"> ISINDEX</a>
    <li> <a href="nextid.html"> NEXTID</a>
    <li> <a href="link.html"> LINK</a>
    <li> <a href="base.html"> BASE</a>
```

```
        </ol>
<li> <a href="body.html"> BODY</a> of an HTML Document

      <ol>

      <li>  <a href="headings.html"> Headings</a> (Hn)

      <li>  <a href="paragraph.html"> Paragraphs</a> (P)

      <li>  <a href="line_break.html"> Line Breaks</a> (BR)

      <li>  <a href="image.html"> Inlined Images</a> (IMG)

      <ol>

      <li>   <a href="image-examples.html"> Examples </a> of Images

      </ol>

      <li>  <a href="anchors.html"> Hypertext Anchors</a> (A)

      <ol>

          <li>  <a href="A_href.html">Link to</A> an object (HREF)

          <li>  <a href="A_name.html">Link from </A>an object (NAME)

          <li>  <a href="A_rel.html">Relationship</A> between objects (REL)

          <li>  <a href="A_rev.html"> Relationship</A> between objects (REV)

          <li>  <a href="A_urn.html"> URN </A>

          <li>  <a href="A_title.html">TITLE </A>

          <li>  <a href="A_methods.html">How</A> to link  (METHODS)

      </ol>

          .

          .

          .

      </ol>
<li> Stepping up to <a
href="http://info.cern.ch/hypertext/WWW/MarkUp/HTMLPlus/htmlplus_1.html">HTML+</a>

<li> <a href="bibliography.html">Bibliography</a>

</ol>

</body>

</html>
```

■■■■■■■■■ **Figure 1.21** HTML source document for the Table of Contents page
htmlindex.html. Some of this document has been omitted to save
space. The rendering of the document is shown in Figure 1.22.

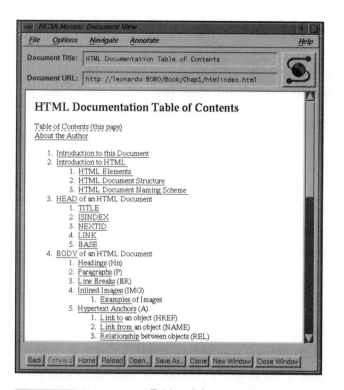

Figure 1.22 Table of Contents page for the HTML document collection that contains the file *hrule.html* (shown in Figure 1.19). This collection of documents can be accessed at:

```
http://www.utirc.utoronto.ca/HTMLdocs/NewHTML/htmlindex.html
```

These documents are not up to date.

ORGANIZATION

Figure 1.22 shows the HTML Table of Contents document for this collection (the listing is in Figure 1.21), although only part of this appears within the displayed window. Notice how this gives a complete overview of the document tree, including the relative placement of the sections in the hierarchy and the hypertext links to each section. This Table of Contents was constructed by hand—a tedious process, to say the least. Fortunately, there are now programs that can automatically generate a hypertext Table of

Contents directly from the HTML document collection, using the headings embedded in the documents to create both section names and a hierarchical organization. This is another good reason to use appropriate heading elements. Information about these indexing tools is provided in Chapter 5.

There are several other organizational features that you may also want to include. Often, a printed version of a document collection is useful. If this is desired, you can combine the documents together and present them as a single, large file that clients can download and read as HTML or print (from their browsers) as a single text file. However, you should let them know what to expect. For example, you can add lines in the Table of Contents or some other page that say something like:

```
<p> This entire archive of documents is also available as a <A
HREF="alldocs.html"> concatenated HTML documents </A> (198 Kbytes), suitable for
printing.  Note, however, that the hypertext links in this document have been
removed.
```

This guides the user to a document that can be both viewed and printed, but also warns that the file is big and that certain facilities available in the discrete files are not present. They can then choose whether to click on the phrase "concatenated HTML documents" and access this resource.

ARCHIVING

In some cases, you might want to make the entire document collection available as an archive. Then, if someone is making extensive use of the documents, they can copy down the entire collection and install it on their own machine, reducing the load on your server and increasing the speed with which they can access the material. If you are using a PC, you most likely will make such an archive using the **PKZIP** package. This allows you to archive files and directories into a single compressed file, usually with the filename extension *.zip*. Thus, you could **pkzip** all the files in the document collection into a file called *alldocs.zip*. On a Macintosh, the canonical program for archiving is **StuffIt:** The resulting archive would be named *alldocs.sit*. UNIX users will use a program called **tar** (for tape archiver), which would result in the archive file *alldocs.tar*. UNIX also has two programs for compressing programs, **compress**, which places a *.Z* at the end of the compressed filename, and **gzip** (for GNU zip, which is distinctly different from **PKZIP**), which places a *.z* at the end of the compressed filename. This would yield the compressed archive files *alldocs.tar.Z* (using **compress**) or *alldocs.tar.z*. (using **gzip**). If you were generous in preparing archives for multiple platforms, you might then have, in your HTML documents, a section pointing to these files. An example of such a document is shown in Figures 1.23 and 1.24.

Many HTTP server programs allow you to control access to certain files or directories on the server and restrict access to files to authorized users. These facilities allow you to control access to archives such as this, should there be copyright problems associated with the archives or other reasons to control access.

As a final HTML aside, note that Figure 1.24 illustrates how lists can be nested. Here, an unordered list element (**UL**) is nested inside an *ordered list* element (**OL**):

```
<UL>
    <LI> <A HREF="alldocs.zip">........

    .

    .

    .

    <UL>
      <LI> (This is a concatenation of the .....
    </UL>
</UL>
```

Recall, however, that you cannot put lists inside headings, or headings inside lists.

```
<HTML>
<HEAD>
<TITLE> Archives of this Documentation </TITLE>
</HEAD>
<BODY>

<H2> Document Archives </H2>

<p> Archives of the document collection are available in the following
formats:

<UL>
<LI> <A HREF="alldocs.zip">  alldocs.zip</A>    (138 Kbytes) -- <EM> DOS PKZIP  </EM>
<LI> <A HREF="alldocs.sit">  alldocs.sit</A>    (532 Kbytes) -- <EM> Macintosh
Stuffit</EM>
<LI> <A HREF="alldocs.tar">  alldocs.tar</A>    (527 Kbytes) -- <EM> UNIX tar </EM>
<LI> <A HREF="alldocs.tar.Z">alldocs.tar.Z</A> (133 Kbytes) -- <EM> UNIX tar
(compressed)</EM>
<LI> <A HREF="alldocs.tar.z">alldocs.tar.z</A> (104 Kbytes) -- <EM> UNIX tar
(gnuzipped) </EM>
<LI> <A HREF="alldocs.html"> alldocs.html </A> (523 Kbytes) -- <EM>
Concatenated HTML documents </EM>
<UL>
<LI> (This is a concatenation of the HTML documents, suitable for
printing from a browser. The Hypertext links have been removed).
</UL>
</UL>
</BODY>
</HTML>
```

■■■■■■■ **Figure 1.23** Example HTML document *src_link.html* that contains links to alternative formats of a document collection. Clicking on the items retrieves the archives to the client's machine.

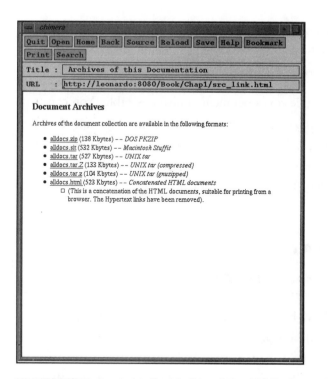

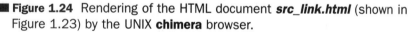

Figure 1.24 Rendering of the HTML document *src_link.html* (shown in Figure 1.23) by the UNIX **chimera** browser.

LESSONS FROM EXAMPLE 4

1. Collections of documents should be consistently designed to make them easy to navigate. You should also try to create a hypertext Table of Contents. There are programs available that can help you do this, some of which are discussed in Chapter 5.

2. You should use navigation icons (or text) as hypertext links to help the user navigate through the document collection. Make sure that you provide a text-only navigation option for users who are using a nongraphical browser.

3. Single HTML documents should be small and self-contained. Larger documents should be broken up into smaller documents to best take advantage of the hypertext facilities.

4. Sometimes a *flat* printable text document is also desirable. You can concatenate your HTML files together to make such a document, and then create a hypertext link from your collection to this document, but be sure to include information about the size of this file (if it is large) next to this link so that the user knows what to expect.

EXAMPLE 5: IMAGES, MOVIES, AND SOUND FILES

As mentioned earlier, WWW browsers can display only GIF or X-Bitmap images and often restrict GIF images to less than 50 or so displayed colors per image. The discussion also stated that small images are advantageous, since large images can take a long time to download and are often irritating for that reason alone.

LINKING LARGE IMAGES

However, sometimes these restrictions are unreasonable. Suppose you need to display a page containing a large image that is an important part of your presentation. For example, it may be an image of a campus map that can be *clicked* on to access information about various campus buildings, in which case, a tiny image is not appropriate. Alternatively, you may have truly high-quality images containing 256 colors, or perhaps non-GIF format images, and want to make them available for viewing. Perhaps you even have movie or sound files. How can these be included in a document and presented to your clients?

Large GIF images can always be added to an HTML document. The key to good document design is simply to warn the user, at the hypertext anchors pointing to a file, that it contains a large image. This is a useful way of directing users to large active images (see creating active images in Chapter 5) and gives the user the option of disabling image loading when accessing the document, or to not access the document altogether. You are still, however, limited to GIF or X-Bitmap images, and by browsers that may limit the numbers of distinct colors that a single image can use.

A *thumbnail sketch* is a particularly useful way of linking to a large image. A thumbnail is simply a reduced size *icon* of the actual image or of some characteristic portion of the image. These are easy to make with almost any commercial or public-domain image editing program. You can then include the thumbnail in your document, and make a hypertext link from the thumbnail to the document containing the large image, or to the image itself. This is what was done in Figures 1.25 and 1.26, where the small images are links to larger images and, in this case, also to movie files. In this example, the thumbnail of the larger GIF image is only 1,500 bytes long, one-tenth the size of the original file. Note that sizes of the linked documents are also given (these are big files!). It is always good practice to give this information when files are large.

You should also indicate the data type of the file, as in Figure 1.26, where the text indicates that the linked image file is in GIF format and that the linked movie is in MPEG format. There are many different movie and image formats, and most clients are capable of displaying only a subset of them. It is always a good idea to give the format of your large data files so that users can avoid downloading files they cannot use.

```
<HTML>
<HEAD>
<TITLE>Simulated Vortex Dynamics in a Porous-Body Wake</TITLE>
</HEAD>

<BODY>
<H1>Simulated Vortex Dynamics in a Porous-Body Wake</H1>

This video presents the result of a numerical simulation on the wake
generated by a porous body.  The wake flow is simulated by inserting
small-scale discrete vortices into a uniform stream,  and  the colors
in the video represent the magnitude of vorticity.   The initial flow
field is subjected to a small perturbation based on experimental data.
The evolution of the wake flow is  manifested  by the merging  and
interactions of the small-scale vortices.<P>

The objective of this investigation is to study the merging and
inter-action processes of vortices and the formation of large eddies in
the flow.  Such an investigation is of importance to many flow-related
industrial and environmental problems, such as mixing, cooling,
combustion and dispersion of air-borne or water-borne contaminants.<P>
<HR>
<B> <A HREF="legend.gif"><IMG SRC="legicon.gif"
ALIGN=Bottom> Initial flow</A> and color legend for vorticity.</B>
(14.5 KB gif image)<p>
<HR>
<B> <A HREF="flow.mpeg"><IMG SRC="vortex.gif" ALT="[movie icon]"
ALIGN=Bottom> Visualization</A> of the evolution of the wake flow.</B>
(0.38 MB mpeg-1 movie)<p>
</BODY>
</HTML>
```

Figure 1.25 The HTML document *vortex.html*, showing links from image icons to full-size images and video sequences. Figure 1.26 shows the rendering of this document by the **Mosaic for X-Windows** browser.

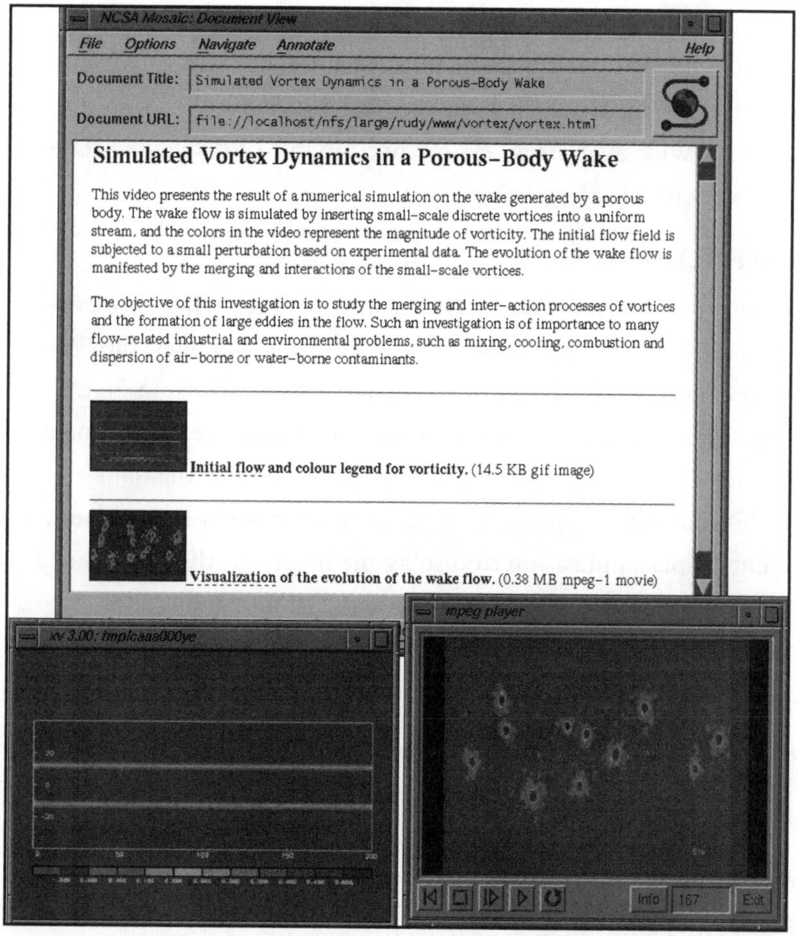

Figure 1.26 The **Mosaic for X-Windows** rendering of the document listed in Figure 1.25, showing thumbnail image icons linked to full-sized image files, movie files, and sounds. The picture overlaid on the browser resulted from clicking on the image icon at the top of the screen, while the movie-playing window was launched by pressing on the icon at the bottom of the screen. This page and the associated images and movies are courtesy of Rudy Ziegler of the University of Toronto Instructional and Research Computing Group, while the displayed data were provided by Z. Huang, J.G. Kawall, and J.F. Keffer of the Department of Mechanical Engineering at the University of Toronto.

So far, our hypertext links have been to HTML documents or to HTML documents containing images via the IMG element. What happens if the links connect to other media, such as image files, movie files, or sound files? Most World Wide Web browsers are not capable of displaying these data formats. So, what do they do?

HELPER APPLICATIONS

The answer lies in so-called *helper* or *viewer* applications, which are programs on the user's computer that can be used to display images, movies, or sounds that cannot be displayed by the browser itself. Thus, in Figure 1.26, the large-screen image was produced by clicking on the upper image icon in the browser window, causing the browser to retrieve the data accessed by this link, acknowledge the data to be an image file, and launch the appropriate helper application to display the image (in this case, the UNIX image viewing program **xv**). In the case of the movie file, the browser knew that the data was an MPEG movie, so it started up the program **mpeg_play** to display the video information.

How does the browser know what a file contains and what to do with it? If the data comes from an HTTP server, then the server, as part of the HTTP protocol, *explicitly tells the browser* the data content. It does this with a special header message that is sent to the client just before the actual data. This message is actually a *MIME content-type* header, which, for the GIF image file, looks like:

```
Content-Type: image/gif
```

and, for the MPEG movie, is:

```
Content-Type: video/mpeg
```

When the browser receives this message, it looks in its own database of *helper* applications to find the program that matches this *MIME type*. If it finds a program to help, it passes the data to the program and lets it do its job.

If the data comes from an FTP server, or if the browser is accessing the file from the local machine and not from a server, then the browser must *guess* at the data content. It does this from the filename extension. Each browser has a database that matches filename extensions to the appropriate MIME type, and uses this database to determine the MIME types of files accessed locally or via FTP. In general, this database will map the *.gif* suffix to the image/gif MIME type, and the suffixes *.mpeg*, *.mpg*, or *.mpe* to the video/mpeg MIME type. These lists have to be updated if you add a new filename extension. With Macintosh and some Windows browsers, the lists can be edited from a pull-down menu.

There are literally dozens of MIME types and dozens of possible filename extensions. A detailed list of MIME types is given in Appendix B, while the usage of MIME types is discussed in more detail in Chapter 4.

LESSONS FROM EXAMPLE 5

1. Warn a user when you present a link to a large image document or file.

2. List the data format for large image, audio, or movie files so that the user can tell if the file is in a format they can actually use.

3. You can use icons to link to larger image or movie files. This lets the user know what to expect and is often a good graphical addition to your document.

EXAMPLE 6: FILL-IN FORMS

This final example looks at the HTML **FORM** element, which allows you to solicit user input by constructing HTML documents containing fill-in forms. Using this element, a designer can build a document containing checkboxes, radio boxes, pull-down lists, text windows, and menus; and can configure this **FORM** to send the data gathered by these buttons and boxes to a program on an HTTP server. For example, FORMs can be used to collect data for a database search; solicit data for an online questionnaire; accept electronic text for submission to a database; or solicit electronic messages for forwarding to a particular user.

The example document in Figure 1.27 shows this latter case: namely, a FORM that allows the user to type in a text message for forwarding to a recipient selected from a list. Figure 1.28 shows how this form is rendered by **Mosaic for X-Windows**, while Figure 1.29 shows the rendering by **lynx**. Finally, Figure 1.30 shows what **MacMosaic** Version 1.0.3 does with this HTML document; this older version of **MacMosaic** does not understand the **FORM** element.

Let's first look to Figure 1.27 and to the <FORM..> tag beginning with the line:

```
<FORM  ACTION="http://side.edu/cgi-bin/send_note">
```

FORM ELEMENT

This line starts the **FORM** element and ties the data of the form to a particular program (*send_note*) on the indicated HTTP server. All a **FORM** element does is collect data: It doesn't do any processing of the data, so the only way you can get a form to do anything useful is to send the data gathered by it to a program on the server. The <FORM...> tag in Figure 1.27 indicates that the data gathered by the form is to be sent to the program *send_note*. Data is sent to this server-side when the user presses the *Send Message* button at the bottom of the page. The FORM and the program *send_note* must be designed together for the program to understand the message sent by the FORM.

The program *send_note* takes the data sent by the client and processes it to complete the task. In this example, the program might take the data sent by the form and compose an electronic mail message to be sent to the intended person. We talk more about gateway programs and how data is actually sent from the FORM to the gateway program in Chapters 4 and 5.

```
<HTML><HEAD>
  <TITLE> Example of an HTML FORM  </TITLE>
</HEAD>
<BODY>
<H1> Example of an HTML FORM  </H1>
<FORM ACTION="no_action">
Data entered into a FORM is sent to a program on the server
for processing.  If you see a button at the end of this sentence
then your browser supports the HTML FORMs element.
--[<INPUT TYPE="checkbox" NAME="button" VALUE="on">]--
If you do not see a button between the square brackets go to the
<A HREF="text_only.html"> text-only interface </A>. </FORM>
<hr>
<FORM  ACTION="http://side.edu/cgi-bin/submit_abstract">
  <p> <STRONG> 1) Send this note to: </STRONG>
  <SELECT NAME="mailto_name" >
    <OPTION SELECTED> Martin Grant
    <OPTION> Jack Smith
    <OPTION> Bruce Lee
    <OPTION> Anna Mcgarrigle
    <OPTION> Kate Bush
    <OPTION> Spike Lee
    <OPTION> Diane Koziol
    <OPTION> Ross Thomson
    <OPTION> Ann Dean
  </SELECT>

  <p> 2) <STRONG>Give your e-mail address: </STRONG>
      This indicates who sent the letter
  <p> <INPUT TYPE="text"  NAME="signature"
      VALUE="name@internet.address" SIZE=60>

  <p> <STRONG> 3) Message Body: </STRONG>
```

```
<p>

<TEXTAREA COLS=60 ROWS=8 NAME="message_body">

 Delete this message and type your message into this

 textbox.  Press the "Send Message" button to send it

 off. You can press the "Reset" button to reset the

 form to the original values.

 </TEXTAREA>

 <P>

 <INPUT TYPE="submit" VALUE="Send Message"> <INPUT TYPE="reset"> (reset form)

 </FORM>

 </BODY>

</HTML>
```

■■■■■■■■ **Figure 1.27** The HTML source code for the document *form.html*.

By comparing the HTML source document in Figure 1.27 and its rendering in Figure 1.28, you can see some of the several input items that can go inside a form. This example shows: a **SELECT** element pull-down menu (where you select the name of the person to whom you wish to send the message—the possible names being given by the **OPTION** element); a single-line text **INPUT** element (where you type in your e-mail address); and a **TEXTBOX** element (where you type the body of your message). Several other input elements are available and are described in Chapter 2. The elements, **SELECT, INPUT, OPTION,** and **TEXTBOX,** can appear only inside a **FORM.**

Every **FORM** input element, namely **INPUT, SELECT,** or **TEXTBOX,** takes one key attribute. This is the **NAME** attribute, which associates a *variable name* to the data associated with this input element; for example, NAME="mailto_name" and NAME="button". These names are used to differentiate between the data associated with the different input elements. Some elements, such as the **INPUT** element, can assign a default initial *value* to the named variable using the **VALUE** attribute. An example is the element:

```
<INPUT TYPE="checkbox" NAME="button" VALUE="on">
```

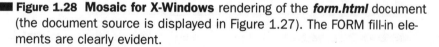

Figure 1.28 **Mosaic for X-Windows** rendering of the **form.html** document (the document source is displayed in Figure 1.27). The FORM fill-in elements are clearly evident.

which assigns the value "on" to the name "button". These values can be subsequently changed by user input, by selecting a different entry from a pull-down menu, typing text into a box, or pushing checkboxes or buttons.

When you press the special *Send Message* button (a special **INPUT** element with the attribute TYPE="submit"), the data in the form is sent to the server as a collection of *name/value* pairs, where *name* is the value assigned to the **NAME** attribute of an element, and *value* is the value assigned by the user's input. For example, the preceding checkbox input element would send the pair *button* and *on*.

```
┌──────────────────────────────────────────────────────────────┐
│ ═══  winterm                                           □ ○ □  │
│                                                                │
│              Example of an HTML FORM     (p1 of 2)             │
│                                                                │
│                    EXAMPLE OF AN HTML FORM                     │
│                                                                │
│       Data entered into a FORM is sent to a program on the     │
│       server for processing. If you see a button at the end of │
│       this sentence then your browser supports the HTML FORMs  │
│       element. --[ ( )]-- If you do not see a button between   │
│       the square brackets go to the text-only interface .      │
│                                                                │
│       ────────────────────                                     │
│                                                                │
│                          +*****************+                   │
│       1) Send this note to: * Martin Grant │   *               │
│                           * Jack Smith       *                 │
│       2) Give your e-mail ad* Bruce Lee      *es who sent the   │
│       letter              * Anna Mcgarrigle *                  │
│                           * Kate Bush        *                 │
│       name@internet.address * Spike Lee     *_____     │
│                           * Diane Koziol     *                 │
│                           * Ross Thomson     *                 │
│       3) Message Body:    * Ann Dean         *                 │
│                          +*****************+                   │
│                                                                │
│       ─────────────────────────────────────────────           │
│       ‾  Delete this message and type your message into this _ │
│       ‾  textbox.  Press the "Send Message" button to send it  │
│       ‾  off. You can press the "Reset" button to reset the __ │
│       ‾  form to the original values._____            │
│       ‾  ─────────────────────────────────────────            │
│       ‾  ─────────────────────────────────────────            │
│       ‾  ─────────────────────────────────────────            │
│                                                                │
│       (Option list) Hit return and use arrow keys and return to select│
│        Arrow keys: Up and Down to move. Right to follow a link; Left to│
│        go back.   H)elp O)ptions P)rint G)o M)ain screen Q)uit /=search│
└──────────────────────────────────────────────────────────────┘
```

Figure 1.29 The **lynx** browser rendering of the *form.html* document (the document source is displayed in Figure 1.27). The FORM fill-in elements are clearly evident: In general, **lynx** gives written instructions at the bottom of the screen to help you properly manipulate the form.

The server program sorts out what the data means by matching the *names* in the message to names the program is designed to recognize. This illustrates why a form and the associated server-side program must be designed simultaneously.

FORM RESTRICTIONS

As with all HTML elements, the **FORM** element has restrictions on where it can be placed. A **FORM** cannot be inside a heading, inside another **FORM,** or inside character emphasis markups, such as a **STRONG** or **EM** element. However, a **FORM** can contain headings, character markup elements, and even lists. Again, the details of the nesting rules are given in Chapter 2.

Figure 1.29 shows the same FORM as displayed by **lynx**. The **lynx** browser can display all the major FORM elements and provides instructions at the bottom of the screen to explain how to fill in the different FORM elements.

The last thing to notice is the little button at the top of Figures 1.28 and 1.29. This button, which does not actually do anything (note that there is no associated <INPUT TYPE="submit" > button), is designed to test the capabilities of the browser. There are still a few commonly used browsers that are unable to process the **FORM** element (an example is **MacMosaic** Version 1.0.3). It is therefore a good idea to test FORM capabilities and let the user know if he or she will be unable to properly view a document. For example, Figure 1.30 displays the same HTML document as Figure 1.28, but by using the **MacMosaic** 1.0.3 browser. You can see that the small box in the first paragraph is missing (as are all the other FORM boxes—in general, browsers simply ignore tags that they do not understand). The first paragraph explains why the rest of the page looks so odd, and can direct users to alternate documents designed for FORM-incapable browsers, should such pages be available.

LESSONS FROM EXAMPLE 6

1. The document developer can use the HTML **FORM** element to solicit user input. However, each FORM document must send the data it gathers to a server-side gateway program designed to analyze the form data. This gateway program is specified by the **ACTION** attribute to the **FORM** element. The program and form must be designed together.

2. An HTML **FORM** can contain several input elements, namely **INPUT**, **SELECT**, and **TEXTBOX**. These elements can appear only inside a **FORM**.

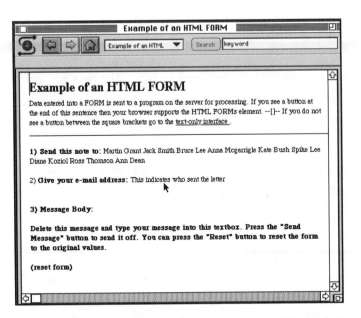

■■■■■■■ Figure 1.30 MacMosaic Version 1.0.3 rendering of the *form.html* document (the document source is displayed in Figure 1.27). This browser cannot display FORM elements

3. A **FORM** cannot be inside a heading element or inside another **FORM**—**FORM**s cannot be nested. However, heading, list, and even **PRE** elements can be inside a **FORM.**

REFERENCES

The WWW USENET newsgroups are a good source of information about HTML and the World Wide Web in general. The newsgroups contain up-to-the-minute information on WWW happenings and are a good place to post HTML questions. The newsgroups are:

comp.infosystems.www.providers   Issues related to publishing material on the Web, such as the HTML language and the development of server gateway programs.

comp.infosystems.www.users	User-related issues, such as configuring browsers, finding browsers, or discussing browsers.
comp.infosystems.www.misc	Other miscellaneous topics.
bionet.software.www	Discusses applications of WWW software in the biological sciences.

Frequently Asked Questions (FAQ) lists are posted regularly to these newsgroups. The entire FAQ list for all the newsgroups is also available in hypertext form at:

```
http://sunsite.unc.edu/boutell/faq/www_faq.html
```

User surveys of WWW software and resources can be found at:

```
http://www.gatech.edu/pitkow/survey/survey-9-1994/Survey_Home.html
```

General References:

```
http://akebono.stanford.edu/yahoo/Computers/World_Wide_Web/HTML/
http://oneworld.wa.com/htmldev/devpage/dev-page.html
http://cbl.leeds.ac.uk/nikos/doc/repository.html
http://coney.gsfc.nasa.gov/www/sswg/candy_style.html
```

HTML IN DETAIL

This chapter is a detailed exposition of the *HyperText Markup Language*; it is written from a document developer's point of view and is designed to help document authors create valid HTML documents. It presents a detailed description of every HTML element and of allowed hierarchical relationships amongst these elements. This section assumes a basic understanding of HTML at the level outlined in Chapter 1 of this book.

INTRODUCTION TO HTML

As mentioned in Chapter 1, the HyperText Markup Language is designed to specify the *logical* organization and formatting of text documents, with extensions to include inline images, fill-in forms, and hypertext links to other documents and Internet resources. HTML is designed to be a platform-independent document representation format that:

- Is not bound to a particular hardware or software environment

- Represents the logical structure of a document, and not its presentation

This emphasis reflects the fact that, in a distributed environment, individuals viewing a document can use many different browser programs of different capabilities. For example, it is of little use specifying that a particular piece of text must be presented with a 14-point Times Roman font if the person viewing the document is sitting in front of a VT-100 terminal. For this reason, HTML does not specify details of the document typesetting and instead marks logical document structure, such as headings, lists, or paragraphs. The details of the presentation of these elements are left to the browser.

HTML is defined in terms of the International Standards Organization (ISO) Standard Generalized Markup Language (SGML). SGML is a complex system for defining types of structured documents and for defining markup languages that can represent these document types. HTML is just one instance of this process. The details of SGML are complex and, fortunately, not important to an HTML document developer. One component that is useful, however, is the SGML *definition* of the HTML syntax, which is contained in a special SGML document called a *Document Type Definition,* or *DTD*. This is a simple text file, often having an imaginative name, such as *html.dtd*. This file can be used, in combination with a program called **sgmls,** to validate the syntax of any HTML document. The "References" section at the end of this chapter suggests places where you can obtain the official DTD file for HTML, while Chapter 6 discusses using **sgmls** to validate HTML documents.

HTML is an evolving language and has undergone substantial evolution over the past few years. The new *"standard"* version of HTML is referred to as HTML Version 2.0, or HTML2.0. This chapter (and this book) describes writing HTML documents using the HTML2.0 specification.

However, it also presents some of the proposed but not yet official HTML features that are already available on a limited number of browsers.

This book is a guide to authoring HTML documents and should not be considered the definitive reference to HTML. For comprehensive details, look at the Internet Engineering Task Force (IETF) documents listed in the "References" section at the end of this chapter.

ALLOWED CHARACTERS IN HTML DOCUMENTS

As illustrated in Chapter 1, an HTML document is just a text document and can be created and edited with any text editor. An HTML document can contain any of the valid printable characters from the 8-bit ISO Latin-1 character set (also known as ISO 8859/1—see Appendix A). The 256 characters of the ISO Latin-1 character set consist of the 128 characters of the 7-bit US-ASCII character set (ISO 646), plus 128 additional characters that use the eighth bit. This extra set of 128 contains many of the accented and other characters commonly used in western European languages.

With most keyboards, it is difficult to type these non-ASCII characters. Partly for this reason, HTML has mechanisms for representing these characters using only 7-bit ASCII characters. These are called *character references* and *entity references*. For example, the character reference for the character "é" is é (the semicolon is necessary and terminates the special reference), while the entity reference for this same character is é. This mechanism is also useful for sending HTML documents by electronic mail, since many electronic mail programs mishandle 8-bit characters. However, transferring HTML documents containing 8-bit characters is not a problem with hypertext servers, since the HTTP access protocol always allows 8-bit transfers and the browsers all understand that the character set is ISO Latin-1.

In addition, some computers, such as a Macintosh or a PC running DOS, do not use the ISO Latin-1 character set for their internal representation of characters (Microsoft Windows does use the ISO Latin-1 set); instead, they use a proprietary mapping between the binary codes and the characters they represent. Fortunately, this affects only the 128 non-ASCII characters so that restricting yourself to ASCII characters ensures an HTML document, while the character and entity reference mechanisms allow you to include characters from the full ISO Latin-1 character set.

Character sets are discussed in more detail in Appendix A. Figure A.1 shows the use of HTML entity references in an HTML document—this document, as displayed by a browser, is shown in Figure A.2.

SPECIAL CHARACTERS

Certain ASCII characters are treated as special in an HTML document. For example: The ampersand character (&) is used to indicate an entity or character reference; the left and right angle brackets (< >) are used to denote the markup tags; and the double quotation mark (") is used to mark literal strings within the markup tags. Since these characters are interpreted in a special manner, they cannot be used as normal characters—the parser will always try to interpret them in a special way. If you want these characters to appear in your text but don't want them to be interpreted as commands, you must include them as character or entity references. The special character and entity references for these four characters are outlined in Table 2.1.

■■■■■■■**Table 2.1** Special Characters in HTML

Character	Character Reference	Entity Reference
Left angle bracket (<)	&#60;	&lt;
Right angle bracket (>)	&#62;	&gt;
Ampersand sign (&)	&#38;	&amp;
Double quotation sign (")	&#34;	&quot;

When a browser parses an HTML file, it looks for the special characters and interprets them accordingly. Thus, when it encounters the string:

```
<H1> Heading string </H1>
```

it interprets the strings in the angle brackets as markup tags and renders the enclosed string as a heading. However, when the parser encounters a string like:

```
&lt;H1&gt; Heading string &lt;/H1&gt;
```

it interprets the < and > as entity references, and produces the string

```
<H1> Heading string </H1>
```

COMMENTS IN HTML DOCUMENTS

Comments are denoted by the special character strings `<!--` and `-->`. The first string starts a comment, while the second ends it; anything between the two is a comment and is ignored. Comments are not displayed by the browser, even if they occur in the **BODY** of a document. There can be spaces between the `--` and the `>` that end a comment, but the string `<!--` that starts a comment must be present without any spaces between the characters.

Comments can span more than one line, but cannot nest or overlap. However, some browsers mishandle comments that span more than one line, so, for safety, you should include comment strings around every line you wish to *comment out*. You should also not use this mechanism to comment out HTML code that would otherwise be displayed, because some browsers mistakenly use the greater than sign (>) in regular HTML markup tags to prematurely terminate the comment.

Here are some examples of comments:

```
<!--    This is a comment -->

<!--    This is also a comment

This comment spans more than one line. Note that many browsers improperly
interpret comments that span multiple lines, so this usage should be
avoided.

    -->
```

HTML AS A MIME TYPE

Finally, we note that HTML is proposed as a MIME content type. MIME, for Multipart Independent Mail Extensions, is a scheme originally designed for sending mixed media mail messages (containing pictures, text, and other formats) using the standard electronic mail protocol. The MIME scheme uses MIME *content-type* headers to define the content of each different type of data being sent. In the World Wide Web, MIME types are used by the HTTP protocol to communicate the *type* of a document being served. When an HTTP server sends a file to a client, it includes, as a header to the data, a MIME content-type header indicating the type of data being sent. For example, a JPEG format image file being sent from a server to a client would have the message string:

```
Content-Type: image/jpeg
```

as part of the HTTP header that precedes the actual data.

HTTP servers treat HTML documents as just another MIME type. When an HTML document is served, it is preceded by the header:

```
Content-Type: text/html
```

which tells the browser that the document is HTML, and not just plain text. HTTP and MIME types are discussed in more detail in Chapter 4 and in Appendix B.

HTML ELEMENTS AND MARKUP TAGS

The overall structure of the HTML was covered in Chapter 1. The following is a review of the basic concepts, using the HTML document in Figures 2.1 and 2.2 as a simple example.

An HTML document is simply a text file in which certain strings of characters, called *tags*, mark regions of the document and assign special meanings to them. In the jargon of SGML, these regions are called *elements*. The tags are strings of characters surrounded by the less than (<) and greater than (>) signs. For example:

```
<H1>
```

is the *start tag* for an **H1** (a heading) element, while

```
</H1>
```

is the *end tag* for a title element. The entire **H1** element is then the string:

```
<H1> Environmental Change Project </H1>
```

Most elements are like this example and mark regions of the document into blocks of text, which, in turn, may contain other elements containing other blocks of text, and so on. You can think of a document as a hierarchy of these elements, with the complete hierarchy defining the entire document. Elements that mark blocks of text are often called *containers*. Some elements do not have any contents and are called *empty* elements. The **IMG** element (which inserts an inline image into a document) or the **HR** element (which draws a horizontal dividing line across the screen) are examples of empty elements that do not affect a block of text.

Each element has a name, which appears inside the tags and which is related to what the element means. For example, the **H1** element is used to mark a level-1 heading. Elements may also have *attributes*, which are quantities that specify properties for that particular element. For example, the **A** (hypertext anchor) element can take the **HREF** attribute, which specifies the target of a hypertext link. Most attributes, like **HREF,** are assigned *values*. For example, **HREF** is assigned the URL of the target document for a hypertext link, as in:

```
<A HREF="http://who.zoo.do/Ozone.html"> Ozone </A> layer
```

Attributes are often optional, in which case, they can be left out.

In some cases, the end tag is optional. This is the case when the end of an element can be unambiguously determined from the surrounding elements. As an example, look at the **LI** element in Figure 2.1. This element defines a single list item inside the **UL** unordered list element and does not require a `</LI>` end tag, even though the element is not empty. This is because the end of a given list item is implied by the next `<LI>` start tag or by the `</UL>` end tag ending the list.

```
<HTML>

<HEAD>

<TITLE> Environmental Change Project </TITLE>

<NEXTID N=33>

</HEAD>

<BODY>

<h1> Environmental Change Project </h1>

<p> Welcome to the home page of the Environmental Change Project.

This project is different from other projects with similar names. In our case
we actually wish to change the climate. For example, we would like hot beaches
in Northern Quebec, and deserts near Chicago.

<p> So how will we do this. Well we do the following

<ul>

<li> <A HREF="burn.html">Burn </A> more forests.

<li> Destroy the <A HREF="http://who.zoo.do/ozone.html">Ozone</A> layer.

<li> Breed more <A HREF="ftp://foo.do.do/cows.gif">cows</a> (for extra

   greenhouse gas).

</ul>

</BODY>
</HTML>
```

Figure 2.1 An example of a simple HTML document.

CASE-SENSITIVITY

The element and attribute names inside the markup tags are case-*insensitive*. Thus, in the above examples, the strings <H1> and <h1>, or

```
<A HREF="http://who.zoo.do/Ozone.html ">
```

and

```
<a hrEF="http://who.zoo.do/Ozone.html ">
```

are equivalent. Element and attribute names are often written in uppercase to make the document easier to read.

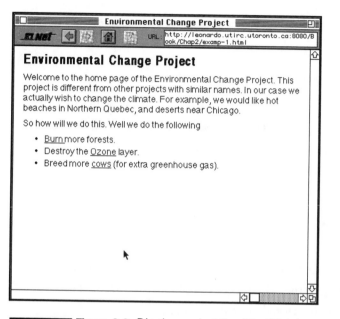

URL: http://leonardo.utirc.utoronto.ca:8080/Book/Chap2/examp-1.html

Environmental Change Project

Welcome to the home page of the Environmental Change Project. This project is different from other projects with similar names. In our case we actually wish to change the climate. For example, we would like hot beaches in Northern Quebec, and deserts near Chicago.

So how will we do this. Well we do the following

- Burn more forests.
- Destroy the Ozone layer.
- Breed more cows (for extra greenhouse gas).

Figure 2.2 Display, using the **MacWeb** browser, of the document listed in Figure 2.1.

Attribute *values*, on the other hand, are often case-*sensitive*. An obvious example is the URL string assigned to the **HREF** attribute. A URL can contain both directory and filename information. Many computers allow both upper- and lowercase characters in file and directory names, so it is crucial that case be preserved. This is accomplished by enclosing the attribute argument in double quotes, as done in the preceding examples and in Figure 2.1. If quotes are omitted, the value may be promoted to uppercase when intepreted by a browser. Some attribute values are case-insensitive, in which case, quotation marks can be omitted.

EMPTY ELEMENTS

Some elements are considered *empty* and do not require end tags, such as the **IMG** and **HR** and **BR** (line break) elements. Formally, you can include end tags to match the start tags, provided you do not place any text between the two tags. In practice, however, several browsers do not function properly when you include end tags for empty elements, so this usage is discouraged.

ELEMENT NESTING

Elements are always *nested*, with this nesting reflecting the structure of the document (for example, emphasized text inside a paragraph inside a form inside the **BODY**). However, elements can *never* overlap. Thus, the structure

```
<A HREF=....> <EM> Burn </EM> </A> more forests
```

is valid HTML markup, while

```
<A HREF=....> <EM> Burn  </A> </EM> more forests
```

is not. In addition, all elements impose restrictions on what can be nested inside them, and on where they themselves can be nested. Details of allowed nestings will be presented later in this chapter.

Some browsers will let you get away with nesting errors so that such errors are often hard to spot. If you are lucky (or unlucky), you will get mail from someone who is wondering why he or she cannot properly view your document.

UNKNOWN ELEMENTS OR ATTRIBUTES

What does a browser do if it encounters tags or attributes within a tag that it does not understand? The HTML specification states that the browser should ignore these tags or attributes. Thus, if a browser does not understand the underline element U, it will take the string

```
<U> text stuff </U>
```

and display it as regular text, without the underline.

OVERALL DOCUMENT STRUCTURE

Every HTML document can be divided into two main parts: the *body*, which contains the part of the document to be displayed by a browser; and the *head*, which contains information about the document but which is not displayed with it. These parts are defined by the **BODY** and **HEAD** elements, respectively. The resulting overall structure of an HTML document should then be:

```
<HTML>
    <HEAD>
        .... elements valid in the document HEAD
    </HEAD>
    <BODY>
        .... elements valid in the document BODY
    </BODY>
</HTML>
```

Note how Figure 2.1 follows this outline. The outer **HTML** element declares the enclosed text to be an HTML document. Directly inside this lies the **HEAD** and the **BODY**. The **BODY** contains the text and associated HTML markup instructions of the material you want displayed. The **HEAD** contains elements that define information *about* the document, such as its title or logical relationships with other documents. Certain elements can appear only in the **HEAD**, while others can appear only in the **BODY**. These elements and the overall structure of the **BODY** and **HEAD** are the focus of the remainder of this chapter.

HYPERTEXT MARKUP LANGUAGE
SPECIFICATION: ELEMENT BY ELEMENT

This section contains a list of each HTML element, a description of the purpose of the element, a list of where the element can go, as well as examples of its use. This element list primarily describes elements from the HTML2.0 specification. Within this specification, there are several attributes that are marked as *proposed*. These are included here, but are marked as proposed to point out their special status; they are less likely to be understood by browsers, so you should be cautious in their use.

Much work is underway on extension and revisions to the HTML—these efforts fall under the rubric HTML+. The HTML+ effort has defined elements for tabular data, sub- and superscripts, margin notes, and so on that will add important functionality to HTML documents. Indeed, several (but not all) browsers already implement some of these HTML+ features. This section mentions these more popular HTML+ elements and attributes, but marks them as HTML+ contributions to denote their experimental nature. In general, if you want your documents to be viewable by a wide audience, do not use these HTML+ elements, or provide alternate HTML documents for those people who are unable to view your more sophisticated creations.

KEY TO THIS SECTION

Because HTML is a hierarchical language, is it important to know not only how to use an element, but also where it can be used. This information is given in the four lines at the beginning of the description of each element. The general format looks like the following:

Usage:	`<NAME> ... </NAME>`
Can Contain:	**element list**
Can Be Inside:	**element list**
Attributes:	**attribute list**

Here is an example, using the **LI** list item element:

LI ELEMENT: LIST ITEM

Usage: `<LI> ... (</LI>)`

Can Contain: **characters, character highlighting, A, BR, IMG, DIR, DL, MENU, OL, UL, BLOCKQUOTE, FORM, P, PRE, [ISINDEX]**

Can Be Inside: **DIR, MENU, UL, OL**

Attributes: (**SRC**: proposed HTML+)

These four fields define the rules for using the different elements. The meanings of the four fields are:

Usage:
Shows how the element is used. An end tag indicates that an element is a container (the *Can Contain* field states what can go inside the element). If the end tag is surrounded by round brackets, then it is optional. If no end tag is given, then the element is empty.

Can Contain:
This field indicates what elements can go inside this element. The string **"characters"** indicates elements that can contain text. If the element is empty, the word "empty" appears here. In several places, the **ISINDEX** name appears enclosed by square brackets. This indicates that the element is allowed but that it should more appropriately appear in the **HEAD**.

| Can Be Inside: | Indicates inside which elements this element can be placed. The preceding example indicates that the **LI** element can be inside a **DIR**, **MENU, OL,** or **UL** element. |
| Attributes: | This lists the names of the attributes that can be taken by the element. The word "none" means that the element takes no attributes. Elements that are proposed as part of the HTML2.0 specifications or as part of HTML+ are so indicated. |

The following short forms are used in the Can Contain and Can Be Inside fields:

Hn:	The six heading elements **H1, H2, H3, H4, H5,** and **H6.**
characters:	Any valid ISO Latin-1 character, character reference, or entity reference.
character highlighting:	**CITE, CODE, DFN** (proposed HTML2.0), **EM, KBD, SAMP, STRIKE** (proposed HTML2.0), **STRONG, VAR, B, I, TT,** and U (proposed HTML2.0).

These are the physical highlighting elements (italics, boldface, etc.) and also the logical highlighting elements that assign to text strings logical meanings that are generally interpreted as changes in text formatting.

The following sections are organized hierarchically. Thus, the first section describes the **HTML** element that contains the entire document. The next section describes the **HEAD** element, and this is followed by descriptions of the elements that can lie inside the **HEAD**. Following this is a description of the **BODY** element, followed by sections describing the elements that go inside the **BODY**.

▬▬▬▬▬▬▬▬▬▬▬▬▬▬▬▬▬▬

HTML ELEMENT: THE HTML DOCUMENT

Usage: <HTML> . . . </HTML>

Can Contain: **HEAD, BODY**

Can Be Inside: nothing

Attributes: none

▬▬▬▬▬▬▬▬▬▬▬▬▬▬▬▬▬▬

The **HTML** element declares the enclosed text to be an HTML document. It may directly contain only two elements: **HEAD** and **BODY**. Although formally optional, you should always include an **HTML** element in new documents.

Example of **HTML**:

```
<HTML>
    <HEAD>
... head content....
    </HEAD>
    <BODY>
... body content....
    </BODY>
</HTML>
```

HEAD ELEMENTS

HEAD Element: Document Meta-information

Usage: `<HEAD> ... </HEAD>`

Can Contain: **TITLE, ISINDEX, BASE, NEXTID, LINK, META**

Can Be Inside: **HTML**

Attributes: none

HEAD contains general information about the document. The information found in the head is not displayed as part of the document text; consequently, only certain elements are appropriate within the **HEAD**. All the head elements are empty, except for **TITLE**, and they can appear in the **HEAD** in any order. The only mandatory **HEAD** element is **TITLE**; all others are optional. The possible **HEAD** elements are, in decreasing level of importance:

TITLE   The title of the document.

ISINDEX   Indicates the document is searchable.

BASE   A record of the original URL of the document.

NEXTID   Used by automated HTML editors to create unique document identifiers.

LINK   Defines a relationship between the document and another document.

META   Used for embedding, within the **HEAD**, information about the document that cannot be expressed in the preceding elements.

You are most likely to see and use the **TITLE, ISINDEX,** and **BASE** elements. The **NEXTID** element is designed for use by special HTML editing tools. The **LINK** element is not widely supported. The **META** element is new to HTML2.0 and is also not widely supported.

The division between the **HEAD** and the **BODY** is important, as there will soon be ways to access just the information in the **HEAD**. This will be much faster than accessing the entire document and extremely useful for generating catalogs or indexes.

BASE ELEMENT: BASE URL

Usage:	<BASE>
Can Contain:	empty
Can Be Inside:	**HEAD**
Attributes	**HREF**

BASE is an empty element and is optional. If present, **BASE** has a single, mandatory attribute, **HREF**, which is assigned the *base URL* of the document. The base URL indicates where a document was originally located. This is useful if a document is moved away from its original URL and related documents, in which case, relative URLs used to reference these neighboring documents are no longer valid. However, if the original URL address is specified in the **BASE** element, then relative URLs from this document are evaluated relative to this *base* URL and will be correctly found.

If the BASE element is absent, the browser assumes the base URL to be that used to access the document, and determines relative URLs with respect to this location. You should note that many browsers, such as **MacWeb** and **lynx,** do not support the **BASE** tag.

Example of **BASE**:

If a document was originally found at the URL:

```
http://somewhere.org/Dir/Subdir/file.html
```

the appropriate **BASE** element is then:

```
<HEAD>
.
<BASE HREF="http://somewhere.org/Dir/Subdir/file.html">
</HEAD>
```

ISINDEX ELEMENT: SEARCHABLE DOCUMENT

Usage: `<ISINDEX>`

Can Contain: empty

Can Be Inside: **HEAD [BODY, BLOCKQUOTE, FORM, LI, DD]**

Attributes: none

ISINDEX is an empty element and is optional. Because there are many older documents that have the **ISINDEX** declaration in the **BODY**, the HTML definition still allows this form. New documents should place **ISINDEX** in the **HEAD**. This element informs the browser program that the document can be examined using a keyword search, and that the browser should query the user for a search or query string.

ISINDEX does *not* mean a search of the text you are reading. Documents containing **ISINDEX** elements are usually sent to the client from server-side gateway programs designed for database searches. You can think of such a document as a *front end* to a gateway program, and the *document* you search as the database *represented* by the document you see.

When you submit the search, the keywords are sent from the client to the server by appending them to the document URL. This mechanism is discussed in the URL portions of Chapters 3 and 4.

Example of **ISINDEX**:

```
<HEAD>
<ISINDEX>
   .
   .
</HEAD>
<BODY>
   .
body of document
   .
</BODY>
```

LINK ELEMENT: RELATIONSHIP TO OTHER DOCUMENTS

Usage:	`<LINK>`
Can Contain:	empty
Can Be Inside:	**HEAD**
Attributes:	Same as **A** (anchor) element:
	HREF, METHODS, NAME, TITLE, URN, (REL, REV: proposed HTML2.0), **(ID, EFFECT, PRINT, TYPE, SIZE, SHAPE**: proposed HTML+)

The **LINK** element describes a relationship between the document and other documents or objects. For example, you might use **LINK** to indicate a related index, a glossary, or perhaps different versions of the same document. Alternatively, you could use it to point to likely *next* or *previous* documents. This could be used by a browser to predict and preload documents it is likely to need (although at present there are no browsers that do this). A document may have any number of **LINK** elements to represent these various relationships to other documents.

LINK is an empty element, and is optional. **LINK** takes the same attributes as the anchor (**A**) element; these are discussed in detail in the anchor element section.

Example of **LINK**:

```
<HEAD>
<LINK HREF="file1.html" TITLE="Title of Related Document" >
</HEAD>
```

LINK is, as yet, rarely used and is largely unsupported.

META ELEMENT: DOCUMENT META-INFORMATION

Usage:	<META>
Can Contain:	empty
Can Be Inside:	**HEAD**
Attributes:	**HTTP-EQUIV, NAME, CONTENT**

The **META** element provides a place to put meta-information that is not defined by the other **HEAD** elements. This allows you to more richly describe the document content for indexing and cataloging purposes, as illustrated in the following. You should not, however, use this as a substitute for the other **HEAD** elements.

The **META** element is optional. If present, it must take the **CONTENT** attribute and one of the **NAME** or **HTTP-EQUIV** attributes (but not both). The meanings of the attributes are:

NAME="name"—This specifies the meta-information name. The client (browser or other program) must understand what this name means.

HTTP-EQUIV="string"—This can be used instead of the NAME attribute. META elements with HTTP-EQUIV attributes are parsed by the HTTP server and are converted into HTTP *response headers*.

CONTENT="string" (mandatory)—This assigns the *content* associated with the META element.

An example using the NAME attribute is:

```
<META NAME="DocumentBranch" CONTENT="Volume1_Branch_4X3">
```

This might tell the client that the document is a derivative in some defined way of Volume 1 of a master text. The client or indexing program that is accessing the HEAD of this document must consequently understand the meanings behind these names and their content.

The attribute HTTP-EQUIV allows the document to pass information to the server delivering the document. An example is:

```
<META HTTP-EQUIV="Last-Modified" CONTENT="23-Sep-94 18:28:33 GMT">
```

By this element, the document is asking the server to take the CONTENT (the string "23-Sep-94 18:28:33 GMT") and include this information as part of the Last-Modified header field that is sent with the HTTP *response header* that precedes the document during an HTTP transaction. (The HTTP protocol and HTTP response headers are discussed in Chapter 4.) HTTP response headers contain information about the document and server, such as the type of data being sent from the server, the date it is being sent, the type of server being used, and so on. The response headers can also contain more descriptive information about the document, comparable to the information found in the document HEAD.

Most servers do not currently parse documents for META or other elements.

NEXTID ELEMENT: COUNTER FOR AUTOMATED EDITORS

Usage: `<NEXTID>`

Can Contain: empty

Can Be Inside: **HEAD**

Attributes: **N**

NEXTID is an empty element and is optional. It is used by HTML editing programs to uniquely identify documents created in the editing process—it is not designed for use by mere humans, by WWW browsers, or by hypertext servers.

NEXTID has a single mandatory attribute **N** that specifies a numeric identifier for the document. Since the numbers should uniquely identify documents, an HTML editor should never reuse old identity numbers.

Example of **NEXTID**:

```
<HEAD>
<NEXTID N=132>

  .

  .

</HEAD>
```

TITLE ELEMENT: DOCUMENT TITLE

Usage: `<TITLE> ... </TITLE>`

Can Contain: **characters**

Can Be Inside: **HEAD**

Attributes: none

The title of a document is specified by the **TITLE** element. Every document must have a **TITLE** and can have only one. The **TITLE** should indicate the document content in a concise and general way. It serves several purposes:

- To label the display window or text screen
- To serve as a record in a history list marking documents you have viewed
- To allow quick indexing of a document, in place of indexing the entire text

The **TITLE** is not part of the document text and cannot contain hypertext links or any other markup commands—it can contain only text, including entity or character references.

The **TITLE** should be short so that it can easily label a window or fit in a history list—preferably less than 60 or so characters. You should also be able to determine the content of the document from the **TITLE** itself. Otherwise, a person reviewing their history will see the **TITLE** but not know to what it refers. Here are some examples:

Good **TITLE**s:

```
<TITLE>Paper on Rings by Baggins and Gandalf, 1989 </TITLE>

<TITLE>Introduction to MIME types </TITLE>
```

Bad **TITLE**s:

```
<TITLE>Introduction</TITLE>

<TITLE>A Summary of the Ring-Ring Interaction Cross-Section Measurement of B.
Baggins, et al. in both Low-Temperature and High-Temperature Studies, including
Water Immersion and Non-Destructive Testing: A Brief Review plus Commentary on
the "Missing Ring" Problem.</TITLE>
```

BODY ELEMENTS

BODY Element: The Displayed Text Body

Usage:	<BODY> ... </BODY>
Can Contain:	Hn, P, HR, DIR, DL, MENU, OL, UL, ADDRESS, BLOCKQUOTE, FORM, PRE, [ISINDEX]
Can Be Inside:	HTML
Attributes:	none

The **BODY** contains the document proper, as opposed to the information about the document found in the **HEAD**. Formally, the **BODY** cannot directly contain text. Instead, it must contain elements that themselves contain the text, because the **BODY** element states only "this is the body of the document" and supplies no additional meaning to its contents. It is the job of the other elements nested within the **BODY** to organize the text and assign it meaning. This is accomplished by the elements that define headings, lists, addresses, paragraphs, and so on.

The contents of the **HEAD** and **BODY** are exclusive—elements that belong inside the **HEAD** cannot go inside the **BODY**, and vice versa.

ADDRESS Element: Provide Address Information

Usage:	<ADDRESS> ... </ADDRESS>
Can Contain:	characters, character highlighting, A, BR, IMG
Can Be Inside:	BLOCKQUOTE, BODY, FORM
Attributes:	none

The **ADDRESS** element is used to mark out information, such as addresses, electronic signatures, lists of authors, and so on. Typically, a document author will use the **ADDRESS** to sign his or her documents. In this case, the **ADDRESS** is often placed at the bottom of the HTML document to keep it separate from the main text. In a family of documents, the **ADDRESS** may contain just the author's initials connected by a hypertext link to a biographical page. Alternatively, a collection of documents may have an introductory document that has **ADDRESS** elements containing detailed contact information for the author or authors, with the remaining documents having **ADDRESS** elements containing hypertext links back to this page.

The rendering of the contents of the **ADDRESS** is left up to the browser. For example, **Mosaic** usually renders the **ADDRESS** in italics. It may also be right-justified (as with **Cello**) or indented.

Figures 2.3 and 2.5 show some typical applications of the **ADDRESS** element. Browser renderings of these documents are shown in Figures 2.4 and 2.6 respectively.

BLOCKQUOTE Element: Block Quotations

Usage:	`<BLOCKQUOTE> ... </BLOCKQUOTE>`
Can Contain:	**Hn, P, HR, DIR, DL, MENU, OL, UL, ADDRESS, BLOCKQUOTE, FORM, PRE, [ISINDEX]**
Can Be Inside:	**BLOCKQUOTE, BODY, DD, FORM, LI**
Attributes:	none

The **BLOCKQUOTE** element is used to mark a block of text as a quotation. Browsers can render this in various ways; for example, by indenting and/or italicizing the **BLOCKQUOTE** contents, and by offsetting it from the preceding and following text. A **BLOCKQUOTE** also causes a paragraph break.

■■■■■■

```
<html>
<head>
<title> Examples of ADDRESS and BLOCKQUOTE elements</title>
</head>

<body>

<h1> Example 2: The Meaning of Life </h1>

<p> How many times have you sat down and asked yourself <quote>
What is the meaning of life? </quote>.  I certainly have.  I've
even read many of the good books, from C.S. Lewis, to Kant, to
Sartre to Zoltan the Magnificent.  But I think the most profound
statement about life was made by Jack Handley, who said:

<BLOCKQUOTE>
I can still recall old Mister Barnslow getting out every morning and
nailing a fresh load of tadpoles to that old board of his.  Then he'd
spin it around and around, like a wheel of fortune, and no matter where
it stopped he'd yell out, "Tadpoles!  Tadpoles is a winner!"
We all thought he was crazy.  But then, we had some growing up to do.
</BLOCKQUOTE>

That pretty well sums it up.

<HR>
<ADDRESS>  <A HREF="about_the_author.html"> C.S.O </A> </ADDRESS>

</body>
</html>
```

■■■■■■ **Figure 2.3** HTML example document illustrating headings, **BLOCKQUOTE,** and **ADDRESS** elements. Figure 2.4 shows this document viewed by **Cello**.

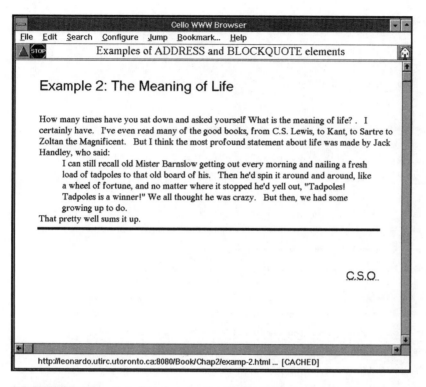

Figure 2.4 Display, by the **Cello** browser, of the document shown in Figure 2.3.

Note that the definition does not allow text directly inside a **BLOCK-QUOTE**; instead, the text must lie inside other elements lying inside the BLOCKQUOTE. Thus, the form:

```
<BLOCKQUOTE>
<P> This is the quotation. ...
..
</BLOCKQUOTE>
```

is correct, while the form:

```
<BLOCKQUOTE>
This is the quotation. ...
..
</BLOCKQUOTE>
```

is not. A typical **BLOCKQUOTE** is shown in Figures 2.3 and 2.4.

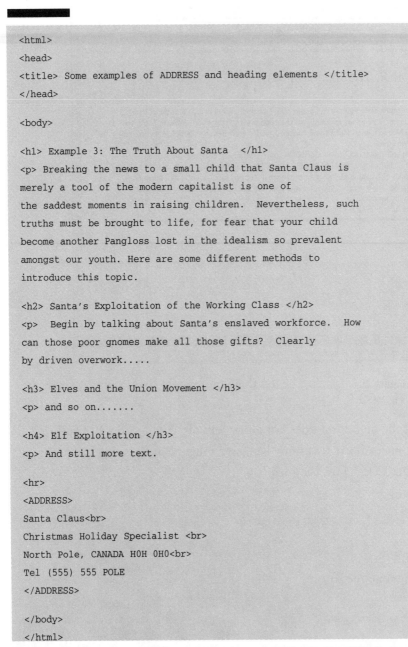

```
<html>
<head>
<title> Some examples of ADDRESS and heading elements </title>
</head>

<body>

<h1> Example 3: The Truth About Santa  </h1>
<p> Breaking the news to a small child that Santa Claus is
merely a tool of the modern capitalist is one of
the saddest moments in raising children.  Nevertheless, such
truths must be brought to life, for fear that your child
become another Pangloss lost in the idealism so prevalent
amongst our youth. Here are some different methods to
introduce this topic.

<h2> Santa's Exploitation of the Working Class </h2>
<p>  Begin by talking about Santa's enslaved workforce.  How
can those poor gnomes make all those gifts?  Clearly
by driven overwork.....

<h3> Elves and the Union Movement </h3>
<p> and so on.......

<h4> Elf Exploitation </h3>
<p> And still more text.

<hr>
<ADDRESS>
Santa Claus<br>
Christmas Holiday Specialist <br>
North Pole, CANADA H0H 0H0<br>
Tel (555) 555 POLE
</ADDRESS>

</body>
</html>
```

■■■■■■■ **Figure 2.5** HTML example document illustrating **TITLE**, heading, and **ADDRESS** elements. Figure 2.6 shows this document viewed by **WinMosaic**.

Figure 2.6 Display, by the **WinMosaic** browser, of the document shown in Figure 2.5.

FORM ELEMENT: FILL-IN FORMS

Usage:	`<FORM> ... </FORM>`
Can Contain:	**INPUT, SELECT, TEXTAREA, Hn, P, HR, DIR, DL, MENU, OL, UL, ADDRESS, BLOCKQUOTE, PRE, [ISINDEX]**
Can Be Inside:	**BLOCKQUOTE, BODY, DD, LI**
Attributes:	**ACTION, ENCTYPE, METHOD**

The **FORM** element marks out the content of an HTML *fill-in form*. This is the element you use to create fill-in forms with checkboxes, radio boxes, text input windows, and buttons. Data from a **FORM** must be sent to server-side gateway programs for processing; recall that **FORM** collects data, but does not process it. In general, a **FORM** and the server-side program handling the **FORM** output must be designed together so that the program understands the data being sent from the **FORM**. Some simple examples showing the variety of possible **FORM**s are shown in Figures 2.7 through 2.10.

The **FORM** element takes three attributes. These determine where the **FORM** input data is to be sent; what HTTP protocol to use when sending the data; and the data type of the content (as a MIME content-type). Note that **FORM**s do not nest—you *cannot* have a **FORM** within a **FORM**.

The attributes are:

ACTION= "*URL*" (mandatory)—The **ACTION** specifies the URL to which the **FORM** content is to be sent. Usually this is a URL pointing to a program on an HTTP server, since only HTTP servers allow significant interaction from the client to the server. However, the **ACTION** can specify other URLs. For example, in the case of a **mailto** URL, the **FORM** content would be mailed to the indicated address.

METHOD= "GET" or "POST" (optional)—When the **ACTION** indicates an **http** URL, the **METHOD** gives the HTTP *method* for sending information to the server. HTTP methods are discussed in Chapter 4. The default value for **ACTION** is GET. With GET, the content of the form is appended to the URL in a manner identical to query data from an **ISINDEX** search. With the POST method, the form content is sent to the server as a message, and not as part of the URL.

ENCTYPE= "*MIME Type*" (optional)—ENCTYPE specifies the MIME-type of data sent, using the POST method. The default value is application/x-www-form-urlencoded. At present, this is the only allowed value.

INPUT Element: Text Boxes, Checkboxes, and Radio Buttons

Usage:	`<INPUT>`
Can Contain:	empty
Can Be Inside:	**FORM**, any nonempty element allowed inside a **FORM**
Attributes:	**ALIGN, CHECKED, NAME, MAXLENGTH, SIZE, SRC, TYPE, VALUE**

The **INPUT** element specifies a variety of *editable fields* inside a form. It takes several attributes that define the type of input mechanism (text field, buttons, checkboxes, etc.), the *variable name* associated with the input data, and the alignment and size of the input element when displayed. Although the **INPUT** element can appear only inside a **FORM** element, **BLOCKQUOTE, P,** and list elements can also be inside a **FORM** and can be used to organize the **INPUT** elements into lists or paragraphs. Some examples of the **INPUT** element, and the organization allowed by these other elements, are shown in Figures 2.7 through 2.10.

The most important attribute to the **INPUT** element is **NAME**, which assigns a *variable name* to the *value* entered into the element. The data entered into a **FORM** are sent to the server as a collection of *name/value* pairs. The program parsing the **FORM** data uses the variable *name* to interpret the contents of the corresponding *value* and must therefore understand the different *names*. This is why a **FORM** and the gateway program that handles the **FORM** data must be designed together.

The other main attribute is **TYPE**, which selects the type of the **INPUT** element. There are several other attributes, but their usage and relevance depends on the **TYPE**.

The attributes are:

NAME = "*name*" (mandatory)—This assigns the variable name "*name*" to the data contents of this **INPUT** element.

TYPE = "checkbox", "hidden", "image", "radio", "reset", "submit", "text" (mandatory):

> "*checkbox*"—*Checkbox* **INPUT** elements are Boolean (*on/off*) quantities; the default value is *off* (this can be modified with the **CHECKED** attribute). The **VALUE** attribute sets the *value* assigned to an *on* checkbox. When you submit a **FORM**, the *name/value* pair is sent only if the checkbox is *on*.

> Different checkboxes may associate different *values* with the same variable *name*. This is convenient, for example, if you have six different databases to search and want to allow the user to select one, two, or all of them. When the **FORM** is submitted, the browser sends all the *values* from the *on* checkboxes yielding several *name/value* pairs with the same *name*. An example is shown in Figure 2.7.

> "*hidden*"—This **INPUT** element is not displayed by the browser and is hence *hidden* from the user. The contents of a "*hidden*" element, set with the **VALUE** attribute, are always sent to the server when the **FORM** is submitted. This is useful for passing information back and forth between the client and server, and is typically used to record the *state* of the client-server interaction. Recall that the HTTP protocol is stateless so that, without such passed information, the gateway program handling the **FORM** data has no record of any past interaction. Typically, a "*hidden*" **INPUT** element is placed in a **FORM** by a server-side gateway program that assembles the **FORM**. This point is discussed in more detail in Chapter 4.

> "*image*"—This **INPUT** element is an active inline image (analogous to the ISMAP attribute of the **IMG** element). The **SRC** attribute specifies the URL of the image.

Clicking on the image immediately submits the **FORM** data, including the coordinates of the mouse pointer (measured in pixels from the upper left-hand corner of the image). The coordinates are sent in two *name/value* pairs. The *name* is created by taking the **NAME** attribute and appending the strings *.x* and *.y* to indicate the *x* or *y* coordinate. Thus, if the **NAME** was set to *"king"*, the coordinates are sent in the *name/value* pairs *king.x/x_coord* and *king.y/y_coord*.

"password"—This **INPUT** element is a single-line text field, but the text typed into the field is obscured by asterisks or by some other method. This is used for password entry. An example password field is shown in Figures 2.9 and 2.10.

"radio"—This **INPUT** element is a radio button. Radio buttons are linked together by assigning them the same **NAME**. By definition, radio buttons can select only one from among all possible values; therefore, when you turn *on* one radio button, any other button associated with the same **NAME** is turned *off*. Each radio button must have a value so that each **INPUT** element of **TYPE=**"*radio*" must have a **VALUE** attribute.

"reset"—This **INPUT** element is a reset button. When pressed, all the fields in the **FORM** are reset to the values given by their **VALUE** attributes.

```
<html>
<head>
<title> Examples of HTML FORMS </title>
</head>

<body>
```

```
<h1> Example 4:  Examples of FORMS</h1>
<p> sends search information to a script.

<FORM  ACTION="http://side.edu/cgi-bin/script">

    <p> Search string: <INPUT TYPE="text" NAME="search_string" SIZE=24>
    <p> Search Type:
          <SELECT NAME="search_type">
              <OPTION> Insensitive Substring
              <OPTION SELECTED> Exact Match
              <OPTION> Sensitive Substring
              <OPTION> Regular Expression
          </SELECT>
    <p> Search databases in:
     [<INPUT TYPE="checkbox" NAME="servers" VALUE="Canada" CHECKED>Canada]
     [<INPUT TYPE="checkbox" NAME="servers" VALUE="Russia">Russia]
     [<INPUT TYPE="checkbox" NAME="servers" VALUE="Sweden">Sweden]
     [<INPUT TYPE="checkbox" NAME="servers" VALUE="U.S.A.">U.S.A.]
     <em>(multiple items can be selected.)</em>
    <p> Niceness:
       <menu>
        <li> <INPUT TYPE="radio" NAME="niceness" VALUE="nicest" CHECKED >Nicest
        <li> <INPUT TYPE="radio" NAME="niceness" VALUE="nice" >    Nice
        <li> <INPUT TYPE="radio" NAME="niceness" VALUE="not nice"> Not Nice
        <li> <INPUT TYPE="radio" NAME="niceness" VALUE="nasty" >   Nasty
       </menu>
    <P> <INPUT TYPE="submit"> <INPUT TYPE=reset>.

</FORM>

<HR>
<ADDRESS>  Form by <A HREF="about_the_author.html"> I.S.G</A> </ADDRESS>

</body>
</html>
```

Figure 2.7 HTML example document illustrating several FORM **INPUT** elements and the **SELECT** element. Figure 2.8 shows this document as displayed by the **Mosaic for X-Windows** browser.

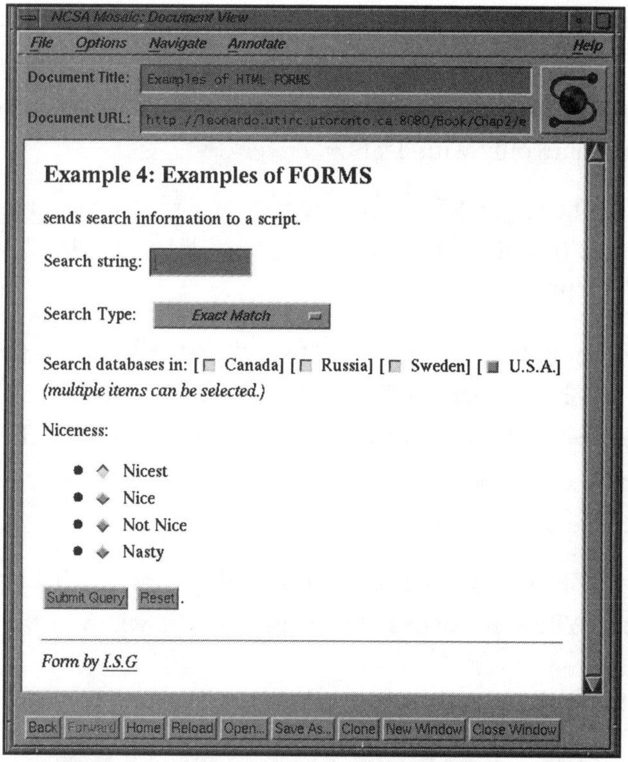

Figure 2.8 Display of the document shown in Figure 2.7 by the **Mosaic for X-Windows** browser.

"submit"—This **INPUT** element is a submit button. Pressing the submit button sends the **FORM** data to the specified URL. A form can have more than one such button, each with different **NAME** and **VALUE** attributes: The **FORM** sends only the *name/value* pair associated with the pressed submit button. The *value* is not editable by the client and is displayed as the button label.

Many browsers do not yet support multiple submit buttons with different *name/value* pairs.

"text"—This **INPUT** element is a single-line text entry field. The physically displayed size of the input field is set by the **SIZE** attribute.

ALIGN="*top*", "*middle*", "*bottom*" (optional)—**ALIGN** specifies the alignment of the image with respect to the surrounding text. The usage is equivalent to the **ALIGN** attribute to the **IMG** element (described later in this section). This is a valid attribute only with **TYPE=**"*image*".

CHECKED (optional)—The **CHECKED** attribute indicates that a checkbox or radio button is selected (turned *on*). This attribute is valid only with **TYPE=**"*checkbox*" or **TYPE=**"*radio.*"

MAXLENGTH="*n*" (optional)—**MAXLENGTH** specifies the length of the character buffer for a text box, where "*n*" is the buffer length. This is a valid attribute only with **TYPE=**"*text*" or **TYPE=**"*password.*" **MAXLENGTH** can be larger than the displayed text box, in which case, the arrow keys may be used to scroll the text. The default length is unlimited.

SIZE="*n*" (optional)—**SIZE** specifies the actual size of the displayed field. When **TYPE=**"*text*" or **TYPE=**"*password*" **SIZE** specifies the width of the input text box in characters.

SRC="*URL*" (mandatory with **TYPE=**"*image*")—**SRC** specifies the URL of the image to be included inline and is valid only with **TYPE=**"*image*".

VALUE="*value*" (mandatory with **TYPE=**"*radio*")—**VALUE** specifies the initial value of the input element.

Figures 2.7 through 2.10 give typical examples of **INPUT** element usage. **FORM**s are also discussed in Chapters 1 and 4.

SELECT ELEMENT: SELECT FROM AMONG MULTIPLE OPTIONS

Usage:	<SELECT> ... </SELECT>
Can Contain:	**OPTION**
Can be Inside:	**FORM**
Attributes:	**MULTIPLE, NAME, SIZE**

The **SELECT** element allows the user to select from amongst a set of values presented as a selectable list of text strings: The possible *values* are specified by the **OPTION** element. The attribute **MULTIPLE** allows multiple values to be selected; otherwise, only one value can be chosen. As with the **INPUT** elements, the selected data is sent to the server as one or more *name/value* pairs.

The attributes are:

MULTIPLE (optional)—If **MULTIPLE** is present, the **SELECT** element allows multiple items to be selected. If **MULTIPLE** is not present, you can select only a single item from the **SELECT** list.

NAME="*name*" (mandatory)—**NAME** specifies the variable name associated with the **SELECT** element.

SIZE="*n*" (optional)—**SIZE** specifies the number of displayed text lines. The default value is 1; consequently, the list is often presented as a pull-down menu. For other values, the list is usually presented as a scrollbox. If **MULTIPLE** is set, browsers choose a minimum **SIZE** greater than 1 and will not let you use **SIZE** to select a smaller value.

Figures 2.9 and 2.10 show typical examples of **SELECT** (and **OPTION**) elements.

OPTION ELEMENT: LIST OF OPTIONS FOR SELECT

Usage: `<OPTION> ... (</OPTION>)`

Can Contain: **characters**

Can Be Inside: **SELECT**

Attributes: **VALUE, SELECTED, (DISABLED: proposed HTML2.0)**

The **OPTION** element sets the different character-string options for a **SELECT** element. This element is not empty but the terminating `</OPTION>` is optional, as the element is by default terminated by the next `<OPTION>` tag or by the `</SELECT>` tag ending the list. **OPTION** can contain characters, character references, or entity references only; it cannot contain markup. The content of **OPTION** is used as the *value* unless a **VALUE** attribute is explicitly set.

The attributes are:

DISABLED (optional) (proposed HTML2.0)—**DISABLED** marks a particular **OPTION** as disabled—if displayed, it may be shown as grayed or faded.

SELECTED (optional)—This marks the **OPTION** as selected. If the **SELECT** element has the **MULTIPLE** attribute, more than one **OPTION** can be marked as **selected.** Figures 2.9 and 2.10 show examples.

VALUE= "*value*" (optional)—Specifies the *value* assigned to the **OPTION**. If absent, the content of **OPTION** is sent as the *value*.

TEXTAREA ELEMENT: INPUT A BLOCK OF TEXT

Usage:	`<TEXTAREA> ... </TEXTAREA>`
Can Contain:	**characters**
Can Be Inside:	**FORM**
Attributes:	**COLS, NAME, ROWS**

TEXTAREA allows the user to enter a block of text. The input block of text can grow to almost unlimited size, and is not limited by the size of the area displayed on the screen. Scrollbars are often present if the text area is bigger than the displayed region.

A **TEXTAREA** window displays characters in fixed-width fonts so that the attributes **COLS** and **ROWS** specify text area window sizes in character widths and heights. **TEXTAREA** can contain any printable characters.

The attributes are:

COLS="n" (mandatory)—**COLS** specifies the width of the **TEXTAREA** in columns.

NAME="$name$" (mandatory)—**NAME** specifies the variable name associated with the **TEXTAREA** contents.

ROWS="n" (mandatory)—**ROWS** specifies the height of the **TEXTAREA** in rows.

Text placed within a **TEXTAREA** is displayed as an initial value. Note that HTML markup tags are not valid here. A browser provides some way to edit the displayed text. Figures 2.9 and 2.10 show a typical example of a **TEXTAREA** element.

▰▰▰▰▰

```
<html>
<head>
<title> Examples of HTML FORMS </title>
</head>

<body>

<h1>Example 5: More Forms Examples</h1>
<p> This might send an abstract for registration to a selection
of databases.

<FORM  ACTION="http://side.edu/cgi-bin/submit_abstract">
   <h2> Please give name and password: </h2>
   <p> Name:      <INPUT TYPE="text"  NAME="userid" VALUE="guest" SIZE=20>
       Password: <INPUT TYPE="password" NAME="password" VALUE="bozo..." SIZE=8>
```

```
<hr>
<h2> Select Databases: </h2>
<p> Physics: <SELECT NAME="physics_database" MULTIPLE SIZE=3>
              <OPTION SELECTED> Condensed-Matter
              <OPTION> High Energy
              <OPTION> Solid-State
              <OPTION> Quantum Cosmology
              <OPTION> Astrophysics
              </SELECT>
   Chemistry: <SELECT NAME="chemistry_database" MULTIPLE SIZE=3>
              <OPTION> Surface Dynamics
              <OPTION> Quantum Chemistry
              <OPTION SELECTED> Polymer Dynamics
              <OPTION> Biochemistry
              <OPTION> Nuclear Chemistry
              </SELECT>
  <h2> Enter Abstract: </h2>
  <p> <TEXTAREA COLS=60 ROWS=4> If you are submitting an abstract, select
the desired databases from the above list, delete this text,
type (or paste) the abstract into this box and press the
"Deposit Abstract" button.
       </TEXTAREA>
  <P> <STRONG> Press </STRONG> <INPUT TYPE="submit" VALUE="Deposit Abstract">
      to deposit, or <INPUT TYPE=reset> to reset form.

</FORM>

<HR>
<ADDRESS>  Form by <A HREF="about_the_author.html"> I.S.G</A> </ADDRESS>

</body>
</html>
```

Figure 2.9 HTML example document illustrating FORM **INPUT**, **SELECT**, and **TEXTBOX** input elements. Figure 2.10 shows this document as displayed by the **Mosaic for X-Windows** browser.

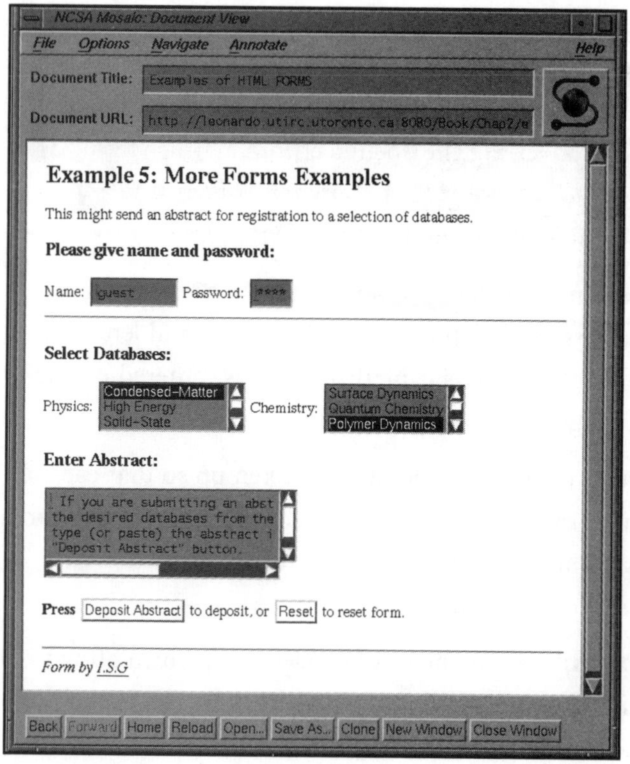

Figure 2.10 Display of the document shown in Figure 2.9 by the **Mosaic for X-Windows** browser.

Hn ELEMENTS: HEADINGS

Usage: `<Hn> ... </Hn>`

Can Contain: **characters, character highlighting, A, BR, IMG**

Can Be Inside: **BLOCKQUOTE, BODY, FORM**

Attributes: **(ID: proposed HTML+)**

HTML allows six levels of headings from **H1** through **H6**. There is no forced hierarchy in these headings, but for consistency you should use the top level (**H1**) for main headings, and lower levels for progressively less important ones. You should also avoid skipping a heading level within a given document, as this breaks the logical structure of the document and may cause problems when converting the document into another form, or if you want to automatically generate HTML Table of Contents documents. **Hn** elements have no attributes under the HTML2.0.

Current renderings of headings are very much browser-dependent. For example, **MacMosaic** renders **H1** headings with a large font and left-justified, while **lynx** renders **H1** headings as capitalized strings centered on the page. Some typical renderings are shown in Figures 2.2 through 2.24.

As a general rule, hypertext documents should be broken up so that each page does not occupy more than one or two browser screen areas. You can then use the **H1** heading to mark the main heading for the collection of documents, and the others to mark subheadings.

HTML+ proposes an **ID** attribute for the heading elements, which allows the heading to be the *named* destination of a hypertext link. The **ID** attribute is similar to the **NAME** attribute of the **A** (anchor) element. The **ID** attribute is optional.

Example:

```
<H1 ID="shops"> Surf Boarding Shops " </H1>
```

This labels the heading as the possible target of a hypertext link and is equivalent to:

```
<H1> <A NAME="shops"> Surf Boarding Shops " </A> </H1>
```

Some browsers, such as **emacs-w3**, support the **ID** attribute in headings but most do not.

HTML+ also proposes the **ALIGN** attribute, which suggests an alignment of the heading on the page. **ALIGN** can take three values: **ALIGN**="left", which left-justifies the heading, **ALIGN**="right", which right-justifies the heading, and **ALIGN**="center", which centers the heading. This attribute is currently supported by the **emacs-w3** and **Netscape** browsers.

HR ELEMENT: HORIZONTAL RULE

Usage: `<HR>`

Can Contain: empty

Can Be Inside: **BODY, BLOCKQUOTE, FORM**

Attributes: none

The **HR** element draws a horizontal line completely across the screen. An `<HR>` terminates any preceding paragraph, so a new paragraph mark should follow an `<HR>` if there is subsequent text. An `<HR>` is commonly used to divide sections within a single document. One common example is to use an `<HR>` at the bottom of a document, followed by an **ADDRESS** element. This is illustrated in Figures 2.4 through 2.10.

The HR element is empty.

LIST ELEMENTS

HTML has several elements for defining different types of lists. They can be divided into two types: glossary lists (the element **DL**) and regular lists (the elements **DIR, MENU, OL,** and **UL**). Lists of the same or different types can be nested. Thus, you can have a regular list within a regular list, a regular list within a glossary list, and so on. Some examples are shown in the following.

DL ELEMENT: GLOSSARY LISTS

Usage: `<DL>` ... `</DL>`

Can Contain: **DT, DD**

Can Be Inside: BLOCKQUOTE, BODY, DD, FORM, LI

Attributes: COMPACT

This list type, also known as a definition list, presents a list of items, each with a descriptive paragraph. This can be used, for example, for traditional glossaries.

DL takes a single optional attribute, **COMPACT,** to signify that the list should be rendered in a physically compact way. You could use this to compact a list of small items, or to compact a large list that would be easier to read if rendered in a compact manner.

A **DL** list can contain two elements:

DT   The term being defined

DD   The definition of the term

DT and DD elements should appear in pairs. The specification allows for successive DT elements without a matching DD, but this use is discouraged. Figures 2.11 and 2.12 show an example of a DL list.

DT ELEMENT: TERM IN A GLOSSARY LIST

Usage: `<DT>` ... `(</DT>)`

Can Contain: **characters, character formatting, A, BR, IMG**

Can Be Inside: **DL**

Attributes: none

The **DT** element contains the term part of a glossary or description list entry. The contents of a **DT** element should be short; typically, a few words and certainly shorter than a line. The element can contain standard character markup, images, line breaks, and hypertext anchors.

The **DT** element is not empty, but the terminating `</DT>` is optional, as it is implied either by the start of another `<DT>` or `<DD>` element or by the `</DL>` ending the list.

___

DD ELEMENT: DESCRIPTION IN A GLOSSARY LIST

Usage:	`<DD>` ... (`</DD>`)
Can Contain:	**characters, character formatting, A, BR, IMG, DIR, DL, MENU, OL, UL, P, BLOCKQUOTE, FORM, P, PRE, [ISINDEX]**
Can Be Inside:	**DL**
Attributes:	none

___

The **DD** element gives the description corresponding to the previous **DT** element. It can be a long description, broken into paragraphs and containing other lists, **FORM**s, quotations, and so on. A **DD** element must always follow a **DT** element; it cannot occur alone.

The **DD** element is not empty, but the terminating `</DD>` is optional, since the end of a **DD** element is implied either by the `<DT>` tag starting another **DT** element or by the `</DL>` tag terminating the list.

```
<html>

<head>
<title> Example of Glossary List elements </title>
</head>

<body>
```

```
<h1> Example 6: Example of Glossary Lists </h1>

<p> Here is an example of a glossary list. The third item in the list
has a regular unordered list nested within it. Note that the first
term (marked by the DT element) does not have a matching description
(marked by the DD element).  This is perfectly legal.  The converse:
a DD without a matching DT, is illegal.


<dl>
<dt> Things to do:
<dt> Things to Avoid:
    <dd> You should not use elements that define paragraph
    formatting within the PRE element. This means you should
    not use <code> &lt;P>, &lt;ADDRESS>, &lt;Hn> </code> and so on.
    You should avoid the use of tab characters -- use single blank
    characters to space text apart.
<dt> Things That are OK:
    <dd>You <em> can </em> use the anchor element A.  A typed carriage
    return will cause a new line in the presented text.
    People you should never let format lists include:
    <ul>
        <li> Bozo the Clown
        <li> Uncle Fester
        <li> Knights who go nii
    </ul>
    as they generally do a poor job.


</dl>


</body>

</html>
```

Figure 2.11 HTML example document illustrating the **DL** glossary list elements, and a **UL** unordered list nested inside a glossary list. Figure 2.12 shows this document as displayed by the **Cello** browser.

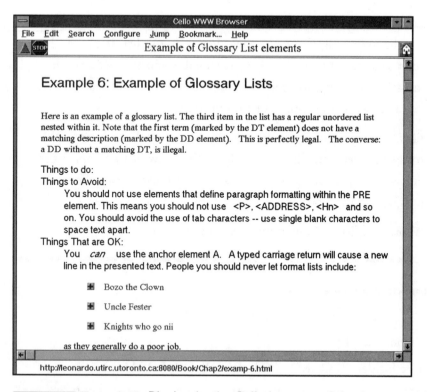

Figure 2.12 Display, by the **Cello** browser, of the document shown in Figure 2.11.

OL ELEMENT: ORDERED LIST

Usage: `<OL> ... </OL>`

Can Contain: **LI**

Can Be Inside: **BLOCKQUOTE, BODY, DD, FORM, LI**

Attributes: (**COMPACT**: proposed HTML+)

The **OL** element defines an ordered list. A browser indicates ordering by numbering the items, assigning them ascending letters, and so on. The **OL** element has no attributes under the HTML2.0 specifications.

Each item in an **OL** list is contained within an **LI** (list item) element; the **LI** element is the *only* thing that can appear inside an **OL** list. Items can be paragraphs of text, but should be kept reasonably short; otherwise, the idea of a list is lost. If the list items are big, perhaps it is not really a list: Try paragraphs with appropriate section headings.

The **HTML+** specifications propose adding the optional attribute **COM-PACT** to the **OL** element. This would direct the browser to compact the list by, for example, reducing white spaces between list entries. This attribute is not understood (and is ignored) by most browsers.

A typical ordered list is show in Figures 2.13 and 2.14.

UL ELEMENT: UNORDERED LIST

Usage: `<UL> ... </OL>`

Can Contain: **LI**

Can Be Inside: **BLOCKQUOTE, BODY, DD, FORM, LI**

Attributes: (**COMPACT, PLAIN, WRAP**: proposed HTML+)

The **UL** element defines an unordered list of items, where each list item is indicated by a special symbol, such as a bullet or an asterisk. The **UL** element has no attributes under the HTML2.0 specifications.

Each item in a **UL** list is contained within an **LI** (list item) element; the **LI** element is the *only* thing that can appear inside a **UL** list. Items can be paragraphs of text, but should be kept reasonably short; otherwise, the idea of a list is lost. If the list items are big, perhaps it is not really a list: Try paragraphs with appropriate section headings.

HTML+ proposes three optional attributes to the UL element:

COMPACT: (optional) (proposed HTML+)—Compact the list, for example, by reducing white spaces between list entries.

PLAIN: (optional) (proposed HTML+) —Leave the list items unmarked (i.e., leave out the bullets).

WRAP= "*horiz*", "*vert*" (optional) (proposed HTML+)—Used for multicolumn lists, and declares how the items should be wrapped on the screen.

These attributes are currently not understood by most browsers.

Figures 2.13 to 2.16 show examples of unordered lists.

DIR ELEMENT: DIRECTORY LIST

Usage:	`<DIR> ... </DIR>`
Can Contain:	**LI**
Can Be Inside:	**BLOCKQUOTE, BODY, DD, FORM, LI**
Attributes:	(**COMPACT**: proposed HTML+)

The **DIR** element defines a directory list: a list of short items, each no more than about 20 characters. If possible, a browser can display the items in columns across the screen, as opposed to one above the other. In HTML2.0 the **DIR** element has no attributes.

Each item in a **DIR** list is contained within an **LI** (list item) element, where the **LI** element is the *only* thing that can appear inside a **DIR** list.

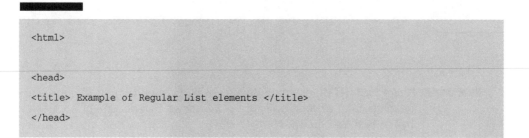

```
<html>

<head>
<title> Example of Regular List elements </title>
</head>
```

```
<body>
<h1> Example 7: Examples of Regular Lists </h1>

<h2> Ordered Lists </h2>
<p> This shows an ordered list, with another ordered list nested
within it.
<OL>
  <LI> First item.  Note that there can be lots of stuff in a list
  item, including images, paragraph breaks, BLOCKQUOTEs, and even
  other lists.
  <LI> A Second item in the list.
  <LI> And a third item.  This item breaks down into some
  subcategories:
      <OL>
      <LI> The first sub-item
      <LI> The second sub-item, and so on.....
      </OL>
</OL>
<hr>
<h2> Unordered Lists </h2>
<p> This also contains an ordered sublist.
<UL>
   <LI> A list item.
   <LI> Another list item; again these can containg IMG elements,
   Paragraphs, and so on.
   <LI> And sub-lists like this:
   <UL>
      <LI> An item in the list.
      <LI> Something else that is important, and so on.
   </UL>
</UL>


</body>
</html>
```

■■■■■■■ **Figure 2.13** HTML example document illustrating **UL** and **OL** lists and the nesting of list elements. Figure 2.14 shows this document as displayed by the **WinWeb** browser.

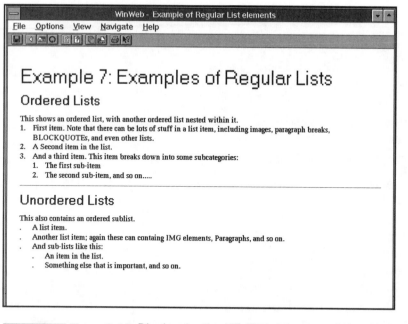

Figure 2.14 Display, by the **WinWeb** browser, of the document shown in
Figure 2.13.

HTML+ proposes the optional attribute **COMPACT**. This would direct the
browser to compact the list by, for example, reducing white spaces between
list entries. This attribute is not understood by most browsers.

An example of a directory list is shown in Figures 2.15 and 2.16.

MENU Element: Menu List

Usage: <MENU> ... </MENU>

Can Contain: **LI**

Can Be Inside: **BLOCKQUOTE, BODY, DD, FORM, LI**

Attributes: none

```
<html>

<head>
<title> Example of Regular List elements </title>
</head>

<body>

<h1> Example 8: Still More Lists </h1>

<h2> Unordered Lists </h2>
<p> This also contains an ordered sublist.
<UL>
    <LI> A list item.
    <LI> Another list item,
    <LI> and still more items.
</UL>
<hr>
<h2> Directory Lists </h2>
<DIR>
    <LI> Abraham - Carbon
    <LI> Cardshark - Elegant
    <LI> Elegiac - Food
    <LI> Foot - Hogs
</DIR>
<hr>
<h2> Menu Lists </h2>
<MENU>
    <LI> First item
    <LI> Second item
    <LI> Third item
    <LI> Fourth item
</MENU>

</body>
</html>
```

Figure 2.15 HTML example document illustrating the **MENU** and **DIR** lists. Figure 2.16 shows this document as displayed by the **MidasWWW** browser.

██████████ **Figure 2.16** Display of the document shown in Figure 2.15 by the
MidasWWW browser.

The **MENU** element defines a list of short menu items, each preferably less than a sentence long. The **MENU** list is designed to work like the **UL** but to be formatted in a more compact manner similar to a <UL COMPACT> list, except that formatting may be optimized to favor short list items.

MENU can contain only the **LI** elements. It is an error to place text directly inside a **MENU**. Figures 2.15 and 2.16 give an example of a **MENU** list.

LI ELEMENT: LIST ITEM

Usage: <LI> ... (</LI>)

Can Contain: **characters, character highlighting, A, BR, IMG, DIR, DL, MENU, OL, UL, BLOCKQUOTE, FORM, P, PRE, [ISINDEX]**

Can Be Inside: **DIR, MENU, UL, OL**

Attributes: (**SRC:** proposed HTML+)

The **LI** element marks an item within a list. The item can contain text, character markup, and hypertext anchors, as well as subsidiary lists and text blocks. In HTML2.0, the **LI** element has no attributes.

HTML+ proposes the attribute **SRC**, for use only when the **LI** element is within list elements **UL, MENU,** or **DIR.** The use of the tag `<LI SRC="image.gif">` would allow the browser to replace the default marker for each list item by the defined image file, as specified by a URL. **SRC** is optional and, in its absence, the browser would use the default marker. Most current browsers ignore the **SRC** attribute.

P ELEMENT: PARAGRAPHS

Usage: `<P> ... (</P>)`

Can Contain: **characters, character highlighting, A, BR, IMG**

Can Be Inside: **BODY, BLOCKQUOTE, FORM, DD, LI**

Attributes: (**ID, ALIGN, WRAP:** proposed HTML+)

The **P** element marks the beginning of a paragraph and implies a paragraph break. This is different from the **BR** element that represents a simple line break. Paragraphs should be thought of as logical blocks of text, similar to a **BLOCKQUOTE, ADDRESS,** or heading **Hn**, while a **BR** is simply a *character* that causes a line break. In HTML2.0, the **P** element has no attributes.

Typically, a paragraph is rendered with extra space between the previous and following blocks of text. Sometimes, the first line is also indented. For historical reasons, an end tag </P> is not required. Instead, the end of a paragraph is implied by the beginning of another paragraph or by another element marking a block of text. An end tag </P> can be used to mark the end of a paragraph, but its use is optional. Examples of the use of paragraph tags are given in Figures 2.1 through 2.24.

You should not use paragraphs to add spacing, for example, by writing:

```
....text
<P>
<P>
<P>
<H2> And another thing of Interest </H2>
```

Formally, a paragraph cannot be empty, so the preceding is illegal. Most browsers will tolerate this, but their interpretations will vary: Some leave extra spaces and some ignore the extra <P> tags completely.

HTML+ suggests the following attributes:

ID (optional) (proposed HTML+)—This marks the paragraph for a possible reference via a URL. (NOTE: In HTML+, **ID** is designed to replace the **NAME** attribute currently used to mark hypertext link targets.) This option works with some current browsers; notably, **emacs-w3**. For example:

```
<P ID="paragraph_1">
```

ALIGN="*center*", "*left*", "*right*", "*justify*", "*indent*" (optional) (proposed HTML+)—Change the paragraph alignment (the default is left) or paragraph justification. This option is implemented on a few browsers; notably, **emacs-w3** and **Netscape**. **ALIGN** is a formatting hint that can be ignored by the browser.

WRAP="*on***", "***off***" (optional) (proposed HTML+)—WRAP** disables or enables wordwrapping. **WRAP="***on***"** enables word wrapping (the default) while **WRAP="***off***"** disables word wrapping. **WRAP** is only supported by **emacs-w3**.

PRE ELEMENT: PREFORMATTED TEXT

Usage:	<PRE> ... </PRE>
Can Contain:	**characters, character highlighting, A**
Can Be Inside:	**BODY, BLOCKQUOTE, FORM, DD, LI**
Attributes:	**WIDTH**

The **PRE** element marks text to be displayed with a fixed-width typewriter font. In particular, the **PRE** environment preserves the line breaks and space characters in the original text. This is the only element in HTML that does so. **PRE** is therefore useful for presenting text that has been formatted for a fixed-width character display, such as a plain text terminal.

With HTML2.0, the **PRE** element is the only mechanism for displaying tabular data or any other information that requires well-defined columns or relative positions of the text. All the other elements format text with variable-width fonts and adjust white spaces between words.

PRE takes the single optional attribute: **WIDTH**. This specifies the maximum number of characters that can be displayed on a single line, and tells a browser that it can wrap the line at this point. A default value of 80 is often assumed, depending on the browser. Graphical browsers often ignore the **WIDTH** attribute completely and let the lines in a **PRE** element be as long as they wish. You can then use a scroll bar to see text that runs off display.

THINGS TO AVOID:

You cannot use elements that define paragraph formatting within the **PRE** element. This means you should not use <P>, <ADDRESS>, <Hn>, and so on. You should avoid tab characters, since different browsers interpret the size of a tab differently. Instead, use space characters to vertically align text.

USEFUL FEATURES:

You can use the **A** (anchor) to create hypertext anchors inside **PRE** and all the character highlighting elements (**STRONG, EM,** and so on). These highlighting elements may be ignored by the browser if appropriate rendering is not possible.

An example of the **PRE** element is shown in Figures 2.17 and 2.18. Note the use of character highlighting. Character highlighting inside a **PRE** element contributes zero character width.

```
<html>
<head>
<title> Example of the PRE elements </title>
</head>

<body>
```

```
<h1> Example 9: The Use of PRE </h1>
<p> The PRE element is often used to include blocks
of plain text.  For example you can use it to include
examples of typed code:
<hr>
<PRE>
/* main program for fitting program */

extern int *sharv;
static char boggle[100];

main (int argc, char *argv)
double x_transpose, y_transpose, f_ack=2.3;
{

  .
</PRE>
<hr>
<p> PRE is also used for <em> tables</em>:  HTML2.0 does not have
elements for defining tables:
<PRE>
   Item            Price     Tax    Total         Category

   fileserver     10000      300    10300              <a href="cat_a.html">A</a>
   disk drive       900       30      930              <a href="cat_b.html">B</a>
  <strong>transmission</strong>      4400    110   4510              C
  <em>fertilizer</em>        5500    100   5600            F
</PRE>
The markup codes take up no space: if you delete everything between the
angle brackets (in the raw HTML) all the columns align perfectly.


</body>
</html>
```

Figure 2.17 HTML example document illustrating the use of the **PRE** element. Figure 2.18 shows this document as displayed by the **Mosaic for X-Windows** browser.

▰▰▰▰▰▰ **Figure 2.18** Display, by the **Mosaic for X-Windows** browser, of the document shown in Figure 2.17.

A ELEMENT: HYPERTEXT ANCHORS

Usage: <A> ... </A>

Can Contain: **characters, character highlighting, BR, IMG**

Can Be Inside: **ADDRESS, Hn, P, PRE, DT, DD, LI, character highlighting**

Attributes: **HREF, METHODS, NAME, TITLE, URN,**

(**REL, REV**: proposed HTML2.0),

(**ID, EFFECT, PRINT, TYPE, SIZE, SHAPE**: proposed HTML+)

The **A**, or *anchor*, element marks a block of the document as the beginning and/or end of a hypertext link. This block can be highlighted text or an image. More complex elements, such as headings, cannot be inside an anchor.

A can take several attributes, where at least one of these *must* be either **HREF** or **NAME**; these specify the destination of the hypertext link or indicate that the marked text can be the target of a hypertext link. Both can be present, indicating that the anchor is both the start and destination of a link.

Anchors containing **HREFs** are rendered differently than plain text: Often, the anchored text or image is underlined, bold-faced, or rendered with a different color. Some browsers change this rendering once a link has been accessed, to inform the user that the link has been *explored*. Anchors with only a **NAME** attribute are usually not rendered in a special way. Several examples of anchor elements are given in Figures 2.2, 2.18, and 2.20.

The element attributes are:

HREF="*URL*" (mandatory if **NAME** is absent)—**HREF** gives the target of a hypertext link. URL is the Uniform Resource Locator referencing the target object.

NAME="*string*" (mandatory if **HREF** is absent)—**NAME** is used to mark a place in an HTML document as a specific destination of a hypertext link. The value "*string*" identifies this destination. For example, the anchor element:

```
<A NAME="poison"> Deadly Toadstools </A>
```

marks this string as a possible hypertext target, referenced by the string "poison". This string is called a *fragment identifier*. Inside this document, the location can be referenced by the hypertext reference:

```
<A HREF="#poison"> Poisonous non-mushrooms </A>
```

Clicking on the phrase "Poisonous non-mushroom" will then link you back to the place in the current document marked by the `<A NAME="poison"> ... </A>` anchor.

From another document, you would write:

```
<A HREF="http://www.site.edu/slimy/toads.html#poison"> Poisonous </A>
```

where

```
http://www.site.edu/slimy/toads.html
```

is the URL for this document.

Clicking on the word "Poisonous" will then link you to the document *toads.html* and to the particular location indicated by the `<A NAME="poison"> ... </A>` anchor.

REL="*string*" (optional) (proposed HTML2.0)—The **REL** attribute gives the relationship(s) described by the hypertext link; consequently, **REL** cannot be used unless an **HREF** is present. The relationship is defined between the two entire documents and is not just related to the particular link. As an example, **REL** could indicate that the linked document is an index for the current one, or that a document is an annotation to the current one (which a browser might want to display as a pop-up), and so on. It is a pity that the **REL** (and **REV**, which is the converse of **REL**) attribute is so little used, as it can impart significant meaning and organization to large sets of related documents.

The value for **REL** is a comma-separated list of case-insensitive relationship values. An example is:

```
<A HREF="http://foo.edu/fe.html" REL="Useindex">sdfsddf</a>
```

This would mean that the document *fe.html*, at the given URL, is an index document related to the current document. Values for the relationships and their semantics will be registered by the HTML registration authority. Here are some other examples:

Example:

```
<A HREF="http://foo.edu/note1.html" REL="annotation">related notes </a>
```

The information in the document **note1.html** is additional and subsidiary to the current document. A browser might display this as margin notes.

Example:

```
<A HREF="http://foo.edu/vers2.html" REL="supersedes">previously </a>
```

The document **vers2.html** is an earlier version of the document containing this link.

At present, the **REL** and **REV** attributes are rarely used, and most browsers do not understand them. They will be of growing importance as HTML documents and document development environments become more sophisticated. For additional information on **REL** and **REV** you should consult the HTML 2.0 draft specification, referenced at the end of this chapter.

REV="*string*" (optional) (proposed HTML2.0)—**REV** is like **REL**, but with the relationship reversed. For example,

```
<A HREF="http://foo.edu/vers2.html" REV="supersedes"> later </a>
```

means that the document **vers2.html** is a later version of the document containing this link. Most browsers do not understand **REV** or **REL**.

URN="*URN*" (optional)—**URN** is designed to specify *Universal Resource Numbers* for the linked document. URNs are designed to be universal document references that do not depend on server specification, as do URLs. Unfortunately, the specification for URNs is still under discussion, so this attribute is not functional.

TITLE="*string*" (optional)—The **TITLE** attribute gives the TITLE of the linked document, and can be used by the browser to *preview* the title before contacting the server for the actual document. Note that you cannot guarantee that the **TITLE** is correct until you actually access the linked document. Alternatively, **TITLE** can be used to give a title to a document that would otherwise not have a title, such as a plain text file, an image file, or a directory accessed via FTP or a Gopher menu. Most browsers do not understand the **TITLE** attribute.

METHOD=*"method"* (optional)—The **METHOD** attribute specifies a comma-separated list of HTTP *methods* supported by the target of the hypertext link. HTTP *methods* specify the way a resource is accessed and are discussed in Chapter 4.

The **METHOD** attribute is only a hint to the browser, as the actual methods that can be used can only be determined after communicating with the HTTP server. The intent is to give the browser a hint of what the link will do so that it can, for example, render the link anchor differently (perhaps using a different font, or apply a special icon) to represent the different methods. Most browsers do not understand the **METHOD** attribute.

The following anchor attributes are part of the HTML+ proposals. Most browsers do not understand these attributes.

ID=*"string"* (optional) (Proposed HTML+)—HTML+ proposes the attribute **ID** in place of **NAME**, to specify identifier strings for hypertext anchors.

EFFECT=*"replace"*, *"new"*, *"overlay"* (optional) (Proposed HTML+)— **EFFECT** tells the browser how to display the linked document upon following the link. *"Replace"* (the default) means replace the current document with the linked one. *"New"* means open a new window (cloned if possible) and display the document there. *"Overlay"* means that the linked document should be displayed in a pop-up window.

PRINT=*"reference"*, *"footnote"*, *"sidebar"*, *"section"*, *"silent"* (optional) (Proposed HTML+)—**PRINT** is used in generating printed versions of HTML documents, and instructs the document generator as to how to represent the hypertext links. "*Reference*" (the default) means to print the URL of the document as a footnoted reference, while "*silent*" means that the reference should be ignored completely. The other options imply including the link document and printing it as a sidebar, footnote, or an inserted section.

TYPE="*MIME_type*" (optional) (Proposed HTML+)—**TYPE** specifies the MIME type of the linked document. This information can be used by the browser to change the link representation (for example, to display an image icon if the link is to an image file).

CHARACTER-RELATED ELEMENTS

There are two character-like elements: **IMG,** which includes an image within a document, and **BR,** which forces a line break in the text. These are both empty elements. In HTML these are treated much like characters and can be inserted almost anywhere that characters are found.

IMG ELEMENT: INLINE IMAGES

Usage:	`<IMG>`
Can Contain:	empty
Can Be Inside:	**character highlighting, A, Hn, P, ADDRESS, DD, DT, LI**
Attributes:	**ALIGN, ALT, ISMAP, SRC**

The **IMG** element includes an image file inline with the text of an HTML document. You cannot use **IMG** to include other HTML text within an HTML document.

There are currently only three image formats that can be included inline by all graphical browsers. These are: GIF format (with the filename suffix *.gif*); X-Bitmaps (with the filename suffix *.xbm*); and X-Pixelmaps (with the filename suffix *.xpm*). To make your documents universally viewable, convert all inlined images into one of these three formats. Note also that the **ISMAP** active image mapping works with GIF images only.

Images within a document are treated like *honorary* words or characters. Almost anywhere you have regular text, you can also have an image. The **PRE** environment is the only place where this is not true: **IMG** elements are not allowed inside a **PRE**. Images can be included within a hypertext anchor; thus, you can make an image icon behave as a button that links other documents.

The **IMG** element can take four attributes: **SRC** is mandatory and specifies the URL of the image file to be included. **ALIGN** specifies the alignment of the image with the surrounding text, while **ALT** gives an alternative text string for browsers that cannot display images. Finally, **ISMAP** indicates that the image is an active image. Examples of the **IMG** element are shown in Figures 2.19 and 2.20.

The attributes are:

SRC="*URL*" (mandatory)—**SRC** gives the URL of the image file.

ALIGN="*bottom*", "*middle*", "*top*" (optional)—**ALIGN** specifies the alignment of the image with the neighboring text. "*Bottom*" aligns the bottom of the image with the bottom of text and is the default. "*Middle*" aligns the middle of the image with the middle of the text, and "*top*" aligns the top of the image with the top of text. The effect of these values is shown in Figure 2.20. Note that text does not wrap around an image, so images within a sentence can leave big gaps between adjacent lines.

ALT="*text alternative*" (optional)—**ALT** provides a text alternative to the image, for use by text-only browsers. This attribute is optional but should be included to let users with text-only browsers know what they are missing. In addition, many graphical browsers can delay image loading and can take advantage of the **ALT** value to *preview* the contents of the image.

```
<html>

<head>
<title> Example of IMG Element </title>
</head>

<body>

<h1> Example 10: Examples of IMG Elements</h1>

<P> <IMG SRC="icon-help.gif" ALT="[Test image]" ALIGN=TOP>
Here is some text related to the test image.    The text is aligned with
the top of the image. Note that the text does not flow around the image.
<P> <IMG SRC="icon-help.gif" ALT="[Test image]" ALIGN=MIDDLE>
Here is some text related to the test image.    The text is aligned with
the middle of the image. Note that the text does not flow around the image.
<P> <A HREF="http://www.bozo.edu/test.html">
<IMG SRC="icon-help.gif" ALT="[Test image]"
ALIGN=BOTTOM> Here is some text </A>  related
to the test image.   The text is aligned with the bottom of
the image, and is also part of the <em> hypertext link</em>.

</body>
</html>
```

Figure 2.19 HTML example document illustrating the **IMG** inline image element. Figure 2.20 shows this document as displayed by the **MacMosaic** browser.

ISMAP (optional)—This attribute marks the image as an *active* image. This allows the user to click the mouse over the image and have different regions of the image cause different actions. When a user clicks on an **ISMAP** image, the browser measures the coordinates of your mouse pointer (relative to the upper left-hand corner of the image) and sends this information to the server for further processing. Typical markup for an active image is:

```
<A HREF="http://www.utirc.ca/cgi-bin/imagemap/map_bozo">
    <IMG SRC="bozo.gif" ISMAP>
</A>
```

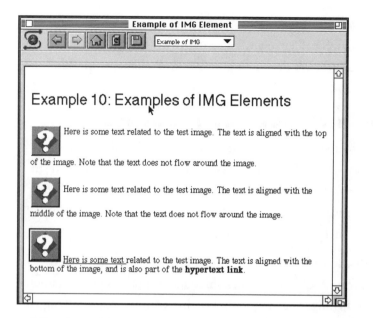

▬▬▬▬▬ **Figure 2.20** Display, by the **MacMosaic** browser, of the document shown in Figure 2.19.

where *imagemap* is a server-side gateway program that can interpret the map coordinates. The details of this procedure are discussed in Chapter 5.

BR ELEMENT: LINE BREAK

Usage:

Can Contain: empty

Can Be Inside: **A, character highlighting, ADDRESS, Hn, P, DD, DT, LI**

Attributes: none

BR indicates a line break. This is fundamentally different from a paragraph mark. A <BR> is treated as a character (like a *hard* carriage return), whereas P defines a block of text as a paragraph element.
 is commonly used in the **ADDRESS** element; an example of this usage is shown in Figure 2.6. **BR** can also break lines in a poem, with **P** elements marking the different verses.

CHARACTER HIGHLIGHTING ELEMENTS

HTML allows you to specify special character highlighting or emphasis (e.g., boldface, italics, etc.). These elements do not cause page breaks or in any way affect the structural layout of the document. Their purpose is to either assign special meanings to the enclosed text, or to request special physical formatting, such as boldface or italics.

These two methods can be described as logical highlighting (also called information-type formatting) and physical highlighting (also called character formatting). Logical highlighting is more in keeping with the markup language model. That is, you can use logical highlighting to mark a block of text as a piece of typed computer code, a variable, or as something to be emphasized. The rendering details are then left to the browser, although hints to appropriate renderings are part of the HTML specifications. You are strongly encouraged to use logical highlighting elements over the physical ones.

Physical highlighting requests a specific physical format, such as boldface or italics. This, of course, gives no clue to the underlying meaning behind the marked-up phrase. Thus, if a browser is unable to implement the indicated markup (e.g., a dumb terminal cannot do italics), it cannot easily determine an alternative logical highlighting.

Logical styles may not be distinct (i.e., different logical styles may be rendered in the same way). Also, some browsers do not support all physical styles. For example, **lynx** does not support italics and renders it as underlined.

LOGICAL HIGHLIGHTING

Here are the different logical highlighting elements, and typical renderings:

CITE	A citation (usually italics)
CODE	Example of typed code (usually fixed-width font)
DFN	(proposed HTML2.0) The defining instance of a term (often, bold or bold italics)
EM	Emphasis (usually, italics)
KBD	Keyboard input (for example, in a manual)
SAMP	A sequence of literal characters
STRIKE	(proposed HTML2.0) Struck-out text. This might be rendered as text with a line drawn through it
STRONG	Stronger emphasis (usually boldface)
VAR	A variable name

HTML+ proposes the following additional elements. These are not understood by most current browsers:

ARG	A command argument (for a computer command: see **CMD** following)
ABBREV	An abbreviation
CMD	A command name (for a computer command)
ACRONYM	An acronym for an organization, protocol, and so on
PERSON	A proper name (e.g., <PERSON> Ian Graham</PERSON>)
Q	A short quotation that could be included inline with the text

You can nest highlighting modes inside one another. This is most often not sensible, given the rather specific meanings assigned to the elements. Also, some browsers misinterpret these nestings and produce inappropriate text formatting.

Examples of the different highlighting elements are shown in Figures 2.21 and 2.22.

■■■■■■

```
<html>

<head>
<title> Example of Highlighting Markup elements </title>
</head>

<body>

<h1> Example 11 - Highlighting Elements </h1>
<h2> Examples of Logical Highlighting </h2>

<ul>
<li> CITE - This is <CITE> citation </CITE>text
<li> CODE - This is <CODE> typed computer code </CODE>text.
<li> DFN - This is <DFN> a defining instance </DFN>text. (Proposed HTML2.0)
<li> EM - This is <EM> emphasized </EM>text.
<li> KBD - This is <KBD> keyboard input </KBD>text.
<li> SAMP - This is <SAMP> literal character </SAMP>text.
<li> STRIKE - This is <STRIKE> strike-out</STRIKE> text. (Proposed HTML2.0)
<li> STRONG - This is <STRONG> strongly emphasized </STRONG>text.
<li> VAR - This is <VAR> a variable </VAR>text.
</ul>

<h2> Examples of Character Highlighting </h2>

<ul>
<li> B - This is <B> boldfaced </B>text.
<li> I - This is <I> italicized </I>text.
<li> TT - This is <TT> fixed-width typewriter font </TT>text.
<li> U - This is <U> underlined </U>text. (Proposed HTML2.0)
</ul>


</body>
</html>
```

■■■■■■ **Figure 2.21** HTML example document illustrating the different text highlighting elements. Figure 2.22 shows this document as displayed by the **MacWeb** browser.

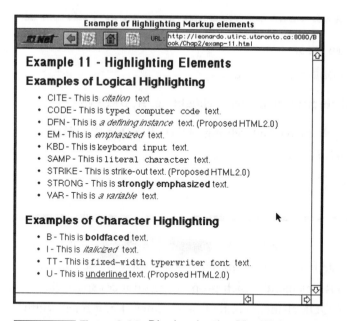

██████ **Figure 2.22** Display, by the **MacWeb** browser, of the document shown in Figure 2.21.

CITE ELEMENT: CITATIONS

Usage:	`<CITE> ... </CITE>`
Can Contain:	characters, character highlighting, A, BR, IMG
Can Be Inside:	A, character highlighting, ADDRESS, Hn, P, PRE, DD, DT, LI
Attributes:	none

The **CITE** element marks a small citation—for example, a book or other document reference. Typically, this block of text will be rendered in italics, subject to the capabilities of the browser.

CODE ELEMENT: TYPED CODE

Usage:	`<CODE> ... </CODE>`
Can Contain:	**characters, character highlighting, A, BR, IMG**
Can Be Inside:	**A, character highlighting, ADDRESS, Hn, P, PRE, DD, DT, LI**
Attributes:	none

The **CODE** element marks a selection of typed computer code—for example, a single line of code from a program. Large selections of code should be displayed using a **PRE** element, which properly reproduces space characters and line breaks. **CODE** element contents are rendered in a fixed-width typewriter font.

DFN ELEMENT: DEFINING INSTANCE (PROPOSED: HTML2.0)

Usage:	`<DFN> ... </DFN>`
Can Contain:	**characters, character highlighting, A, BR, IMG**
Can Be Inside:	**A, character highlighting, ADDRESS, Hn, P, PRE, DD, DT, LI**
Attributes:	none

The **DFN** element marks the defining instance of a term. This is useful for generating indexes of definitions, or for searching through documents for defining instances. A browser will typically render this in italics or bold italics. Note that this element is not understood by all browsers.

EM Element: Emphasis

Usage: <EM> ... </EM>

Can Contain: **characters, character highlighting, A, BR, IMG**

Can Be Inside: **A, character highlighting, ADDRESS, Hn, P, PRE, DD, DT, LI**

Attributes: none

The **EM** element marks a block of text for emphasis. Typically, the marked block of text is rendered in italics, subject to the capabilities of the browser. For example, **lynx** represents **EM** emphasized text by an underline.

KBD Element: Keyboard Input

Usage: <KBD> ... </KBD>

Can Contain: **characters, character highlighting, A, BR, IMG**

Can Be Inside: **A, character highlighting, ADDRESS, Hn, P, PRE, DD, DT, LI**

Attributes: none

The **KBD** element marks a block of text as keyboard input. Typically, this is displayed with a fixed-width typewriter font.

SAMP Element: Literal Characters

Usage: <SAMP> ... </SAMP>

Can Contain: **characters, character highlighting, A, BR, IMG**

Can Be Inside: **A, character highlighting, ADDRESS, Hn, P, PRE, DD, DT, LI**

Attributes: none

The **SAMP** element marks a block of text as a sequence of literal or *sample* characters. Typically, this is rendered in a fixed-width typewriter font.

STRIKE ELEMENT: STRUCK-OUT TEXT (PROPOSED: HTML2.0)

Usage: `<STRIKE> ... </STRIKE>`

Can Contain: **characters, character highlighting, A, BR, IMG**

Can Be Inside: **A, character highlighting, ADDRESS, Hn, P, PRE, DD, DT, LI**

Attributes: none

The **STRIKE** element marks a block of text to be *struck out.* An example would be a legal document, where a sentence or section is struck out but should be left present in the text for reference purposes. Typically, this block of text is rendered in a normal font but with a line drawn horizontally through the text. Other renderings are necessary on text-only browsers, such as **lynx**. The **STRIKE** element is not understood by most browsers.

STRONG ELEMENT: STRONG EMPHASIS

Usage: `<STRONG> ... </STRONG>`

Can Contain: **characters, character highlighting, A, BR, IMG**

Can Be Inside: **A, character highlighting, ADDRESS, Hn, P, PRE, DD, DT, LI**

Attributes: none

The **STRONG** element marks a block of text for strong emphasis. Typically, this is rendered in boldface, although text-only browsers, such as **lynx,** use an underline (with **lynx, EM** and **STRONG** emphasis are displayed in the same way).

VAR ELEMENT: A VARIABLE

Usage: `<VAR> ... </VAR>`

Can Contain: **characters, character highlighting, A, BR, IMG**

Can Be Inside: **A, character highlighting, ADDRESS, Hn, P, PRE, DD, DT, LI**

Attributes: none

The **VAR** element marks a variable name. This is typically rendered in italics or bold italics.

PHYSICAL HIGHLIGHTING

Physical highlighting elements request physically desired renderings. Physical styles are useful when translating from another document to HTML, where the only information available may be physical markup instructions. Use logical highlighting in new documents whenever possible.

Physical highlighting elements can be nested and, unlike the case with most logical highlighting elements, these nestings make sense. Therefore, requesting that a block of text be rendered in Underlined-Boldface-Italics is entirely reasonable. However, be aware that some browsers (for example, **Mosaic For X-Windows**) presently mishandle these nestings.

The physical style elements, and their renderings, are:

B   Boldface (where possible)

I   Italics (may be rendered as slanted in some cases)

TT   Fixed-width typewriter font

U   Underlined (proposed: HTML2.0)

Examples of the renderings of these styles are shown in Figure 2.22.

HTML+ proposes the following additional physical highlighting elements:

S   Strike-through. This does not have the logical meaning associated with the **STRIKE** logical highlighting element.

SUB   Subscript

SUP   Superscript

B ELEMENT: BOLDFACE

Usage: `<B> ... </B>`

Can Contain: **characters, character highlighting, A, BR, IMG**

Can Be Inside: **A, character highlighting, ADDRESS, Hn, P, PRE, DD, DT, LI**

Attributes: none

The **B** element marks a section to be rendered in boldface. If this is impossible, the browser can render this in some other way (**lynx** uses an underline).

I ELEMENT: ITALICS

Usage:	`<I> ... </I>`
Can Contain:	**characters, character highlighting, A, BR, IMG**
Can Be Inside:	**A, character highlighting, ADDRESS, Hn, P, PRE, DD, DT, LI**
Attributes:	none

The **I** element marks a section to be rendered in italics. If this is impossible, the browser can render this in some other way (**lynx** uses an underline).

TT ELEMENT: FIXED-WIDTH TYPEWRITER FONT

Usage:	`<TT> ... </TT>`
Can Contain:	**characters, character highlighting, A, BR, IMG**
Can Be Inside:	**A, character highlighting, ADDRESS, Hn, P, PRE, DD, DT, LI**
Attributes:	none

The **TT** element marks a section to be rendered with a fixed-width typewriter font.

U ELEMENT: UNDERLINE (PROPOSED: HTML2.0)

Usage:	`<U> ... </U>`
Can Contain:	**characters, character highlighting, A, BR, IMG**

Can Be Inside: **A, character highlighting, ADDRESS, Hn, P, PRE, DD, DT, LI**

Attributes: none

The U element marks a section to be rendered with an underline. This element is not understood by all browsers.

HTML+ ELEMENTS

The following elements are part of the HTML+ proposals, and are not understood by most WWW browsers. However, there is a particular push to implement the **TABLE** element so that this will soon be available on aggressively designed browsers. Other elements that are implemented on some browsers are the **FOOTNOTE** and **MARGIN** elements (implemented on **emacs-w3**), and the **SUP** and **SUB** (superscript/subscript) elements implemented on **Mosaic for X-Windows** Version 2.5.

TABLE Element: Tables (Proposed HTML+)

Usage: `<TABLE> ... </TABLE>`

Can Contain: **CAPTION, TH, TD, TR**

Can Be Inside: not yet specified; probably:

BLOCKQUOTE, BODY, FORM, DD, LI

Attributes: **BORDER**

The **TABLE** element contains tabular data; the structure and contents of the table are defined by additional elements that can appear only inside the **TABLE**. The **TABLE** element has one optional attribute:

BORDER (optional)—The border attribute tells the browser to draw a box around each cell in the table, if possible.

The **TABLE** element can contain four table description elements:

CAPTION	Gives the caption or title of the table.
TH	Table Header: Gives the headings for a particular row or column.
TD	Table Data: Gives the data contents of a table cell.
TR	Table Row: Defines the end of a row and the start of a new row.

The design of HTML **TABLE**s will be familiar to those who have used the tabular environment in LaTeX. Tables are defined as *cells,* where a cell is an item within the table. Cells can be of various sizes, specified by the number of table rows or columns that are spanned by the cell. It is the author's responsibility to ensure that the number of cells in a given row (or column) add up to the correct table size. An example of a **TABLE** is shown in Figures 2.23 and 2.24.

CAPTION Element: Table Caption (Proposed HTML+)

Usage:	`<CAPTION> ... </CAPTION>`
Can Contain:	not yet specified; probably: **characters, character highlighting, A, BR, IMG**
Can Be Inside:	**TABLE**
Attributes:	none

The **CAPTION** element specifies the table caption or title. Each **TABLE** can have at most one **CAPTION**. The **CAPTION** can contain text, character highlighting elements, and the **IMG** element, along with hypertext anchors.

Example:

```
<CAPTION> Profits In each Year: 1983-1993 </CAPTION>
```

TH ELEMENT: TABLE HEADING (PROPOSED HTML+)

Usage: `<TH> ... (</TH>)`

Can Contain: not yet specified; probably: **characters, character highlighting, A, IMG, BR, TABLE**

Can Be Inside: **TABLE**

Attributes: **ALIGN, COLSPAN, ROWSPAN**

The **TH** element specifies a Table Header cell—the cell that defines the contents of a row or column. The **TH** element is not empty, but the end tag `</TH>` is optional, as its existence is implied by the next `<TH>`, `<TR>`, or `<TD>` tag. The **TH** element can be present with no contents, which simply means that the cell is blank. **TABLES** can have more than one **TH** for a given row or column: It is up to you, the **TABLE** designer, to ensure that table headings are placed appropriately. The **TH** element has three optional attributes that define the centering of the contents of the header, and that define how many columns or rows of the entire table are to be spanned by the *cell*.

The attributes of the **TH** element are:

ALIGN = "*left*", "*right*", "*center*" (optional)—**ALIGN** specifies the alignment of the table cell contents within the cell: **ALIGN**="*left*" aligns the contents flush-left within the cell; **ALIGN**="*right*" aligns the contents flush-right within the cell; **ALIGN**="*center*" centers the contents within the cell.

ROWSPAN = "*n*" (optional)—**ROWSPAN** specifies how many table rows are spanned by the cell—the default value is 1. Counting of rows starts from the top of the table. It is the author's responsibility to ensure that the cells in each column sum to the correct number of rows.

COLSPAN = "*n*" (optional)—**COLSPAN** specifies how many table columns are spanned by the cell—the default value is 1. Counting of columns starts from the left side of the table. It is the author's responsibility to ensure that the cells in each row sum to the correct number of columns.

Example:

```
<TH ALIGN=LEFT> Housing Prices: </TH>
```

This example specifies a table heading cell that spans one row and one column and that contains the heading "*Housing Prices*:." **TH** cells need not contain simple text strings. They can also contain other **TABLE**s, lists, images, hypertext anchors, and so on.

```
<html>

<head>
<title> HTML+ Features>: TABLEs, SUB and SUP</title>
</head>

<body>

<h1> Example 12 HTML+ Features</h1>

<p> HTML+ proposed several new elements. among them are
<ul>
<li> superscript element: hello<sup>2</sup>
<li> subscript element: sub<sub>script</sub>.
```

```
</ul>

<p>

Also defined are TABLE elements that allow you to construct
formatted tables.  Here is an example:

<p>

<table border>
<caption>Table Caption </caption>
<th rowspan=2>  Item                        </th>
<th colspan=2>  Breakdown Costs            </th>
<tr>
<th align=left> Pre- </th>
<th align=left> Post- </th>
<tr>
<td> Carbuncles                             </td>
<td align=left>      0.00                  </td>
<td align=left>  $12,000                   </td>
<tr>
<td>Klystrons (a)                          </td>
<td rowspan=2 align=left>$13,000           </td>
<td align=left>$8,000                      </td>
<tr>
<td>Klystrons (b)                          </td>
<td align=left><em>  $8,000</em></td>
<tr>
<td>Sticks                                 </td>
<td align=left> 23&#162;                   </td>
<td align=left> 13&#162;                   </td>
</table>

</body>
</html>
```

Figure 2.23 HTML example document illustrating the **TABLE**, **SUP**, and **SUB** elements. Figure 2.24 shows this document as displayed by the **Mosaic for X-Windows** Version 2.5 browser.

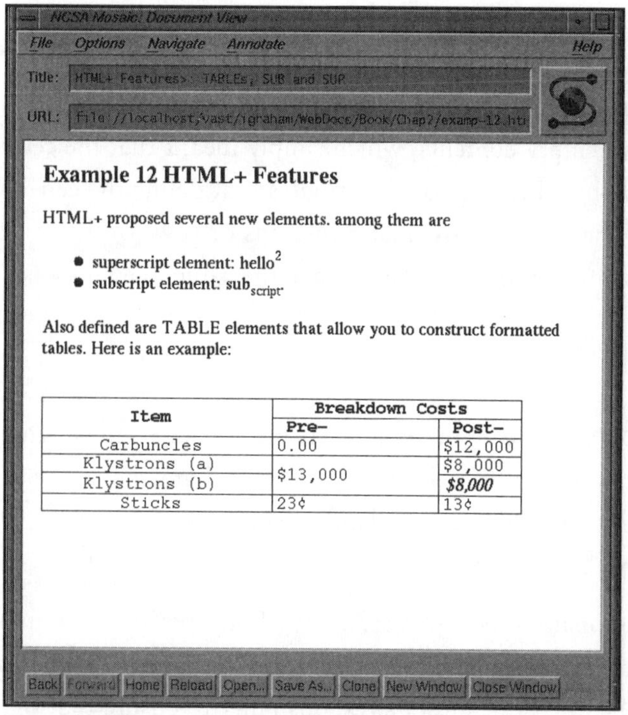

Figure 2.24 Display, by the **Mosaic for X-Windows** Version 2.5 browser, of the document shown in Figure 2.23.

TD ELEMENT: TABLE DATA (PROPOSED HTML+)

Usage: <TD> ... (</TD>)

Can Contain: Not yet specified; probably: **characters, character highlighting, A, BR, IMG, TABLE**

Can Be Inside: **TABLE**

Attributes: **ALIGN, COLSPAN, ROWSPAN**

The **TD** element specifies a Table Data cell, which is a cell that contains the tabular data. The **TD** element is not empty, but the end tag `</TD>` is optional, as its existence is implied by the next `<TH>`, `<TR>`, or `<TD>` tag. The **TD** element can have empty contents, which simply means that the cell is blank. The **TD** element has three optional attributes that define the centering of the contents of the cell and how many columns or rows of the entire table are to be spanned by the cell. These have the same meanings as with the **TH** element.

Attributes:

ALIGN = "*left*", "*right*", "*center*" (optional)—**ALIGN** specifies the alignment of the table cell contents within the cell: **ALIGN**="*left*" aligns the content flush-left within the cell; **ALIGN**="*right*" aligns the contents flush-right within the cell; **ALIGN**="*center*" centers the contents within the cell.

ROWSPAN = "*n*" (optional)—The **ROWSPAN** attribute specifies how many rows are spanned by this cell—the default value is 1. Counting of rows starts from the top of the table. It is the author's responsibility to ensure that the cells in each column sum to the correct number of rows.

COLSPAN = "*n*" (optional)—The **COLSPAN** attribute specifies how many columns are spanned by this cell—the default value is 1. Counting of columns starts from the left-hand side of the table. It is the author's responsibility to ensure that the cells in each row sum to the correct number of columns.

Example:

```
<TD center colspan=1, rowspan=2> 23.22 </TD>
```

This example specifies a table data cell that spans one column and two rows, and that contains the data value 23.22. **TD** cells need not contain numbers, or even simple text strings; they can also contain other **TABLE**s, lists, images, hypertext anchors, and so on.

TR ELEMENT: END OF TABLE ROW (PROPOSED HTML+)

Usage: `<TR>`

Can Contain: empty

Can Be Inside: **TABLE**

Attributes: none

The **TR** element indicates the end of a table row. Thus, a row in a table might be coded:

```
<TH> Heading <TD> data 1 <TD> data2 <TD> data3 <TD> data4 <TR>
```

which indicates a row containing five columns; the first column containing a table heading, and the rest containing table data. Every row must be terminated by a `<TR>`, except for the final row, where the final `<TR>` is implied by the `</TABLE>` tag ending the table.

ABSTRACT ELEMENT: ABSTRACTS (PROPOSED HTML+)

Usage: `<ABSTRACT> ... </ABSTRACT>`

The **ABSTRACT** element is used to give an abstract of a document. This would be part of the **BODY** and hence would be displayed, probably with an indent and a noticeably different font.

FIG ELEMENT: FLOATING FIGURES (PROPOSED HTML+)

Usage: `<FIG> ... </FIG>`

The **FIG** element is designed to be a more sophisticated way of including images within documents. The **FIG** element would indicate the desired image as an attribute to the **FIG** (e.g., `<FIG SRC="image.gif">`, just as with the **IMG** element), but would also allow for an image **CAPTION** and for typed text associated with the image. The resulting **FIG** element is then treated as a paragraph, with the image and associated **CAPTION** floating within the paragraph for most appropriate formatting, and with the text allowed to flow around the image.

FIG images can also be **ISMAP** active images, as with the **IMG** elements. Another proposed extension is to make **FIG** images active by including geometry information about the active region with the document itself. This would allow you to click on a region and access a document without first having to access a server to parse the image map. The **FIG** element is not currently implemented.

FOOTNOTE ELEMENT (PROPOSED HTML+)

Usage: `<FOOTNOTE>  ...  </FOOTNOTE>`

The **FOOTNOTE** element would be used to include footnote annotations within a document. This may appear in the document as a special footnote icon or symbol indicating the presence of a footnote; it does not have to appear at the bottom of the document page. Clicking on the button should *pop up* the footnote, displaying it next to or on top of the current document. **FOOTNOTE**s should be small and could contain images and text highlighting elements.

The **emacs-w3** browser supports the **FOOTNOTE** element.

LIT ELEMENT: LITERAL TEXT (PROPOSED HTML+)

Usage: `<LIT> ... </LIT>`

In HTML2.0, preformatted text can be displayed only using the **PRE** environment. This forces the text into a fixed-width typewriter font. This preformatted mode is certainly not ideal for such text as poetry or other prose, for which the line breaks and indents are important, and where you want easier to read variable-width fonts.

The **LIT** element is proposed for presenting such information. The **LIT** element would preserve line breaks in the typed text and preserve the special meanings of **TAB** characters (presently, **TAB**s are treated as simple white space and are ignored). The actual indent to associate with a **TAB** would be specified as an attribute of **LIT** (for example, `<LIT AT=10 AT=20 > .. </LIT>`).

MARGIN ELEMENT: MARGIN NOTES (PROPOSED HTML+)

Usage: `<MARGIN> ... </MARGIN>`

The **MARGIN** element would be used to include a margin note for a particular paragraph. This might appear in the document as a special icon note next to the **MARGIN**ed paragraph. Clicking on the icon would pop up the margin note in a small overlay window, and would retain the current document in the main viewing window. **MARGIN** notes should be small, but could contain images and text highlighting elements. The **emacs-w3** browser supports the **MARGIN** element.

MATH ELEMENT: MATHEMATICAL EXPRESSIONS (PROPOSED HTML+)

Usage   `<MATH> ... </MATH>`

The **MATH** element is proposed to allow for the construction (and correct display on graphically capable terminals) of complex mathematical expressions, such as equations, integrals, and so on. Unfortunately, this is not currently implemented.

The best way currently to present equations in HTML documents is to convert the equations or other mathematical symbols into small image files and include them inline with the text. The program **latex2html** does this automatically when converting LaTeX documents into HTML. **Latex2html** is discussed in more detail in Chapter 6.

NOTE ELEMENT: EXCLAMATORY NOTES (PROPOSED HTML+)

Usage: `<NOTE> ... </NOTE>`

The **NOTE** element would be used when you want to display an exclamatory note. This could be displayed highlighted from the regular text, indented, and perhaps with a special notifying icon. The **NOTE** element can take two attributes: the **SRC=**"*URL*" attribute, which could specify an optional notifying icon to be used to mark the **NOTE**, while **ROLE=** "*tip*", "*note*", "*warning*", or "*error*" could be used to specify the nature of the **NOTE**.

ONLINE/PRINTED ELEMENTS: (PROPOSED HTML+)

Usage: `<ONLINE> ... </ONLINE>`

                      `<PRINTED ... </PRINTED>`

The **ONLINE** and **PRINTED** elements would be used to give two different representations for the same piece of the document: one to be used with the interactive electronic format (**ONLINE**), and the other for use with a printed version (**PRINTED**). This may be useful for giving a printed text alternative to a hypertext link so that the printed version would give more details about the link or the related reference.

REFERENCES

An introduction to SGML:

`http://etext.virginia.edu/bin/tei-tocs?div=DIV1&id=SG`

The HTML 2.0 draft specification:

`http://www.hal.com/products/sw/olias/Build-html/CGQLOZBEfmg24aK.html`

The HTML2.0 Document Type Definition (DTD):

`http://www.hal.com/%7Econnolly/html-spec/html.decl`

`http://www.hal.com/%7Econnolly/html-spec/html.dtd`

HTML references:

`http://akebono.stanford.edu/yahoo/Computers/World_Wide_Web/HTML/`

HTML+ references:

`http://akebono.stanford.edu/yahoo/Computers/World_Wide_Web/HTML/HTML_/`

UNIFORM RESOURCE
LOCATORS (URLS)

This chapter explains the structure and syntax of the *Uniform Resource Locator*, which is the addressing scheme used in HTML documents to indicate the target of hypertext links. The URL scheme allows WWW browser clients to send search data to servers for further processing. This mechanism is explained here, aand also in Chapter 4.

Uniform Resource Locators, or *URLs*, are a scheme for specifying Internet resources using a single line of printable ASCII characters. This scheme encompasses all major Internet protocols, including FTP, Gopher, HTTP, and WAIS. URLs are one of the foundation tools of the World Wide Web and are used within HTML documents to reference the targets of a hypertext link. However, URLs are not restricted to the World Wide Web and can be used to communicate information about Internet resources in e-mail letters, handwritten notes, or even books.

A URL contains the following information:

- The *protocol* to use when accessing the server (e.g., HTTP, Gopher, WAIS).

- The Internet *Domain Name* of the site on which the server is running, along with any required username and password information.

- The *Port Number* of the server; if this is omitted, the browser assumes a commonly understood default value of the indicated protocol.

- The *location* of the resource in the hierarchical (often, directory) structure of the server.

Here is a typical example; in this case, for the HTTP protocol:

```
http://www.cern.ch/hypertext/WWW/RDBgate/Implementation.html
```

This references the file ***Implementation.html*** in the directory ***/WWW/RDBgate,*** accessible at the server ***www.cern.ch*** using the HTTP protocol.

ALLOWED CHARACTERS IN URLS

Every URL must be written using printable ASCII characters (the bottom half of the ISO Latin-1 character set, as discussed in Appendix A, and excluding the ASCII control characters), and *cannot* be written using the full ISO Latin-1 character set. This restriction ensures that URLs can be sent by electronic mail; many electronic mail programs mishandle characters from the upper half of the ISO Latin-1 character set. In a URL, any ISO Latin-1 character can be represented using a *character encoding* scheme. This is analogous to the character entities used with HTML. However, the schemes are distinctly different: You must *never* use HTML characters or entity references in a URL.

The mechanism is simple: Any ISO Latin-1 character can be represented by the encoding:

```
%xx
```

where the percent sign is a special character indicating the start of the encoding and where *xx* is the *hexadecimal code* for the desired ISO Latin-1 character (the *x* represents a hexadecimal digit in the range [0-9,A-F]). Table A.1 (Appendix A) lists all the ISO Latin-1 characters alongside their hexadecimal codes. As an example, the encoding for the character *é* (the letter *e* with an acute accent) is %E9.

DISALLOWED CHARACTERS

Several ASCII characters are disallowed in URLs and can be present only in encoded form, because these characters often have special meanings in a non-URL context and may be misinterpreted. For example, HTML documents use the double quotation mark (") to delimit a URL in a hypertext anchor so that a quotation mark inside the URL would end the URL prematurely. Therefore, the double quote is disallowed. The space character is also disallowed, since many programs will consider the space as a break between two separate strings. Space characters often appear in Macintosh file or folder names. For example, the filename Network Info (where there is a single space between the words Network and Info) must be encoded in a URL as:

```
Network%20Info
```

The disallowed characters are summarized in Table 3.1.

■■■■■■■ **Table 3.1** Disallowed ASCII Characters in URLs

Character	Hex	Character	Hex
TAB	09	SPACE	20
"	22	<	3C
>	3E	[	5B
\	5C	]	5D
^	5E	`	60
{	7B	|	7C
}	7D	~	7E

SPECIAL CHARACTERS

In a URL, several ASCII characters have special meanings, such as the percent character that denotes character encodings. The forward slash character (/) is also special and denotes a change in hierarchy, such as a directory change. These special characters must be encoded if you want them to appear as regular uninterpreted characters. Thus, to include the string:

```
ian%euler
```

in a URL, you must encode it as:

```
ian%25euler
```

where `%25` is the encoding for the percent character. If you do not do this, a program parsing the URL will try and interpret `%eu` as a character encoding. Conversely, you must not encode a special character if you require its special meaning. For example, the string:

```
dir/subdir
```

indicates that `subdir` is a subdirectory of `dir`, while:

```
dir%2Fsubdir
```

is just the character string `dir/subdir` (`%2F` is the encoding for the slash).

The general rule is: Encode any character that might be special if you do not want to use its special meaning. The more common special characters are listed in the following:

- The percent sign (%). This is the escape character for character encodings.

- The slash (/). This is used to indicate hierarchical structures, such as directories.

- The hash (#). This is used to separate the URL of a resource from the *fragment identifier* for that resource. A fragment identifier references a particular location within a resource (special in HTTP URLs only).

- The question mark (?). This indicates a *query string*; everything after the question mark is query information to be passed to the server (special in Gopher, WAIS, and HTTP URLs only).

EXAMPLE OF A
UNIFORM RESOURCE LOCATOR

Figure 3.1 shows a typical URL (in this case, for the HTTP protocol) with the different parts and the associated meanings. The different parts are discussed in subsequent sections.

1. PROTOCOL

The first string in the URL specifies the Internet *protocol* to use in accessing the resource; this example requests the HTTP protocol. The protocol is indicated by the name appearing before the first colon in the URL. URL schemes are defined for most Internet protocols, including FTP, Gopher, HTTP, telnet, and WAIS. The details of the different schemes are presented later on.

2. ADDRESS AND PORT NUMBER

The second part of this URL is the Internet address of the server; this information lies between the double forward slash (//) and a terminating forward slash (/). This example gives the *domain name* of the server and the *port number* to contact. Omitting the port number implies the default value for the given protocol. Numeric IP addresses can be used instead of domain names; for example:

```
//132.206.9.22:1234/
```

You can include username and password information if this is needed to access a resource. The format is:

```
//username:password@www.address.edu:1234/
```

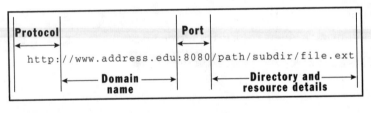

Figure 3.1 Example of a URL.

Note that the password can be read by anyone who reads the URL, so this is not a secure way to allow access to a resource.

3. RESOURCE LOCATION

The forward slash after the host and port number field indicates the beginning of the *path* information required to locate the resource on the server. This field varies considerably, depending on the service being accessed. Often, this resembles a directory path leading down to a file, as in Figure 3.1. In this context, the forward slash character (/) is used in place of *all* system-dependent symbols, such as the backslash (\) on DOS or Windows computers; the colon (:) on Macintoshes; and the [dir.subdir.subsubdir] expressions used by VAX/VMS systems.

PASSING SEARCH STRINGS

The URL syntax allows you to pass query strings to the designated server, in situations (typically, Gopher, HTTP, or WAIS) that support such service. This is accomplished by appending the query strings to the URL, separated from the URL by a question mark. Two examples are:

```
gopher://gopher.somewhere.edu/77/searches.phone?bob+steve
http://www.somewhere.edu/cgi-bin/srch-data?archie+database
```

SPECIAL CASES

In some cases, Internet domain names are not part of a URL. This is the case for protocols that are not dependent on a particular server, such as sending electronic mail or accessing USENET newsgroup articles.

Some Simple URL Examples

```
http://info.cern.ch/hypertext/WWW/Addressing/URL/Overview.html
```

This references the file *Overview.html* in the directory */hypertext/WWW/Addressing/URL/* from the server *info.cern.ch* using the HTTP protocol and the default port number (80 for HTTP).

```
gopher://gumby.brain.headache.edu:151/7fonebook.txt
```

This references the searchable index *fonebook.txt* from the Gopher server at *gumby.brain.headache.edu* running on port number 151.

```
news:alt.rec.motorcycle
```

This references the newsgroup *alt.rec.motorcycle*.

```
mailto:ross@physics.mcg.ca
```

This indicates sending an electronic mail message to the indicated e-mail address.

PARTIAL URLS

Within a given HTML document, you do not need to specify the entire URL to locate a second, neighboring document. This is because being *in* the document already implies information about the current URL, so that you can reference neighboring documents or resources using a *partial* URL that gives the location *relative* to the current document.

Suppose you originally access the document *file.html* using the full URL:

```
http://www.stuff.edu/main/docs/file.html
```

Within this document there is a hypertext reference containing a *partial* URL:

```
<A HREF="stuff.html"> anchor text </A>
```

Where is this file? From inside *file.html,* any information not present in a URL reference is considered the *same* as that used to access the current document. Thus, the partial URL stuff.html is transformed into a full

URL by appropriating the missing information from the URL used to access *file.html*. The completed URL is then:

```
http://www.stuff.edu/main/docs/stuff.html
```

which indicates, as expected, that *stuff.html* is on the same server and in the same directory as *file.html*. Other equivalent partial URLs are then:

```
/main/docs/stuff.html

//www.stuff.edu/main/docs.html
```

The former appropriates http://www.stuff.edu from the current URL to complete the reference, while the latter appropriates only the http: part from the *base* URL of the current document.

You can also use partial URLs to reference files in other directories; for example, from the example *file.html* the relative URL:

```
../../main.html
```

indicates the file *main.html* in the root HTTP directory, namely:

```
http://www.stuff.edu/main.html
```

Partial URLs are very useful when constructing large collections of documents that will be kept together. Of course relative URLs become invalid if a document is moved to a new directory or a new Internet site. This problem can be mitigated using the **BASE** element of the HTML, which is used to record the correct **BASE** URL of a document. If the document is moved, all relative URLs are determined relative to the URL recorded by the **BASE** element.

URL SPECIFICATIONS

We now look at the details of the different URL forms. The protocols most commonly referenced by URLs are:

```
ftp:

gopher:

http:
```

```
mailto:

news:

telnet:/rlogin:/tn3270:

wais:

file: (local file access)
```

FTP URLS

Ftp URLs designate files and directories accessible using the FTP protocol. In the absence of any username and password information, anonymous FTP access is assumed. This connects you to the designated server as user *anonymous* and uses your Internet mail address as the password. Here is a typical example, referencing the file *splunge.txt* located in the directory *path* at the Internet site *internet.address.edu*:

```
ftp://internet.address.edu/path/splunge.txt
```

You can specify an FTP access of a directory using a URL such as:

```
ftp://internet.address.edu/path/
```

In this case, FTP servers provide a list of directory contents. WWW browsers display this information as a menu, allowing the user to navigate through the filesystem or select particular files for downloading.

NON-ANONYMOUS FTP ACCESS

You can reference non-anonymous FTP resources by specifying, as part of the URL, the username and password of the account you wish to access. For example,

```
ftp://joe_bozo:bl123@internet.address.edu/dir1/Dir2/file.gz
```

allows a user to access files on machine *internet.address.edu* belonging to user joe_bozo with password bl123. This is, however, not a secure way of giving access to this file, since anyone who reads the URL knows joe_bozo's password. If you have information you want to make available via FTP, set up a proper anonymous FTP service.

FTP DIRECTORY PATHS

Directory paths in FTP accesses are defined relative to a home directory. This home directory is different, depending on how you accomplish the FTP connection. If someone connects to a machine via anonymous FTP, they are placed in the anonymous FTP home directory and have restricted access to the server filesystem. This is a security feature that allows you to make files available to the public without exposing your system to unauthorized users. On the other hand, if someone connects to the same machine as a registered user, their home directory will be that of the user, entirely different from the anonymous FTP directory.

All of this means that the path you use to access a file as a regular user can be quite different from the path used to access a file by anonymous FTP. You must keep this in mind when archiving data into anonymous FTP archives and when creating URLs that point to these data.

MODES FOR FILE TRANSFERS

The FTP protocol allows several modes for transferring files. The most important is *image* or *binary* mode, which makes a byte-by-byte copy of the file. This is the mode to use when transferring programs, compressed data, or image files. Also common is *ASCII* mode, which should be used to transfer plain, printable text files. This mode is useful because it *corrects* for the fact that PCs, Macintoshes, and UNIX computers use different characters to mark the end of a line of text. In particular, Macintoshes use the carriage-return character CR; UNIX computers use the line-feed character LF; and DOS/Windows computers use both CR and LF (often written CRLF). In ASCII mode, FTP automatically converts between these three end-of-line markers to ensure that the received file has the new line codes appropriate to the local system. You cannot use this mode to transfer programs, however, since programs and data files will contain bytes with the same codes as CR or LF characters, and, under ASCII mode, these codes will be converted into the new line codes appropriate to the local system, which destroys the data content of binary data files.

The FTP protocol has no knowledge of the data contents of a file and must be told what mode to use in a file transfer. Thus, your WWW browser must have some way of determining the data type of a file being accessed via an **ftp** URL. In general, the browser *guesses* the type from the suffix of the filename. All WWW clients maintain a local database that maps file-name extensions onto data types. For example, **Mosaic for X-Windows** maintains this database in a file called *mime.types*. WWW browsers use this information to guess the contents of a file and to select the appropriate transfer mode.

TROUBLESHOOTING FTP URLS

At times, an **ftp** URL request may fail, either because the network is down or because the machine you are trying to access is overloaded with FTP accesses and refuses your request. Alternatively, the server may be configured to restrict access to only certain Internet sites. WWW browsers are notoriously terse in handling FTP connections, and say very little if a connection has failed. You can check for the cause of the problem by using an FTP connection outside of your WWW application. A stand-alone FTP program provides much more commentary on the state of your connection and will often give you a message explaining why the connection cannot be made.

GOPHER URLS

Gopher servers can be accessed via URLs in a manner that looks superficially similar to that of FTP or HTTP servers, but is, in fact, quite different. This is because Gopher resources are accessed using a combination of *resource identifier* codes and *selector strings*, so a **Gopher** URL is quite different from an **ftp** or **http** URL. Resource identifiers are single-digit codes that specify the *type* of the Gopher resource; for example, that it is a text file, a directory, or a searchable index. The Gopher selector string is just a name associated with this resource. This can be a directory or filename, but can also be a redirection to a database search procedure or a telnet session.

Sometimes, the selector string has, as its first character, a duplicate of the single-character resource type identifiers. Table 3.2 summarizes the Gopher resource identifier codes.

Table 3.2 Gopher Resource Identifier Codes

Code	File/Resource Type
0	Text file
1	Directory
2	CSO Name/phone book server
3	error
4	Macintosh binhexed (*.hqx) file
5	DOS binary file of some type
6	UNIX uuencoded file
7	Full text index search
8	Telnet session
9	Binary file

GENERAL FORM OF A GOPHER URL

The general form for a Gopher URL is:

```
gopher://domain.name.edu/Tselector_string
```

where T is the Gopher type code and `selector_string` is the Gopher selector string. The root information of a Gopher server can be obtained by leaving out all type and selector string information. Thus, the root information of the preceding Gopher server is available through the URL:

```
gopher://domain.name.edu/
```

Hierarchical relationships are possible. For example:

```
gopher://domain.name.edu/1stuff
```

would retrieve the Gopher contents of the indicated directory, while the URL

```
gopher://domain.name.edu/7stuff/index
```

means access to the *index* search in the directory *stuff*.

PASSING SEARCH INFORMATION

Search information is sent to the Gopher server by appending the search strings to the URL, separated from the URL by a question mark. Thus, to pass the strings `bob`, `carol`, and `ted` to the Gopher search index noted above, the URL is:

```
gopher://domain.name.edu/7stuff/index?bob+carol+ted
```

Note that the URL syntax for Gopher queries uses a plus (+) sign to separate different search strings. Therefore, if you want to send a plus sign as part of a string, it must be encoded. The encoding for a plus sign is `%2B`.

CLIENT CONSTRUCTION OF QUERY STRINGS

Inserting plus sign separators and converting plus signs in query strings into encoded values is done by the WWW or Gopher client. When a user accesses a Gopher search from a WWW browser, he or she is prompted for search strings. These are generally entered in a text box, using space characters or tabs to separate the different strings. When you submit the search, the strings are appended, with appropriate encodings, to the URL. The client software is responsible for replacing space characters by plus signs and for encoding characters in your search string that might be incorrectly interpreted.

GOPHER URL EXAMPLES

```
gopher://gopher.utirc.utoronto.ca/
```

Retrieve the home menu from the Gopher server running on the machine *gopher.utirc.utoronto.ca* running on the default port number (70).

```
gopher://gopher.utirc.utoronto.ca/11adaptive.technology
```

Retrieve the adaptive technology menu from the indicated Gopher server running on the default port number. The selector string for this directory is 1adaptive.technology.

```
gopher://gumby.brain.headache.edu:151/7fonebook.txt?bob+carol+ted+alice
```

Access the searchable index fonebook.txt from the named Gopher server, running on port number 151, and pass to it the four indicated search strings. The Gopher selector string is fonebook.txt.

The Gopher protocol is currently being enhanced, and more sophisticated URLs will be needed to access these newer Gopher features. For more information, please consult the References at the end of this chapter.

HTTP URLS

Http URLs designate files, directories, or server-side programs accessible using the HTTP protocol. **Http** URLs follow the general form indicated in Figure 3.1. Here are some examples:

```
http://www.site.edu:3232/cgi-bin/srch-example
```

> References the program *srch-example* at the site *www.site.edu*, accessible through the HTTP server running on port 3232.

```
http://www.utirc.utoronto.ca/
```

> Access the root directory of the indicated HTTP server. The server can be configured to deliver a standard HTML document, a listing of the directory contents, or an error message.

An **http** URL must always point to a file (text or program) or a directory. A directory is indicated by terminating the directory name with a forward slash, such as:

```
http://www.site.utoronto.ca/HTMLdocs/
```

The following reference to this directory is an error and implies that you are referring to a file, and not a directory:

```
http://www.site.utoronto.ca/HTMLdocs
```

PASSING PARAMETERS TO THE SERVER IN A URL

Http URLs can pass strings to be passed to the server. These strings are appended to the URL separated by a question mark, as with Gopher query strings. Two common examples follow:

```
http://some.site.edu/cgi-bin/foo?arg1+arg2+arg3
```

This is equivalent to the Gopher mechanism discussed in the previous section, and passes the three strings arg1, arg2, and arg3 to the server.

```
http://some.site.edu/cgi-bin/imagemap?ix,iy
```

This mechanism is used by active images. For example, this URL is implied by the following HTML markup:

```
<A HREF=http://some.site.edu/cgi-bin/imagemap>
        <IMG SRC="image.gif" ISMAP>
</A>
```

The **ISMAP** directive declares this image to be an active image map, while the surrounding hypertext anchor indicates the URL to which the image coordinates should be sent. When the user clicks the mouse over the image, the coordinates of the mouse pointer relative to the upper left-hand corner of the image (`ix` and `iy`) are sent by appending them to the indicated URL. The *imagemap* program must know how to interpret this information. This is discussed in more detail in Chapter 5.

In these examples, the information is passed to a resource in the */cgi-bin* directory. In general, HTTP servers do not handle query data directly and instead pass it on to other *gateway* programs for further processing. The directory name */cgi-bin* is a symbolic name used by several servers to reference a directory containing gateway programs.

FRAGMENT IDENTIFIERS

A single HTML document can use the **NAME** attribute of the anchor element to specify distinct targets of hypertext references. For example:

```
<A NAME="raw"> hypertext link target </A>
```

marks the string as a possible target of a hypertext link. In URLs, these named locations are called *fragments* and can be referenced in a URL by appending the *fragment identifier* to the document URL, separated from it by the hash (#) sign. For example, suppose the preceding anchor is found in the document:

```
http://site.world.edu/dir/data.html
```

The string "`hypertext link target`" is then explicitly referenced by the URL:

```
http://site.world.edu/dir/data.html#raw
```

You can also use fragment identifiers from within a single document by using a partial URL that references only the fragment identifier, prepended by the hash sign. Thus, within the document *data.html*, the string "hypertext link target" is referenced with the URL #raw. For example:

```
<A HREF="#raw"> raw data </a>
```

SERVER ISSUES: SPECIAL PROGRAM DIRECTORIES

URL resource specification strings beginning with the strings /cgi-bin or /htbin are often special and refer to directories containing programs and scripts (this is an HTTP server feature and these names can be changed in the server configuration files). When a server is contacted via a URL referencing a gateway program, the server launches the program and passes data from the client (if any) to this program for further processing. This is discussed in more detail in Chapter 4. However, here are two simple examples, with brief explanations:

```
http://some.site.edu/cgi-bin/srch-example
```
> The server executes the program *srch-example* found in the *cgi-bin* directory. Any output from *srch-example* is sent back to the client.

```
http://www.site.edu/cgi-bin/srch-example/path/other?srch_string
```
> The server again executes the program *srch-example* found in the *cgi-bin* directory. The extra *path information* path/other is passed as a parameter to *srch-example*, as is the query information srch_string.

SERVER ISSUES: PERSONAL HTML DIRECTORIES

Users who have accounts on a machine running the NCSA HTTP server can have world-accessible HTML documents in their own home directories, distinct from those files in the server hierarchy. With the NCSA server, these *personal* HTTP document directories are indicated in a URL by a tilde (~) character prepended in front of the path information (the first item in the path hierarchy following the tilde must be the account name of the user). The tilde tells the server that this is not a regular directory, but a *redirection* to a personal document archive of the user with the indicated account. For example, if the user `iang` has a personal document directory, this could be accessed using the URL:

```
http://site.world.edu/~iang/
```

MAILTO URLS

The **mailto** URL indicates that mail is to be sent to the designated electronic mail address. The format for **mailto** is straightforward:

```
mailto:mail_address
```

where `mail_address` is the address to which the message should be sent. Typically, this is of the form `name@host`, where `name` is the username of the person, and `host` is the name of the machine. A browser will allow the user to type in the mail message.

Some mail addresses contain the percent character. This character must be encoded, since it is a special character (marking the beginning of a character encoding string). As an example, the e-mail address:

```
jello%ian@utirc.utor.ca
```

must be converted into the **mailto** URL:

```
mailto:jello%25ian@utirc.utor.ca
```

Several browsers, such as **Mosaic**, **WinWeb**, and **MacWeb**, do not support **mailto** URLs.

NEWS URLS

News URLs reference USENET newsgroups or individual USENET news articles. Newsgroups are specified via the URL:

```
news:news.group
```

where `news.group` is the name of a particular newsgroup. Note that this does not specify an NNTP server from which news can be accessed. This must be specified elsewhere and in a browser-specific manner. For example, **MacWeb** users can configure this with a pull-down menu, while UNIX

Mosaic for X-Windows users must set the NNTPSERVER environment variable to the name of the desired server.

TELNET/TN3270/RLOGIN URLS

You can use a **telnet** URL to indicate a telnet link to a remote machine. An example is:

```
telnet://flober.rodent.edu
```

If you are connecting to a machine that requires IBM 3270-terminal emulation, you can substitute `tn3270` for `telnet`, provided your own machine has a tn3270 client program and that your WWW client is configured to know about this program. Note that you cannot include username and password information in a telnet URL.

Rlogin connections can be indicated using the **rlogin** URL. The specification is:

```
rlogin://username@flober.rodent.edu
```

where `username` is the account name on the remote machine. You will be prompted for a password in the resulting window unless one is not required. Many browsers emulate **rlogin** URLs using a telnet connection.

WAIS URLS

WAIS servers can be accessed via URLs in a manner similar to HTTP servers. The major difference is in the file specification: Here, we must pass the correct search instructions to the WAIS server, in addition to information about what is to be searched.

The standard form for accessing a WAIS server is:

```
wais://wais.server.edu/database?search
```

where `wais.server.edu` is the Internet domain name of the host running the WAIS server (including a port number, if required); `database` is the name of the WAIS database to be searched; and `search` is a list of search instructions to pass to the database. Another form is:

```
wais://wais.server.edu/database
```

which designates a particular searchable database. A browser will understand that this URL references a searchable database and will prompt for query string input.

FILE URLS

File URLs are specific to a local system and should not be used in documents to be accessed over the Internet. A **file** URL represents access of files from computers on a network, particularly from the local computer, but does not specify a protocol for accessing these files. The general form for a **file** URL is:

```
file://hostname/path/file
```

where `hostname` is the domain name for the system, and `path/file` is the locator of the file. The **file** URL is most commonly used to represent local file access. All browsers allow local file access, often with a pull-down menu, and represent the location of the selected file using a **file** URL. The domain name for local file access can be either the special string `localhost` or an empty field. For example, if you are accessing the local file */big/web/docs.html*, the **file** URL could be either of the following:

```
file://localhost/big/web/docs.html
file:///big/web/docs.html
```

Note that the path is the absolute path to the file from the root of the file system.

REFERENCES

IETF working draft specification for URLs:

```
ftp://ds.internic.net/internet-drafts/draft-ietf-uri-url-08.txt
```

(If this file is not available you can check the status of the IETF draft document from the document:)

```
ftp://ds.internic.net/internet-drafts/1id-abstracts.txt
```

Hypertext URL documentation:

```
http://info.cern.ch/hypertext/WWW/Addressing/URL/Overview.html
http://info.cern.ch/hypertext/WWW/Addressing/Addressing.html
```

THE HTTP PROTOCOL AND THE COMMON GATEWAY INTERFACE

To develop interactive HTML documents, you need to understand the interaction between the WWW clients and an HTTP server. This interaction involves two distinct but closely related issues. The first is the HTTP protocol used for communication with HTTP servers. This protocol has several specific communication *methods* (for example, GET, POST, or HEAD) that allow clients to request data from the server and send information to the server.

The second issue is the way HTTP servers handle a client's requests. If the request is for a file, the server simply locates the file and sends it, or sends an appropriate error message if the file is unavailable. Of interest here is the situation when the client wants to send information to the server for more complicated processing. In general, servers do not do this processing themselves and instead *hand off* the work to other programs called *gateway programs.* The *Common Gateway Interface (CGI)* specification defines the mechanisms by which HTTP servers communicate with gateway programs. You therefore need to understand both the HTTP protocol and the CGI specification to write server-side gateway programs and client HTML documents that use these programs.

Gateway programs are referenced using URLs, as with files. When a client accesses a URL pointing to a gateway program, the server activates the program and uses the CGI mechanisms to pass to the program data sent by the client (if any). The gateway program acts on the data and returns its response back to the server, again using the CGI mechanisms. The server then forwards the data to the client that initiated the request using the HTTP protocol, completing the transaction.

This chapter begins with a description of the HTTP protocol, followed by an examination of the Common Gateway Interface specification, including examples of gateway programs that receive data from clients via HTML FORM and ISINDEX search interfaces. The chapter concludes with references to the IETF working draft documents on the HTTP protocol and the CGI specification, should you be interested in further details.

THE HTTP PROTOCOL

HTTP is an Internet client-server protocol designed for the rapid and efficient delivery of hypertext materials. HTTP is a stateless protocol, which means that a client can make several requests of a server but that each request is treated independently, with the server having no recollection of previous connections. This statelessness is an important feature if the server is to be fast.

All HTTP communication uses 8-bit characters, which ensures safe transmission of all forms of data, including HTML documents containing 8-bit ISO Latin-1 characters.

An HTTP connection has four stages:

1. Open the connection—The client contacts the server at the Internet address and port number specified in the URL (the default port is 80).

2. The request—The client sends a message to the server, requesting service. The request consists of HTTP *request headers* that define the *method* requested for the transaction and provide information about the capabilities of the client, followed by the data being sent to the server (if any). Typical HTTP methods are *GET*, for getting an object from a server, or *POST*, for posting data to an object on the server.

3. The response—The server sends a response to the client. This consists of *response headers* describing the state of the transaction (for example, the status of the response—successful or not—and the type of data being sent), followed by the actual data.

4. Close the connection—The connection is closed.

This procedure means that a connection can download only a single document or process a single transaction, while the stateless nature of the transaction means that each connection knows nothing about previous connections. The implications of this are illustrated in the following example HTTP transactions.

Single Transaction per Connection

Suppose HTTP is being used to access an HTML document containing ten inline images. Composing the entire document then requires 11 distinct connections to the HTTP server: one to retrieve the HTML document itself, and ten more to retrieve the ten image files.

Statelessness of the Connection

Suppose a user retrieves a fill-in HTML FORM from a server and enters his or her username and password information to access a restricted server-side resource. When the user submits the FORM data to the server, this username/password information is sent to the server gateway program as part of the data contents (the URL of the gateway program is specified as an attribute to the **FORM** element, as discussed in Chapter 2).

This CGI program returns the results as an HTML document, along with a second FORM allowing further requests. But, this FORM doesn't contain a place for passwords. Since the server is stateless and has no memory of your first connection, how does it know who the user is the second time around? It does not. To keep track of this information, the CGI program must place the username/password information in an `<INPUT TYPE ="hidden">` element, within the returned FORM, as a record of the *state* of the client-server transaction. This information is then passed back and forth between the client and server, preserving knowledge of the username and password for each transaction.

EXAMPLE HTTP CLIENT-SERVER SESSIONS

The easiest way to understand the HTTP protocol is through simple examples. The following section documents five examples covering the most important HTTP methods. Each presentation shows both the data sent from the client to the HTTP server and the data returned from the server to the client. First a few words about how this *eavesdropping* was accomplished.

MONITORING CLIENT-SERVER INTERACTION

It is not difficult to monitor the interaction between HTTP servers and World Wide Web clients, because the communication is entirely in character data sent to a particular port, so that all you need is the ability to *listen* at a port or talk to a port. You can listen at a port using the program **listen**, given in Appendix D, while you can talk to a port using the telnet program.

You use **listen** to find out what a Web client sends to a server. To obtain this information, you run the **listen** program on a computer; for example, *leonardo.subnet.ca.* When you start **listen**, it prints out the port number it is listening at, for example:

```
listening at port 1743
```

and then falls silent, waiting to print any data that arrives at that port. You now configure a WWW client to send HTTP requests to this port. You do this by *pointing* the browser to port 1743 on *leonardo.subnet.ca,* using a URL, such as:

```
http://leonardo.subnet.ca:1743/Tests/file.html
```

The client dutifully sends the HTTP request headers to port number 1743 on *leonardo.subnet.ca*, where **listen** receives the data and prints it to the screen.

Determining what the server sends in response to the client takes a bit more work. In this case, you can use the telnet program to connect to the server and then must enter by hand the HTTP request headers that were sent by the client (and that you intercepted using the **listen** program, as just described). Suppose, for example, that the server is running at port 80 on *leonardo.subnet.ca*. To connect to this server, simply make a telnet connection to this port. On a UNIX system, type (the PC or Macintosh versions are slightly different):

```
leonardo:> telnet leonardo.subnet.ca 80
Trying 128.100.121.33...
Connected to leonardo.subnet.ca
Escape character is '^]'
```

The string you type is in boldface. Telnet gives three lines of information to let you know what it is doing and then falls silent. Whatever you type is sent to the server running on *leonardo.subnet.ca*, so you now type in the required request headers. Whatever the server sends in response is sent to the telnet program and printed on the screen.

These tools are used in the following five examples to determine the information passed between the client and server in typical HTTP transactions.

These five examples look at:

1. A GET method request for a file

2. A GET method request to a gateway program, with a query string appended to the URL

3. An HTML FORM accessing a server gateway program using the GET method

4. An HTML FORM accessing a server gateway program using the POST method

5. An HTTP HEAD method request of a file

These examples build on an understanding of URLs and of the way data are gathered by an HTML form. These topics were covered in Chapters 2 and 3.

EXAMPLE 1: A SIMPLE GET METHOD REQUEST

This request accesses the server and requests that a document be sent to the client. This could be initiated by clicking on a hypertext anchor pointing to the file. For example:

```
<A HREF="http://some.server.edu/Tests/file.html">
   anchor text
</A>
```

The transaction can be broken into two parts: the passing of the request to the server, and the response information sent by the server back to the client.

Passing the Request ■ Figure 4.1 shows the actual data sent by a **Mosaic for X-Windows** Version 2.4 client to the server. Other clients send qualitatively the same information. The dots indicate Accept headers that were omitted to save space.

```
GET /Tests/file.html HTTP/1.0
Accept: text/plain
Accept: application/x-html
Accept: application/html        .
Accept: text/x-html
Accept: text/html
Accept: audio/*

  .

  .

  .

Accept: text/x-setext
Accept: */*
User-Agent: NCSA Mosaic for the X Window System/2.4 libwww/2.12 modified
        [a blank line, containing only CRLF ]
```

Figure 4.1 Data sent from a client to an HTTP server during a simple GET request. *Comments are in italics.*

This request message consists of a *request header* containing several *request header fields*. Each field is a text line, terminated by a carriage-return linefeed character pair (CRLF). The blank line (containing only a CRLF pair) at the end indicates the end of the headers and the beginning of any data being sent from the client to the server. This example transaction does not send data to the server, so the blank line is the end of the request.

The request message contains two parts: the *method* field, which is the first line of the request and which specifies the HTTP method to be used and the location of the desired resource on the server, followed by HTTP *request* fields, which pass information to the server about the capabilities of the client.

The method field contains three text fields, separated by white space (white space is any combination of space or tab characters). In this example, the method header is:

```
GET /path/file.html HTTP/1.0
```

The general form of this field is:

```
HTTP_method  identifier  HTTP_version
```

These three strings contain:

HTTP_Method   The HTTP method specification—GET in the preceding example. The method specifies what is to be done to the object specified by the URL. Some other common methods are HEAD, which requests header information about an object, and POST, which is used to send information to the object.

identifier   The identifier of the resource. Here, this is the URL stripped of the protocol and Internet domain name strings. If this were a message to a *proxy server*, this would be the entire URL. Proxy access is discussed later in this chapter.

HTTP_Version   The HTTP protocol version used by the client, currently HTTP/1.0.

The example shows several additional request headers. The Accept field passes to the server a list of data representation schemes acceptable to the client. These are given as MIME content-types and simply tell the server what type of data the client can handle. MIME types are discussed in more detail in Appendix B. The meanings are relatively straightforward. For example, the line Accept: text/plain means that the client can accept plain text files, while the line Accept: audio/* means that the client can accept any form of audio data.

There are several other possible request fields. The only other one used in the preceding example is the User-agent header:

```
User-Agent: NCSA Mosaic for the X Window System/2.4 libwww/2.12 modified
```

This provides information about the client making the request. The string libwww/2.12 refers to the CERN common-code library for WWW applications, which is a software library used in developing WWW software. Other possible request headers are summarized at the end of this section.

Server Response ■ When the server receives the request, it tries to apply the designated method to the specified object (file or program) and passes the results of this effort back to the client. The returned data are preceded by a response header made up of *response header fields*, which communicate information about the state of the transaction back to the client. As with the request header fields sent from the client to the server, these are single lines of text terminated by a CRLF. The end of the response header is indicated by a single blank line containing only a CRLF. The data of the response comes after the blank line.

Figure 4.2 shows the data sent from the server to the client in response to the request of Figure 4.1.

The first seven lines are the response headers. The end of the response headers is indicated by the single blank line. The data response of the request (in this case, the requested HTML document) follows this blank line.

The first line in the response header is a status line that lets the client know what protocol the server uses and whether the request was successfully completed. In our example, this line is:

```
HTTP/1.0 200 OK
```

The general format for this line is:

```
http_version status_code explanation
```

The `HTTP_version` field gives the protocol version used by the server, currently HTTP/1.0. The `status_code` is a number between 200 and 599 that gives the status of the connection, while the `explanation` field is a text string that provides more descriptive information about the status. Explanation strings may vary from server to server, whereas status codes are explicitly defined by the HTTP specifications. Status codes between 200 and 299 indicate successful transactions. Numbers 300 to 399 indicate redirection, which means that the object specified by the URL has moved and that the server is also sending the client the new URL of the object (the server sends the new URL in a `Location` header). Numbers 400 to 599 are error messages. When you encounter an error, the server usually sends a small HTML document to explain the error. Figure 4.3 gives more details about the different status codes.

```
HTTP/1.0 200 OK
Date: Friday, 23-Sep-94 16:04:09 GMT
Server: NCSA/1.3
MIME-version: 1.0
Content-type: text/html
Last-modified: Friday, 23-Sep-94 16:03:27 GMT
Content-length: 145
     [a blank line, containing only CRLF ]
<html>
<head>
<title> Test HTML file </title>
</head>


<body>


<h1> This is a test file</h1>
<p> So what did you expect, art?


</body>
</html>
```

Figure 4.2 Data returned from the server to the client subsequent to the GET request of Figure 4.1. *Comments are in italics.*

The remaining response headers contain information about the server and about the response being sent. The example in Figure 4.2 returned six lines of response header information. The first three, the `Date`, `Server`, and `MIME-version` fields, describe the server and the details of the transaction, while the `Content-type`, `Last-modified`, and `Content-length` fields pass information specific to the document being returned. The formats and meanings of these header fields are:

`Date: date_time`—Contains the time and date when the current object was assembled for transmission, in the format `Friday, 23-Sep-94 16:04:09 GMT`. Note that the time must be Greenwich Mean Time (GMT) to ensure that all servers share a common time zone.

`MIME-version: version_number`—Gives the MIME protocol version. The current version is 1.0.

`Server: name/version`—This gives the name and version of the server, with a slash character separating the server name from the version number; for example, `NCSA/1.3` or `CERN/3.0pre6`.

`Content-length: length`—Gives the length in bytes of the data portion of the message (in this case, `145`). In some cases, the length is unknown (for example, if it is output from a gateway program), in which case, this field is absent.

`Content-type: type/subtype`—Gives the MIME `Content-type` of the data being sent. This tells the client what type of data is being sent by the server. In this example, the MIME type is `text/html`, which informs the browser that the data is an HTML document.

`Last-modified: date_time`—Gives the date and time that the document was last modified, in the format `Friday, 23-Sep-94 16:03:27 GMT`. As with the `Date` field, the date must be given in Greenwich Mean Time.

How are these headers generated? If the request is for a file, the HTTP server constructs these headers itself. If the request is to a CGI gateway program, then the gateway program must provide headers that specify details about the returned data, such as the Content-type, that cannot be otherwise determined by the server. The server parses these headers and adds some of its own to construct a complete collection of server response headers. Alternatively, the gateway program can return all the response headers and bypass the server. This *nonparsed header* option is described in the discussion of the CGI specification.

A complete list of commonly used HTTP response headers is given at the conclusion of the HTTP protocol section.

■■■■■■

A) Successful Transactions

200   The request was fulfilled.

201   The request was a POST method and was completed successfully.

202   The request has been accepted for processing, but the results of this processing are unknown. This would be returned, for example, if the client deposited data for batch processing at a later date.

203   The request was fulfilled but has returned partial information.

B) Redirection Transactions

301   The data requested has been permanently moved to a new URL. If this status is returned, the server should also send the client the URL of the new location via the header

```
Location: URL comments
```

where URL is the new document URL. Browsers that understand the Location field will automatically connect to the new URL.

302   The data was found but it actually resides at a different URL. If this status is returned, the server should also send the client the correct URL via the header

```
Location: URL comments
```

Browsers that understand the `Location` field will automatically connect to the new URL. You will get a 302 Redirection if a URL pointing to a directory is missing the trailing slash character.

304   A GET request was sent containing the `If-Modified-Since` field. However, the server found that the document had not been modified since the date specified in this field. Consequently, the server responds with this code and does not resend the document.

C) Error Messages

400   The request syntax was wrong.

401   The request required an `Authorization:` field, and the client did not specify one. The server also returns a list of the allowed authorization schemes using `WWW-Authenticate` response headers. This mechanism is used by a client and server to negotiate data encryption and user authentication schemes.

402   The requested operation costs money, and the client did not specify a valid `Chargeto` field in the request header.

403   You have requested a resource that is forbidden.

404   The server cannot find the URL you requested.

500   The server has encountered an internal error and cannot continue with the request.

501   The request you have made is legal, but the server does not support this method.

Figure 4.3 HTTP status codes.

LESSONS FROM EXAMPLE 1

1. When a client contacts an HTTP server, it sends the server a collection of *request headers*. These headers include the *method field*, which specifies the HTTP method being requested by the client and the *location* on the server of the resource being requested, followed by other request header fields that pass information about the capabilities of

the client. The collection of request headers is terminated by a single blank line.

2. The server responds with a message consisting of a *response header* followed by the requested data. The response header fields communicate information about the state of the transaction, including a MIME *content-type* header that explicitly tells the client the type of data being sent. The collection of response headers is terminated by a single blank line. The data being sent to the client follows after the blank line.

EXAMPLE 2: A GET METHOD REQUEST WITH SEARCH STRINGS

The second example is a GET method, but with query information appended to the URL. As discussed in Chapter 2, query information is appended to the URL, separated by a question mark. This is done automatically by World Wide Web browsers when you submit ISINDEX queries or HTML FORMs data using the GET method.

A typical URL might be:

```
http://www.stuff.ca/cgi-bin/srch-example?item1+item2+item3+item4
```

which passes four items to the program *srch-example*.

Figure 4.4 shows the request headers sent by the **MacWeb** browser when it accesses this URL. Again, some accept headers are omitted to save space.

This GET method is also known as the HTTP *TEXTSEARCH* method, even though it is constructed using GET and a modified URL. This request header is essentially the same as in Figure 4.1, the major difference being the query strings added to the locator string. The server's interpretation of this string is described in the second half of this chapter.

```
GET /cgi-bin/srch-example?item1+item2+item3+item4 HTTP/1.0

Accept: video/quicktime

Accept: video/mpeg

Accept: image/x-xbitmap

Accept: image/pict

Accept: image/jpeg

.

.

.

Accept: text/plain

Accept: text/html

User-Agent: MacWeb/1.00ALPHA2 libwww/2.13

   [a blank line, containing only CRLF ]
```

▬▬▬ **Figure 4.4** Data sent from a **MacWeb** client to an HTTP server during a GET request, with query strings appended to the URL. *Comments are in italics.*

LESSON FROM EXAMPLE 2

Query data appended to a URL during a GET request to a server is passed as part of the locator string in the HTTP *method field* of the request headers. All other request headers are the same as those for a standard GET request, as described in Example 1. A GET request with an appended query string is also called the HTTP TEXTSEARCH method.

EXAMPLE 3: SUBMITTING A FORM USING THE GET METHOD

This example examines how an HTML FORM submits the form data contents to a server, using the HTTP GET method. The example HTML FORM is shown in Figure 4.5. The actual rendering of this form by a WWW browser is shown in Figure 4.6.

```
<FORM ACTION="http://leonardo.utirc.utoronto.ca:8080/cgi-bin/form1" METHOD=GET>
<p> Search string: <INPUT TYPE="text" NAME="srch" VALUE="dogfish">
<p> Search Type:
  <SELECT NAME="srch_type">
    <OPTION> Insensitive Substring
    <OPTION SELECTED> Exact Match
    <OPTION> Sensitive Substring
    <OPTION> Regular Expression
  </SELECT>
<p> Search databases in:
  <INPUT TYPE="checkbox" NAME="srvr" VALUE="Canada" CHECKED> Canada
  <INPUT TYPE="checkbox" NAME="srvr" VALUE="Russia"  > Russia
  <INPUT TYPE="checkbox" NAME="srvr" VALUE="Sweden" CHECKED> Sweden
  <INPUT TYPE="checkbox" NAME="srvr" VALUE="U.S.A."  > U.S.A.
  <em>(multiple items can be selected.)</em>
<P> <INPUT TYPE="submit"> <INPUT TYPE=reset>.
</FORM>
```

Figure 4.5 Example HTML FORM that uses the GET method to submit data to a server.

The FORM element is discussed in detail in Chapter 2. This FORM defines the three variable names, *srch*, *srch_type*, and *srvr*. These have been assigned values *srch=dogfish*, *srch_type=Exact Match*, *srvr=Canada*, and *srvr=Sweden*. **Mosaic for X-Windows** Version 2.4 is again used, as in Example 1. Figure 4.7 shows the data sent by this FORM to the server. The dots indicate accept headers that were deleted to save space.

As discussed in Chapter 2, submitting a FORM sends the data to the server as a collection of *name/value* pairs. In practice, this is accomplished by sending the data as a collection of strings, name=value, with the ampersand character (&) separating the strings. In addition, blank characters are encoded into plus signs. With the GET method, this string is appended to

Figure 4.6 Mosaic for X-Windows browser rendering of the FORM example in Figure 4.5.

the URL and separated from it by a question mark. When the HTTP server receives these data, it forwards the entire *query string* to the gateway program *form1*. These details are discussed in Example 9 in the CGI section of this chapter.

LESSON FROM EXAMPLE 3

When an HTML FORM submits data to an HTTP server using the GET method, the FORM data are appended to the URL as a query string. Consequently, the FORM data are sent to the server in the query string part of the locator string in the request header method field. The FORM data are encoded according to the URL syntax.

```
GET /cgi-bin/form1?srch=dogfish&srch_type=Exact+Match&srvr=Canada&srvr=Sweden HTTP/1.0
Accept: text/plain
Accept: application/x-html
Accept: application/html
Accept: text/x-html
Accept: text/html
Accept: audio/*
   .
   .
   .
Accept: text/x-setext
Accept: */*
User-Agent: NCSA Mosaic for the X Window System/2.4 libwww/2.12 modified
   [a blank line, containing only CRLF ]
```

Figure 4.7 Data sent from a client to an HTTP server during a FORM-based GET request.

EXAMPLE 4: SUBMITTING A FORM USING THE POST METHOD

This example again uses the FORM shown in Figure 4.6 but with one subtle change: It uses the HTTP POST method, not GET. Therefore, this example sends the same data to the server but by a different method.

As in Example 3, this form has variable names *srch*, *srch_type*, and *srvr*. These have been assigned values *srch=dogfish*, *srch_type=Exact Match*, *srvr=Canada*, and *srvr=Sweden*. Figure 4.8 shows the data sent to the server, again from the **Mosaic for X-Windows** browser.

The POST method sends data in a message *body*, not in the URL. The difference is indicated in three places. The first is in the method header, which now specifies the POST method and which has no data appended to the URL. The second is in the two new request header fields: Content-type and Content-length. Last, it is indicated by the line of data following the headers. This line is the data being sent to the server via the POST method.

```
POST /cgi-bin/form1 HTTP/1.0
Accept: text/plain
Accept: application/x-html
Accept: application/html
Accept: text/x-html
Accept: text/html
Accept: audio/*

  .

  .

  .

Accept: text/x-setext
Accept: */*
User-Agent: NCSA Mosaic for the X Window System/2.4 libwww/2.12 modified
Content-type: application/x-www-form-urlencoded
Content-length: 58


srch=dogfish&srch_type=Exact+Match&srvr=Canada&srvr=Sweden
```

▬▬▬▬▬▬ **Figure 4.8** Data sent from a client to an HTTP server during a FORM-based POST request.

The two new headers tell the server that there will be data following the request headers. The content-length header gives the length in bytes of the message, while the content-type header specifies the MIME-type of the message being sent to the server. There is currently only one valid content-type for FORM data being sent to a server, namely:

```
Content-type: application/x-www-form-urlencoded
```

This header indicates that the data is from a FORM and that it is encoded in the same manner as when appended to a URL. You can compare the message body at the bottom of Figure 4.8 with the data appended to the URL in Figure 4.7 to verify this equivalence. The details of how the data are passed from the server to the CGI program are described in the second half of this chapter.

LESSON FROM EXAMPLE 4

When an HTML FORM submits data to an HTTP server using the POST method, the FORM data are sent to the server as a *message body* that follows the request headers. This message body is encoded in the same manner as when appended to the URL. Additional request headers tell the server the content-type of the arriving message (`application/x-www-form-urlencoded`) and the length of the message. No data are appended to the URL.

EXAMPLE 5: ACCESSING A
DOCUMENT WITH THE HEAD METHOD

The HEAD method is often used by programs that automatically search for documents on WWW servers. This method requests that the server send the response headers relevant to the requested URL, but not the referenced object. This is a quick way of seeing if a document or gateway program is actually present and of obtaining some general information about it, such as its MIME content-type, without downloading an entire document.

For example, suppose you access the document in Example 1, but using the HEAD method. This request is written:

```
HEAD /Tests/file.html HTTP/1.0
User-Agent: HEAD Test Agent
From: name@domain.name.edu
```

You do not need all the accept headers, since you are not requesting a complete document. The new `From` field gives the server the electronic mail address of the person making the HEAD request. The response to this request (in this case, the NCSA Version 1.3 HTTP server) is:

```
HTTP/1.0 200 OK
Date: Saturday, 24-Sep-94 23:10:55 GMT
Server: NCSA/1.3
MIME-version: 1.0
```

```
Content-type: text/html

Last-modified: Sunday, 18-Sep-94 19:44:28 GMT

Content-length: 0
```

This indicates that the document is there (the status code 200 implies a valid URL), and includes information about the document type and the date it was last modified. In principle, the HTML **META** allows the server to parse the document and include additional information about the document in these header fields, but few servers currently implement this feature.

LESSON FROM EXAMPLE 5

A HEAD request retrieves the response headers for the indicated URL only—the document itself is not retrieved. If the HEAD request is for an HTML document, some servers parse the *document* **HEAD** for information to include in the response headers—this server feature is not widely implemented.

The preceding discussion and examples provided an overview of the HTTP protocol. You can, if you wish, skip to the CGI specifications section of this chapter. The next section looks briefly at more complex features of the HTTP protocol, such as user authentication, format negotiation, and other less used methods, and gives a summary of commonly used request headers, response headers, and HTTP methods.

USER AUTHENTICATION, DATA ENCRYPTION, AND ACCESS CONTROL

So far, we have not discussed controlling access to an HTTP server, or the encryption of data for transmission between client and server. There are several mechanisms available for doing these things, but as yet no well-established standard. This section briefly discusses the different options open to a server administrator, and refers the interested reader to more advanced documentation on this topic.

For low-level security, you can configure the server to allow access only to machines in an authorized Internet domain. For example, several servers can be configured to allow access only to machines with Internet domain names ending with a string such as .domain.site.edu. This feature is available on several servers. Often, access can be restricted on a per-file or per-directory basis. This is not very secure, however, since a clever cracker can *spoof* a domain name and access the data. It is also not very specific, since anyone can access the restricted material, provided they can access one of the allowed machines.

A somewhat finer control is possible when accessing server-side CGI programs. For example, you can connect an HTML FORM to a server-side program and have the FORM request identification and password information for authentication on the server. This is still not very secure, since the information being sent is not encrypted so that anyone intercepting the messages can read the username and password information.

Truly secure communication requires negotiated encryption of the data being sent from client to server and from server to client. Negotiated encryption means that the server and client must negotiate the scheme to be used and must also exchange information allowing each of them to send encrypted information that can be decoded by the receiver. This requires that both client and server contain encryption/decryption software and that they both understand the same encryption schemes. Currently, the NCSA and CERN HTTP servers have these capabilities, as do certain client programs, such as **Mosaic for X-Windows**. The references at the end of this chapter describe the details of the CERN and NCSA authentication/encryption implementations. Authentication is an important feature for most commercial providers of WWW software products, so, if encryption is important, you may want to consider commercial providers of server and browser software.

PROXY SERVERS AND SERVER CACHING

Proxy servers are used by local area networks (LANs) that want to protect themselves from unauthorized entry over the Internet. This can be done by installing *firewall* software on the gateway machine that links the local network to the outside world. A firewall keeps TCP/IP packets from entering the local network from the outside world and thereby protects the LAN from the dangerous world outside.

Unfortunately, a firewall means that users inside the LAN cannot access WWW resources outside, since communication is blocked by the firewall. The solution is to install a *proxy server* on the firewall, and to configure your WWW browsers to refer to this proxy server instead of the real servers outside your LAN. A proxy server has access to both the inside and outside worlds, and can safely pass information back and forth across the firewall. When your browser wants to request information from outside the firewall, it sends this request to the proxy server on the firewall. The proxy server then *proxies* the request—that is, it completes the request on your behalf and forwards to you the result.

This two-stage process can be slow. To speed up service, proxy servers can *cache* the retrieved files. Thus, the first time you request a document, the server goes to the outside world and fetches it, but subsequently retains a copy on its own local disk. If you make another request for this same file, the proxy server gives you the locally cached copy of the document and does not refetch it. This saves time and can also significantly reduce the load on the network connection.

This can be a problem, however, if the file is one that changes with time. This can be the case for pages containing periodically updated data or for documents created dynamically by CGI programs. This problem can be solved using the `Expires` server response header, which is used to inform a proxy server how long it can keep a cached copy of a downloaded document. When the proxy server retrieves a document from the primary server outside the firewall, the primary server can place in the server response headers the line:

```
Expires: date
```

This tells the proxy server how long it can keep the document before it must be updated from the original server.

CERN HTTP PROXY SERVER

There are two ways of implementing proxy servers on a LAN. The CERN HTTP proxy server was explicitly designed to be an HTTP server, and also to support proxy access outside a firewall-protected network. The CERN HTTP server also implements document caching, and is the best choice for implementing HTTP service in a secure environment. More details about the CERN HTTP server are given in Chapter 8.

SOCKS PROXY SUPPORT

The SOCKS package is another proxying package, but was not designed specifically for HTTP service and does not have caching capabilities. However, this is an ideal choice if you do not also need an HTTP server, and is significantly easier to implement than the full CERN HTTP server. Additional information about SOCKS can be found at:

```
ftp://ftp.nec.com/pub/security/socks.cstc
```

A proxy server is useful only if your browser can be configured to use it. Chapter 7, which discusses the different WWW browsers, notes browsers that support proxy service. Additional information about proxy support is found in the References at the end of this chapter.

HTTP METHODS AND HEADERS REFERENCE

The following three sections summarize the currently implemented HTTP methods, request headers, and response headers. A more detailed list can be found in the References at the end of this chapter.

HTTP METHODS

The most common methods are the GET/TEXTSEARCH, HEAD, and POST methods just discussed. The following is a slightly more complete list of these methods:

GET — Retrieve the indicated URL.

HEAD — Retrieve the HTTP header information for the indicated URL.

TEXTSEARCH — Access the indicated URL and query the URL. This is done using a GET method and a URL that contains appended query data.

LINK — This method links an existing object to another object. For an HTML document, this would imply editing the document and adding LINK information to the document HEAD.

UNLINK — Remove the link information inserted, for example, by a LINK method.

POST — Send the data to the indicated URL. The URL must already exist.

PUT — Place the data being sent by the client in the indicated URL, replacing the old contents. The URL must already exist. The CERN HTTP server has an implementation of PUT.

HTTP REQUEST HEADERS

`Accept: type/subtype`—This field contains a list of MIME content-types that are acceptable to the client, separated by semicolons.

`Accept-Encoding: encoding_type`—Lists the data encoding types acceptable to the client. For example, `Accept-Encoding: x-compress` tells the server that the client can accept compressed data in the compress format.

The only current encoding types are `x-compress` and `x-gzip`. If a server sends a document in compressed format, it must include the `Content-Encoding` response header.

`Authorization: scheme data`—This passes user authentication and encryption scheme information to the server.

`Content-length: length`—Gives the length (in bytes) of the message being sent to the server.

`Content-type: type/subtype`—This gives the MIME content-type of the message being sent to the server.

`From: mail_address`—This contains the address, in Internet mail format, of the user accessing the server.

`If-Modified-Since: date`—This request header is used with the GET method to make the GET request conditional: If the requested document has not changed since the indicated time and date, the document is not sent. The date must be in Greenwich Mean Time and of the format `Friday, 23-Sep-94 18:28:33 GMT`. If the document is not sent, the server should send the response header message 304 (not modified).

`Pragma: directives_for_server`—Pragma directives are designed for passing special-purpose information to servers. Currently, there is only one server directive, `Pragma: no-cache`, which instructs a proxy server to always fetch the document from the actual server, and to never use a locally cached copy.

`Referer: URL`—This gives the URL of the document from which the request originated. This can be a partial URL, in which case, it is interpreted relative to the URL of the document being requested. If a document contains an HTML **BASE** element, then the contents of this should be sent instead.

`User-Agent: program/version comments`—Provides information about the client software making the request.

HTTP RESPONSE HEADERS

The following is a list of currently implemented HTTP response headers. A more detailed list can be found in the References listed at the end of this chapter.

`Content-Encoding: encoding_type`—Specifies the encoding type mechanism used in generating the results. The only currently valid types are `x-compress` and `x-gzip`. You can have only one type per header. This allows compressed files to be uncompressed on-the-fly by the client.

`Content-length: xxx`—Gives the length (in bytes) of the message being sent to the client.

`Content-Transfer-Encoding: encoding_type`—This is a MIME protocol header and gives the encoding mechanism used for the MIME messages. The default is 8-bit character encoding.

`Content-type: type/subtype`—This gives the MIME content-type of the message being sent to the client.

`Expires: date_time`—Gives the time and date after which the information being sent should be considered invalid. This can allow clients to automatically refresh data that should be periodically updated. Proxy servers use this field to determine when a cached copy of a document should be refreshed.

`Title: title`—The title of the document. This should be identical to the contents of the document's **TITLE** element.

`WWW-Authenticate: scheme scheme_message`—This passes information to the client stating the encryption and authorization schemes the server wants to use. This is used only for directories, files, or CGI programs that require user authentication. `Scheme` gives the name of the authorization scheme, while `scheme_message` gives related data.

`WWW-Link:`—This should contain the information from the **LINK** elements of an HTML document. This allows the HTTP header to contain information about an HTML document, and would allow clients using HEAD methods to access information about the document useful for cataloging and indexing purposes.

THE COMMON GATEWAY INTERFACE

The Common Gateway Interface (CGI) is the specified standard for communication between HTTP servers and server-side gateway programs. When you access a gateway program, the server activates the program and passes it any ISINDEX query, FORM, or other data that was sent from the client. When the gateway program has finished processing the data, it sends the result back to the server and, from there, back to the client. The CGI specifications define how these data are passed from the server to the gateway program, and vice versa.

Gateway programs can be compiled programs written in languages such as C, C++, or Pascal, or they can be executable scripts written in scripting languages such as perl, tcl, and the various shell programs. In fact, most gateway programs are scripts, since these are easy to write and modify and are inherently transportable from machine to machine. In addition, execution speed is often not an important factor when writing a gateway program, since the slowest part is usually the resource the gateway connects to, and not the gateway program itself.

SENDING DATA FROM
THE CLIENT TO THE SERVER

There are three ways data is sent from the client to the server. The first is via a URL query string, such as:

```
http://some.site.edu/cgi-bin/ex_prog?query_info
```

This passes the query string `query_info` to the server. The server, in turn, launches the gateway program *ex_prog* and passes it the query string.

The second way is as *extra path* information, which is placed in the URL by adding directory-like information to the URL just after the name of the gateway program. For example:

```
http://some.site.edu/cgi-bin/ex_prog/dir/file?query_info
```

The string `/dir/file` is interpreted by the server as extra path information, while the string `query_info` is once again interpreted as a query string. When the server launches the gateway program *ex_prog*, it passes to *ex_prog* both the query string `query_info` and the extra path string `/dir/file`.

Third, data can be sent to the server in a message body. This is possible with the HTTP POST method and is often used with HTML FORMs. When a server receives a POST method message from a FORM, it sends the POSTed data to the designated gateway program.

SENDING DATA TO THE
GATEWAY PROGRAM FROM THE SERVER

The CGI specifications define the mechanisms by which data are forwarded to a gateway program. There are three mechanisms:

1. Command-Line Arguments—The server launches the gateway program with command-line arguments.

2. Standard Input—The server passes data to the gateway program such that it is read as input (from standard input) by the gateway program client.

3. Environment Variables—The server puts information in special *environment variables* before starting the gateway program. The gateway program can then access these variables and obtain their contents.

The mechanisms that are used during a particular transaction depend on the HTTP method of the request (GET or POST), and also on the nature of the query string appended to the URL (ISINDEX versus non-ISINDEX queries). Later sections use examples to illustrate typical cases.

RETURNING DATA FROM THE
GATEWAY PROGRAM TO THE SERVER

There are two ways in which a CGI program can send information back to the server:

1. Write to standard output—The gateway program passes data back to the server by writing data to standard output. This is the *only* way that gateway programs can return data to a client.

2. The name of the gateway program—Gateway programs with names beginning with the string *nph-* are called *nonparsed header* programs and are treated specially by the server. In general, the server parses the output of a gateway program looking for headers that it can use to create the HTTP response headers it will send to the client with the returned data. If a gateway program name begins with *nph-*, the server sends the gateway program directly to the client and does not add any header information.

These methods are illustrated with several examples. The first of these, Example 6, looks at an HTML ISINDEX document request. Example 7 demonstrates nonparsed header gateway programs, which send data directly back to the client, bypassing any server processing. Example 8 shows how environment variables are passed to the gateway program and explains the contents of these variables. Examples 9 and 10 show how HTML FORMs data—using the GET and POST methods, respectively— are passed to a gateway program.

EXAMPLE 6: ISINDEX SEARCHES

ISINDEX queries is the *only* query method that passes data to a gateway program as command-line arguments. It is a simple technique and a useful starting point for understanding client-server-gateway interactions.

This example accesses the gateway program *srch-example* listed in Figure 4.9. This is a Bourne-shell script designed to search a phone-number database using the search program *grep*. This script searches for names in a phone-listings database and uses the **ISINDEX** element to prompt for the search string. In this example, the search string is just the list of names you want to search for. When this script receives this data, it searches the database for the indicated names and returns the names and phone numbers of any matches. The script is designed both to prompt for search strings and to return the results of the search.

From Chapter 2, you will recall that ISINDEX sends data to the server by appending the query data onto the URL being viewed; for example:

```
http://some.where.edu/cgi-bin/srch_program?query_string
```

When this information reaches the server, the URL is decoded and, if it is an ISINDEX query, the server takes the query strings and passes them to the indicated gateway program as command-line arguments.

How does the server know if a query is an ISINDEX query? The convention is that an ISINDEX query string *does not contain* any unencoded equal signs (=). As noted in Example 3, FORM data is passed as a collection of name=value strings, which always contains equal signs. Therefore, the presence of an equal sign indicates that the query does not come from an ISINDEX query, in which case, the server does not convert the query data into command-line arguments.

Step 1: First Access of the URL ■ In the example, we first access the script *srch-example* using the URL:

```
http://leonardo.utirc.utoronto.ca:8080/cgi-bin/srch-example
```

Note that there is no query information attached to this URL; this is an important factor in the behavior of the script.

■■■■■

```
01 #!/bin/sh
02 echo Content-TYPE:  text/html
03 echo
04
05 if [ $# = 0 ]            # is the number of arguments == 0 ?
06 then                     # do this part if there are NO arguments
07   echo "<HEAD>"
08   echo "<TITLE>Local Phonebook Search</TITLE>"
09   echo "<ISINDEX>"
10   echo "</HEAD>"
11   echo "<BODY>"
12   echo "<H1>Local Phonebook Search</H1>"
13   echo "Enter your search in the search field.<P>"
14   echo "This is a case-insensitive substring search: thus"
15   echo "searching for 'ian' will find 'Ian' and Adriana'."
16   echo "</BODY>"
17 else                     # this part if there ARE arguments
18   echo "<HEAD>"
19   echo "<TITLE>Result of search for \"$*\".</TITLE>"
20   echo "</HEAD>"
21   echo "<BODY>"
22   echo "<H1>Result of search for \"$*\".</H1>"
23   echo "<PRE>"
24    for i in $*
25    do
26       grep -i $i /vast/igraham/Personnel
27    done
28   echo "</PRE>"
39   echo "</BODY>"
40 fi
```

■■■■■ **Figure 4.9** Bourne-shell script CGI gateway program *srch-example*.

Line 1 tells the computer to interpret this script using the **/bin/sh** program, which is the traditional location and name for the Bourne shell. The second two lines *echo* information to standard output (echo is the Bourne-shell command for printing to standard output). Standard output information is sent back to the server and, from there, back to the client. These two lines provide HTTP response header information about the data to come. This is necessary, as the server has no other way of knowing the type of data the gateway program will send. The first line in this script prints the header:

```
Content-type: text/html
```

to tell the client and server that the data to follow is an HTML document. The next line of the script prints a blank line. Per the HTTP protocol, this indicates the end of the header fields and that subsequent output is message data.

Line 5 tests the number of command-line arguments. In this case, there is no query string, so there are no arguments and the first branch of the if is executed. This first branch prints to standard output a simple HTML document explaining the nature of the search; this is shown in Figure 4.10. The document also contains the **ISINDEX** element, which instructs the browser to prompt for search information; this results in the query box shown in Figure 4.10. The names *ian* and *bradley* are already typed into this box, separated by a single space. These are the names to be used in the search.

Step 2: Second Access of the URL ■ Submitting this ISINDEX search information accesses the same URL, but appends the names *ian* and *bradley* to the URL as query strings. Thus, in this second phase, the accessed URL is:

```
http://leonardo.utirc.utoronto.ca:8080/cgi-bin/srch-example?ian+bradley
```

where the space between *ian* and *bradley* has been encoded as a plus sign.

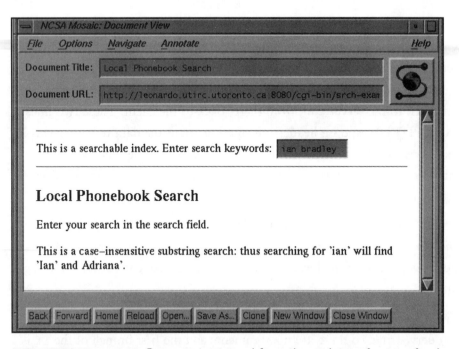

■■■■■■ **Figure 4.10** Document returned from the script ***srch-example*** when accessed *without* a query string appended to the URL.

When the server receives this URL, it parses the query string and finds that there are no unencoded equal signs, so it knows that this is an ISINDEX query. It therefore takes the query string and breaks it into individual strings, using the plus signs to mark the string separators. This yields two strings: `ian` and `bradley`. The server next launches the gateway program ***srch-example***, using the names `ian` and `bradley` as command-line arguments. If you were to type the command yourself, this would look like:

```
srch-example ian bradley
```

Figure 4.11 shows the results of this second access to the Bourne-shell program and, by following Figure 4.9, you can see how this was generated. As before, the first two lines print the MIME content-type of the message and the blank line separating the HTTP headers from the data. At line 5, the program checks for command-line arguments. This time, there are arguments, so the second branch of the script is executed starting at line 18.

This section prints a different HTML document: this time, including output from the program *grep*. Lines 24 through 27 loop the variable i through all the different command-line arguments. The contents of the variable i (denoted by $i) are given as an argument to the program *grep*, which scans the file */vast/igraham/Personnel* for names matching the pattern given by the argument i. *Grep* prints the matches to standard output. The result of the searches is shown in Figure 4.11. Note that there is now no query box. The second branch through the script in Figure 4.9 did not include an **ISINDEX** element, so no query box is presented.

EXAMPLE 7: HEADERS AND GATEWAY PROGRAMS

In this example, we look at how the HTTP server adds header information to the document returned by the gateway program. Consider first (see Figure 4.12) the actual data sent by the server to the client when it first accessed the *srch-example* (these are the data that produced Figure 4.10).

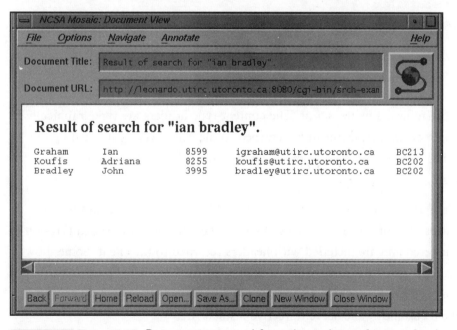

Figure 4.11 Document returned from the script ***srch-example*** when accessed *with* a query string appended to the URL.

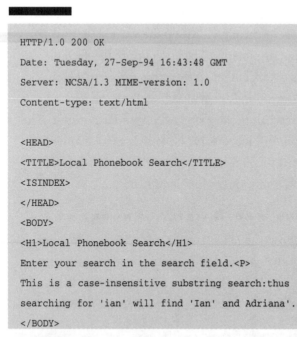

```
HTTP/1.0 200 OK

Date: Tuesday, 27-Sep-94 16:43:48 GMT

Server: NCSA/1.3 MIME-version: 1.0

Content-type: text/html


<HEAD>

<TITLE>Local Phonebook Search</TITLE>

<ISINDEX>

</HEAD>

<BODY>

<H1>Local Phonebook Search</H1>

Enter your search in the search field.<P>

This is a case-insensitive substring search:thus

searching for 'ian' will find 'Ian' and Adriana'.

</BODY>
```

Figure 4.12 Data returned to the client upon accessing the URL `http://leonardo.utirc.utoronto.ca:8080/cgi-bin/srch-example`. These are the data used to generate Figure 4.10.

Comparing with Figure 4.9, you will see that the headers are not, in fact, those returned by the script: The content-type headers are typographically different. In fact, the headers returned to the client were generated by the HTTP server, with help from the headers passed from the gateway program.

The server takes the header data returned by the gateway program and parses each of the header fields. Most of these headers are passed through unaltered and are included with headers returned to the client. Some, however, are treated as *server directives* and are used by the server to *modify* the HTTP response headers it adds to the returned response headers. The three currently valid server-directive headers are:

1. `Content-type: type/subtype`—This gives the MIME-type for the data being sent by the gateway program. The server replaces its default Content-type server response header with the type/subtype values given here.

2. `Location: URL`—This tells the server that the gateway program is specifying the URL to which the client should be redirected. The server adds this header to the server response and also changes its header status line from:

   ```
   HTTP/1.0 200 OK
   ```

   to:

   ```
   HTTP/1.0 302 Redirection
   ```

   which tells the client that there is redirection information in the response headers, and that it should use the `Location` field to access the desired document.

3. `Status: code string`—This passes an HTTP status string to the server for use in place of the standard value. For example, if the *srch-example* gateway script returned the header:

   ```
   Status: 444 four-fourty-for
   ```

   as a result, the response headers returned to the client would look like:

   ```
   HTTP/1.0 444 four-fourty-for
   Date: Tuesday, 27-Sep-94 16:43:48 GMT
   Server: NCSA/1.3
   MIME-version: 1.0
   Content-type: text/html
   ...
   ```

NONPARSED HEADERS

It is possible to return gateway program output directly to the client without it being parsed by the HTTP server. This is done by appending the string *nph-*, for *nonparsed headers*, to the name of the script. When the server sees gateway program names beginning with *nph-*, it knows to pass the gateway program output directly to the client. For example, Figure 4.13 shows the data returned from the gateway program *nph-srch-example*; this is an exact duplicate of the program *srch-example*, the only change being the string *nph-* added to the program filename.

Comparing Figure 4.13 with Figure 4.9 shows that the response now contains just the data printed by the gateway program, with nothing added or changed by the server. The advantage of nonparsed header gateway programs is speed, since the server is not required to parse the returned data and generate appropriate headers. In exchange, the gateway program itself must produce all the required headers. Thus, an *nph-* script must also print, at a minimum, the following response headers (with values appropriate to the script):

```
HTTP/1.0 200 OK
Date: Tuesday, 27-Sep-94 16:43:48 GMT
Server: NCSA/1.3
MIME-version: 1.0
```

EXAMPLE 8: ENVIRONMENT VARIABLES

The preceding examples would imply that the server passes very little information to the gateway programs. In fact, the server is not so ungenerous. Before launching the gateway program, the server initializes several *environment variables* that are subsequently accessible to the gateway programs. In particular, this mechanism is used to pass extra path information to the gateway program. The names and contents of the environment variables are shown in Figures 4.14 and 4.15. Figure 4.14 shows the gateway script *srch-example-2*; this is the same ISINDEX script shown in Figure 4.9, modified to print the contents of the environment variables. The HTML document generated upon accessing this script at the URL:

```
http://leonardo.utirc.utoronto.ca:8080/cgi-bin/srch-example-2/dir/file?ian+bradley
```

is shown in Figure 4.15. Accessing this URL passes both query string and extra path information to the referenced gateway program.

```
Content-TYPE: text/html

<HEAD>
 <TITLE>Local Phonebook Search</TITLE>
<ISINDEX>
</HEAD>
<BODY>
<H1>Local Phonebook Search</H1>
Enter your search in the search field.<P>
This is a case-insensitive substring search: thus
searching for 'ian' will find 'Ian' and Adriana'.
</BODY>
```

Figure 4.13 Nonparsed header output returned upon accessing the URL: `http://leonardo.utirc.utoronto.ca:8080/cgi-bin/nph-srch-example.`

```
#!/bin/sh
echo Content-TYPE:  text/html
echo
 if [ $# = 0 ]    # is the number of arguments == 0 ?
then              # do this part if there are NO arguments
  echo "<HEAD>"
  echo "<TITLE>Local Phonebook Search</TITLE>"
  echo "<ISINDEX>"
  echo "</HEAD>"
  echo "<BODY>"
  echo "<H1>Local Phonebook Search</H1>"
  echo "Enter your search in the search field.<P>"
  echo "This is a case-insensitive substring search: thus"
  echo "searching for 'ian' will find 'Ian' and Adriana'."
  echo "</BODY>"
else              # this part if there ARE arguments
  echo "<HEAD>"
  echo "<TITLE>Result of search for \"$*\".</TITLE>"
```

```
echo "</HEAD>"
echo ""<BODY>"
echo "<P> Number of Command-line Arguments = $#. They are:"
for i in $*
do
        echo " <code> $i </code> "
done
echo "<h2> The Environment Variables </h2>"
echo "<pre>"       # print the environment variables
echo " SERVER_SOFTWARE = $SERVER_SOFTWARE"
echo " SERVER_NAME = $SERVER_NAME"
echo " GATEWAY_INTERFACE = $GATEWAY_INTERFACE"
echo " SERVER_PROTOCOL = $SERVER_PROTOCOL"
echo " SERVER_PORT = $SERVER_PORT"
echo " REQUEST_METHOD = $REQUEST_METHOD"
echo " HTTP_ACCEPT = $HTTP_ACCEPT"
echo " PATH_INFO = $PATH_INFO"
echo " PATH_TRANSLATED = $PATH_TRANSLATED"
echo " SCRIPT_NAME = $SCRIPT_NAME"
echo " QUERY_STRING = $QUERY_STRING"
echo " REMOTE_HOST = $REMOTE_HOST"
echo " REMOTE_ADDR = $REMOTE_ADDR"
echo " REMOTE_USER = $REMOTE_USER"
echo " AUTH_TYPE = $AUTH_TYPE"
echo " CONTENT_TYPE = $CONTENT_TYPE"
echo " CONTENT_LENGTH = $CONTENT_LENGTH"
echo "</pre>"
echo "<H2>Result of search for \"$*\".</H2>"
echo "<PRE>"
for i in $*
do
    grep -i $i /vast/igraham/Personnel done
echo "</PRE>"
echo "</BODY>"
fi
```

Figure 4.14 Bourne-shell script *srch-example-2*. This is a modification of the script in Figure 4.7 to explicitly print the environment variables and the command-line arguments.

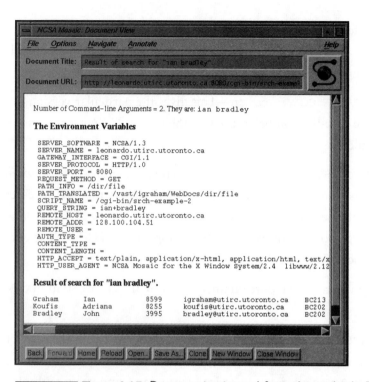

▬▬▬▬▬ **Figure 4.15** Document returned from the script in Figure 4.14 after accessing the URL: `http://leonardo.utirc.utoronto.ca:8080/cgi-bin/ srch-example-2/dir/file?ian+bradley`.

Most of the environment variables shown in Figure 4.15 are easy to understand. Some are set by default and do not depend on the nature of the request, while others are set only when particular client-server-gateway interactions are involved. The following is a list of the different variables and their contents, discussed with reference to the data displayed in Figure 4.15.

SERVER_SOFTWARE=server_name/version—The name and version of the server software answering the request. The format is name/version, as in NCSA/1.3 for this example.

SERVER_NAME=domain.name—The Internet domain name of the server; here, leonardo.utirc.utoronto.ca. If the domain name is not available, this will be the numerical IP address.

GATEWAY_INTERFACE=CGI/version—This gives the particular version of the CGI interface specification being used by the server. The current version is 1.1, so this should be CGI/1.1.

SERVER_PROTOCOL=HTTP/version—This specifies the protocol being used, namely HTTP, and the related version number. This allows the CGI specification to be used with servers that support protocols other than HTTP, or that support multiple protocols (for example, both Gopher and HTTP). The current HTTP protocol version is 1.0, so this should be HTTP/1.0.

SERVER_PORT=number—The port number called by the client: 8080 in this example.

REQUEST_METHOD=HTTP_method—The method associated with the request. For HTTP server access, this will be GET, HEAD, POST PUT, and so on. This allows you to write a single gateway script or program supporting multiple methods; the script can use the contents of this variable to decide which portions of the program to execute.

PATH_INFO=extra_path—This contains any extra path information found in the URL. In our example, this contains the string: PATH_INFO=/dir/file.

PATH_TRANSLATED=/transl/extra_path—This contains the *PATH_INFO* path translated into an *absolute* document path on the local system. For example, suppose the server document directory (the directory under which all documents are kept) is */vast/igraham/WebDocs*. The translated path is then:

PATH_TRANSLATED=/vast/igraham/WebDocs/dir/file
Note that this is not related to where the gateway program is physically kept. The translated path can be used to locate configuration files for use by the gateway program.

SCRIPT_NAME=/path/script_name—The path and name of the script being accessed as it would be referenced in a URL. This can be used to construct URLs, for insertion in script-generated HTML documents that refer back to this same script. For example, the concatenated string

```
http://$SERVER_NAME:$SERVER_PORT$SCRIPT_NAME
```

(the *$NAME* here refers to the contents of the environment variable *NAME*) generates the URL of the script from information contained in the environment variables.

QUERY_STRING=query_string—This contains the query string that follows the question mark in a URL; in this case, ian+bradley. It is still encoded so that blanks are represented by plus signs and FORM name=value pairs will be separated by the ampersand character. The person writing the gateway program must write code to interpret the information in the query string. If this string results from an ISINDEX search request, then *QUERY_STRING* information is also passed to the program as command-line arguments. However, you can access the same information from the *QUERY_STRING* variable.

REMOTE_HOST=domain.name—This contains the Internet domain name of the host making the request. If the domain name is unavailable, this field is left blank. The numerical IP address is available in the *REMOTE_ADDR* variable. In this example, I accessed the server on leonardo from leonardo itself.

REMOTE_ADDR=xxx.xxx.xxx.xxx—This contains the numeric IP address of the remote host accessing the server.

AUTH_TYPE=type—This lists the authentication method required to authenticate a user who desires access, and is used only with scripts that are so protected. Many servers contain configuration files to indicate which gateway programs (or regular files) require authentication prior to access. If authentication is not required, this variable is empty.

REMOTE_USER=name—This is set only if authentication is required, and contains the authenticated name of the user gaining access. This can be used to record the name of the user and to control access, depending on the user's identity. This field is left blank if authentication is not required.

REMOTE_IDENT=name—This contains the remote username retrieved from the server using the *identd* identification daemon.

CONTENT_TYPE=MIME_type—If the client is POSTing or PUTting data to the server, this variable contains the MIME content-type of the data. If no data is being sent, this is left blank. The data itself is available to the gateway program by reading from standard input.

CONTENT_LENGTH=length—If the client is POSTing or PUTting data to the server, this variable contains the length of the data message. If no data is being sent, this is left blank. The gateway program does not have to read all the data before returning data to the client or before exiting.

In addition to these server-specific environment variables, every piece of information found in the HTTP request headers (the headers sent from the client to the server to access the script) is passed to the gateway program as an environment variable. These variable names are constructed by capitalizing the name in the request header field and adding the prefix *HTTP_*. Thus, the accept headers becomes the environment variable *HTTP_ACCEPT*. In the examples, the browser sent only two types of request headers; namely, the accept and User_Agent headers (see, for example, Figures 4.1 or 4.4), so there are only two *HTTP_* environment variables:

HTTP_ACCEPT =type/subtype, type/subtype ....—This contains a comma-separated list of all the MIME-types acceptable to the client, as indicated by the Accept headers sent from the client to the server.

HTTP_USER_AGENT=program/version—This contains the contents of the User_Agent field in the request headers. This information can be used to modify the behavior of a gateway program, depending on the capabilities of the client.

THE POST METHOD AND STANDARD INPUT

The next two examples look at the data passed to the program shown in Figure 4.16 from an HTML form. The examples access this script using the two HTML FORM examples discussed in Examples 3 and 4 (the FORM is shown in Figure 4.5, and shown rendered by a browser in Figure 4.6). The script prints out the relevant environment variables, and also reads data from the input (the `read var` command on the seventh line from the bottom) and prints the resulting input to standard output.

EXAMPLE 9: FORM-BASED GET REQUEST

This example accesses the program shown in Figure 4.16, using the FORM template shown in Figure 4.5—that is, a GET request. Figure 4.6 shows the browser display of this FORM prior to sending the query to the server, while Figure 4.7 shows the data that is sent to the server and shows how the FORM data are encoded for transmission and appended to the URL.

Figure 4.17 shows the results returned by the script in Figure 4.16. You will note that there are no command-line arguments. In parsing the URL, the server detected equal signs in the query string. This implies a non-ISINDEX query, so the server does not create command-line arguments. The remaining quantities are obvious. The *REQUEST_METHOD* environment variable is set to GET, and the query string is placed in the *QUERY_STRING* environment variable. The *CONTENT_TYPE* and *CONTENT_LENGTH* variables are empty, since there is no data sent in a GET method, while the *PATH_INFO* and *PATH_TRANSLATED* variables are also empty, since there was no extended path information in the query.

▬▬▬

```sh
#!/bin/sh
echo Content-TYPE:  text/html
echo
```

```
# is a FORMs test script -- it prints the environment variable
# contents generated by a FORM access to this script.
echo "<HEAD>"
echo "<TITLE>FORMs Test Page </TITLE>"
echo "</HEAD>"
echo "<P> Number of Command-line Arguments = $#. They are:" for i in $*
do
    echo " <code> $i </code> "
done
echo "<h2> The Environment Variables </h2>"
echo "<pre>"
echo "SERVER_NAME = $SERVER_NAME"
echo "SERVER_PORT = $SERVER_PORT"
echo "REQUEST_METHOD = $REQUEST_METHOD"
echo "PATH_INFO = $PATH_INFO"
echo "PATH_TRANSLATED = $PATH_TRANSLATED"
echo "SCRIPT_NAME = $SCRIPT_NAME"
echo "QUERY_STRING = $QUERY_STRING"
echo "CONTENT_TYPE = $CONTENT_TYPE"
echo "CONTENT_LENGTH = $CONTENT_LENGTH"
echo
if [ -n "$CONTENT_LENGTH" ]; then # Read/print input data (if any).
  echo "<H2>data at Standard Input is:</h2>"
  echo "<PRE>"
  read "var"  # read data from standard input into "var"
  echo "$var" # print var to standard output
  echo "</PRE>"
else
  echo "<h2> No Data at standard input </h2>"
fi
echo "</BODY>
```

Figure 4.16 Test script *form1* accessed by the HTML **FORM** in Figure 4.5. This script returns an HTML document listing the script command-line arguments (if there are any), the contents of all the environment variables, and any data read from standard input (if any exists).

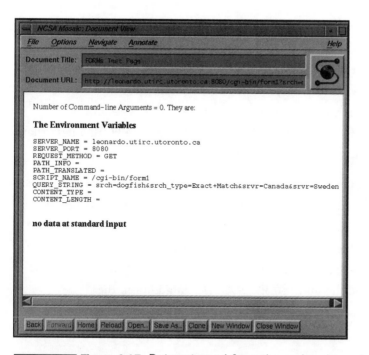

Figure 4.17 Data returned from the script shown in Figure 4.16 when accessed by the **FORM** shown in Figure 4.7 using the GET HTTP method.

Further processing requires more sophisticated programming tools to parse the *QUERY_STRING* and break it into its component parts. This is not difficult, recalling that: the ampersand character divided the different segments; the equal sign is used to relate FORM variable names to the assigned values; and spaces in the query strings are translated into plus signs. Finally, you must unencode all the special characters that may have been encoded, using the URL encoding scheme discussed in Chapter 3. Chapter 5 lists some useful CGI libraries that can help you do this processing.

EXAMPLE 10: FORM-BASED POST REQUEST

This example again accesses the program shown in Figure 4.16 using the FORM shown in Figure 4.5, but, this time, using the POST method.

Figure 4.8 shows the data actually sent to the server. In this case, the data is sent to the server as an encoded message following the headers. There are two extra headers: the content-length header, which tells the server the length of the following message; and the content-type header, which tells the server that this is an `application/x-www-form-urlencoded` MIME-type. This is a special MIME-type used to indicate FORM data that has been encoded using the URL encoding scheme.

Figure 4.18 shows the results returned by the script in Figure 4.16, and displays the data that arrived at the script. There are no command-line arguments—this time, because there is no query string. Most of the environment variables are the same as with the GET request shown in Figure 4.17. Obvious differences are the *REQUEST_METHOD* variable that is now POST instead of GET, and the null *QUERY_STRING*. In addition, the *CONTENT_TYPE* and *CONTENT_LENGTH* are not empty but contain the length of the message and the content-type, as indicated in the fields sent by the client.

Where is the query data? With the POST method, this is sent to the gateway program as an input stream, which the program reads from standard input. The script in Figure 4.16 reads this standard input and prints the results back to standard output. This is printed at the bottom of Figure 4.18 and is just the query data sent by the client (and shown at the bottom of Figure 4.8). This is encoded using the URL encoding mechanisms. To further process this data, you must parse it to separate the fields. Again, there are CGI libraries, discussed in Chapter 5, that can help in the processing of these data.

Example 10 may seem similar to Example 9 but is, in fact, different in important ways. First, many systems have a finite data space for environment variables so that large messages passed via GET URLs can be truncated. In addition, the POST method allows for complicated MIME messages to be sent from client to server, something that is difficult if not impossible with the GET method.

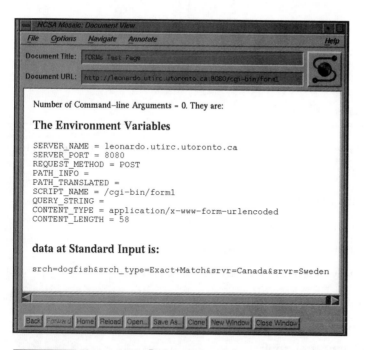

Figure 4.18 Data returned from the script shown in Figure 4.16 when accessed by the **FORM** shown in Figure 4.7 and modified to use the POST HTTP method.

SECURITY CONSIDERATIONS

There is always a security risk associated with running a gateway program on a server, since a rogue program can easily corrupt the data files being managed by the server. Most HTTP servers can restrict executable programs to special URLs (typically, those pointing to the directories */cgi-bin* or */htbin*). The server administrator can maintain strict control over the installation of programs in these areas, and can verify that installed gateway programs will not be dangerous to the integrity of the server database.

The details of these security features depend strongly on the server that you are using. In general, most servers allow significant customization of these features. Chapter 7 gives a brief review of different servers and their capabilities in this regard.

REFERENCES

The HTTP specifications are currently under development. Some useful reference documents are:

Working Draft on the HTTP protocol:

```
http://info.cern.ch/hypertext/WWW/Protocols/HTTP/HTTP2.html
```

CERN data encryption and user-authentication notes:

```
http://info.cern.ch/hypertext/WWW/AccessAuthorization/Overview.html
```

NCSA data encryption and user-authentication notes:

```
http://hoohoo.ncsa.uiuc.edu/docs/PEMPGP.html RFC931 References
```

NCSA Mosaic authentication tool:

```
http://wintermute.ncsa.uiuc.edu:8080/auth-tutorial/tutorial.html
```

CERN proxy HTTP server:

```
http://info.cern.ch/hypertext/WWW/Daemon/User/Proxies/Proxies.html
```

Using proxy gateways (Mosaic for X-Windows):

```
http://www.ncsa.uiuc.edu/SDG/Software/Mosaic/Docs/proxy-gateways.html
```

CGI specifications:

```
http://hoohoo.ncsa.uiuc.edu/cgi/overview.html
```

Demonstration CGI documents:

```
http://hoohoo.ncsa.uiuc.edu/cgi/ex mples.html
```

HTML AND CGI TOOLS

This chapter discusses programs or tools that are useful in developing or presenting HTML documents on the World Wide Web. The first half covers tools useful in developing HTML documents, such as image processing tools, the active image map facility, and programs for automatically generating a Table of Contents from a collection of HTML documents. The second half of the chapter looks at useful CGI programs. This includes programs for sending mail messages, for accessing databases, and for processing query data. The chapter concludes with some references to CGI gateway program archive sites and to sites containing up-to-date information on World Wide Web database techniques.

IMAGES IN HTML DOCUMENTS

Inlined images are one of the most useful features of HTML. The image tag `<IMG SRC="image_url">` allows you to include images within your document and have them displayed with the text, provided the browser is capable of doing so. But, don't forget about clients using text-only browsers. Adding an `ALT="description"` attribute to an image element is only a little extra work and is well worth the effort.

Although some browsers support multiple image formats, there are only three formats that are always viewable. These are the GIF format images (GIF87 and GIF89), X-Bitmaps, and X-Pixelmaps. The different file types can usually be inferred from the filename suffix: GIF image files usually have the suffix *.gif*; X-Bitmaps, the suffix *.xbm;* and X-Pixelmaps, the suffix *.xpm*.

X-BITMAP IMAGES

X-Bitmaps are a common format on UNIX workstations, and you will often find them in image and icon libraries. These simple black-and-white bitmaps are useful, as most browsers interpret the white portion of the image as *transparent*. This means that the black part of the image is displayed in black, while the white part is treated as transparent and takes on the color of the underlying window. This makes for much more attractive graphics, since the square box surrounding the black image is invisible to the user. However, X-Bitmaps are an inefficient way to store an image and are uncommon outside the UNIX environment.

X-PIXELMAPS

X-Pixelmaps are similar to X-Bitmaps but assign 8 bits to each pixel. This allows for images containing 256 distinct colors, and X-Pixelmaps are often used for X-Windows icons. The main drawback of X-Pixelmaps (and X-Bitmaps) is size: X-Pixelmaps are an inefficient way of storing image information so that the image files tend to be much larger than corresponding GIF images.

GIF IMAGE FILES

GIF is the most common image format in World Wide Web applications. This format can store black-and-white or color images, although it is limited to a maximum of 256 colors per image. The GIF format codes the image information using a *color indexing* scheme. When you create a GIF image, the software takes the raw image data and tries to find the best set of 256 (or fewer) colors for representing the image, and creates a *color table* containing these colors. For example, if the picture were of a red sunset, this table might contain mostly reds; whereas if it were a picture of a forest, it might mostly be greens. The software then goes through the image and assigns to each pixel the number from 0 to 255 corresponding to the color in the color table that comes closest to the actual color of the pixel. The result is a GIF image file consisting of an array of color indices, plus a *color map* table that maps each of these indices onto a particular color. The combination can yield a breathtakingly successful rendering of the original image, even though there are only 256 colors present.

There are two versions of the GIF format: GIF87 and GIF89. The GIF89 format is more sophisticated than the GIF87, and particularly allows you to select one of the colors in the image as *transparent*. The use and creation of transparent GIFs are described later on.

REDUCING IMAGE FILE SIZE: THE COLOR MAP

Color images are much bigger than black-and-white images, since they contain a lot more information: 8 or more bits of information per pixel, as opposed to only 1 bit per pixel for black and white. Also, files of images that contain more colors are often bigger than those that contain only a few colors, even if they are physically the same size. This is because the GIF format is clever enough to know, if an image has only eight colors instead of 256, that it needs fewer bits per pixel to map each color properly. Thus, if you want to make your image files small (which is always a good thing on the World Wide Web), you should use as few colors as possible. Often, you can use image-processing programs, such as **Adobe Photoshop**, **Paintshop Pro** (a shareware program for Windows PCs), **Graphic Converter** (a shareware program for the Macintosh), or the **pbmplus** package (a collection of shareware programs for UNIX workstations), to process images and reduce the number of colors they contain.

There is another reason to reduce the size of the color map in an image, due to the limitations of the color display capabilities of many computers. Most computers are equipped with graphics cards capable of displaying at most 256 colors. If your WWW browser tries to display a 256-color GIF image, things will look fine. However, suppose your browser is displaying two GIF images at the same time, each containing 256 colors, and each image with its own color map. Clearly, this is a problem—both color maps cannot be used, since this requires 512 colors, not 256. Most browsers try to *dither* the color—that is, they try to find an average color map that is acceptable to both images. This works sometimes, and sometimes fails miserably, resulting in poor-quality color images.

You can alleviate this problem in two ways: by ensuring that the images you have created for simultaneous display all use the same color map, or by limiting each image to at most 40 or 50 colors. The former solution is useful, but difficult to implement. The second option can be accomplished using a number of image-processing programs, including the ones previously listed. Almost all of them allow you to reduce the size of the color table and then dither the remaining colors to make the image look as good as possible. This allows you to display four or five images together before you *run out* of space in the color map. It also has the side effect of reducing the size of the image files, which is a nice bonus.

REDUCING IMAGE SIZE: RESCALING IMAGES

There are other image-processing tricks to consider. For example, you may want to reduce the size of an image either because the original is just too big, or because you want to create a small icon of the image and link it to the bigger version. You can create reduced image sizes with a variety of programs, including the ones listed previously. When you *shrink* an image you may also want to *smooth* it at the same time. Smoothing reduces edge sharpness created by the size reduction process. Some programs do this automatically, while others let you turn on and off this feature. Note that you want to smooth while doing the size reduction—not after—since, once the image is shrunk, the smooth function simply blurs what's left.

TRANSPARENT GIF IMAGES

Unlike X-Bitmaps, there is no implicit transparent color for a GIF image. The background of a GIF image is simply another color which is displayed as such when the image is viewed by a WWW browser. This is inconvenient if the image is simply a black-and-white logo, a color *bullet* on a plain background, or an equation to be presented inline with the text. Fortunately, the GIF89 format allows you to declare one of the color indexes as transparent, giving the same transparency features as the black-and-white X-Bitmaps. To enable transparency, you find the color index value that corresponds to the part of the image you want to make transparent (usually, the background color) and then use a special program to modify the image file to make this color index transparent. The procedure is outlined in the following section.

TRANSPARENCY (MACINTOSH)

Aaron Giles of Cornell University Medical College has developed an elegant and useful program called **transparency**. This simple, graphically oriented program allows you to easily edit GIF images and make one of the colors transparent.

You operate **transparency** by either dragging a file to the transparency icon or by double-clicking on the transparency icon and opening the desired GIF image file. To select the transparency color you simply place the mouse pointer inside the image and hold down the mouse button. You are then presented with the color palette for the image, and can select the color you wish to make transparent by putting the mouse pointer over the desired color and releasing the button. You can choose to have no transparent color by selecting the NONE bar at the top of the palette. Upon releasing the mouse button, there is a short pause, after which the image is redrawn with the selected color rendered transparently. You now select the Save as GIF89... menu from the pull-down File menu to save the newly transparent version.

Transparency is available at a number of anonymous FTP sites, including:

```
ftp://ftp.med.cornell.edu/pub/aarong/transparency/
```

The program is found in a file named *transparency*sit.hqx*, where the star represents the version number. Additional information about **transparency** can be found at:

```
http://www.med.cornell.edu/~giles/projects.html
```

GIFTRANS (UNIX AND PC-DOS)

Giftrans is a simple C-language program, written by Andreas Ley, that can convert any GIF files into the GIF89 format. While making this conversion, **giftrans** also allows you to make one of the colors transparent. It is currently available in source code (for compilation on any platform, but most specifically for UNIX workstations) and as an executable program for PCs running DOS. **Giftrans** is a command-line program, so it does not need Windows or a GUI to run. If you have the correct information, you can run **giftrans** from a simple text terminal.

Typically, **giftrans** is used as follows:

```
giftrans -t xx image.gif > transparent_image.gif
```

which translates the file *image.gif* into *transparent_image.gif* and makes the color labeled by xx transparent. There are several ways of labeling the colors, the most common being to:

- Specify the absolute RGB value for the color (as a 24-bit RGB value). For example, the command

  ```
  giftrans -t #ffffff image.gif > transparent_image.gif
  ```

  makes the color white transparent (`ffffff` is the RGB code for white).

- Specify the color index value. For example, the command

  ```
  giftrans -t 21 image.gif > transparent_image.gif
  ```

  makes the color found in color index 21 transparent.

How do you find the color index or RGB value of the color you want transparent? To find this information, you need a graphics program that can tell you the color indices or RGB values for a given pixel. Several shareware graphics programs can do this: **xv** is a common UNIX program suitable for this task. With **xv**, you load the image file, place the mouse over the desired color, and depress the left mouse button. This gives the mouse coordinates with respect to the upper left-hand corner of the image, plus color information for the pixel. This is presented in the following manner:

```
132, 34  5 = 203, 203, 203 (0, 1, 79 HSV)
```

The first two numbers are the x and y coordinates of the pixel. The number just before the equal sign is the color index, while the next three numbers are the RGB values for this color (in decimal numbers). The three numbers in brackets are an alternative color coding scheme.

To make this color transparent, you turn to **giftrans**. You have two ways to make the preceding color transparent, using the color index:

```
giftrans -t 5 image.gif > transparent_image.gif
```

or the RGB value:

```
giftrans -t #cbcbcb image.gif > transparent_image.gif
```

where cb is the hexadecimal code for the decimal number 203. If you run **giftrans** without any arguments, the program prints out a list of possible arguments and their meanings.

Giftrans is available from a number of anonymous FTP sites. Its original home is:

```
ftp://ftp.rz.uni-karlsruhe.de/pub/net/www/tools/
```

which contains the files:

giftrans.exe	DOS executable version of **giftrans**
giftrans.c	Source code for **giftrans** (if you are compiling on a PC, you also need the file *getopt.c*)
giftrans.1	UNIX-style manual page for **giftrans**; useful also with DOS

The program **xv** is available from many anonymous FTP sites. You will need both a C compiler and the standard X11 libraries to compile **xv** on your machine. **Xv** is available at:

```
ftp://ftp.cis.upenn.edu/pub/xv/xv-3.00a.tar.Z
ftp://ftp.ira.uka.de/pub/x11/xv-3.00.tar.Z
ftp://sunb.ocs.mq.edu.au/X11/Graphics/xv-3.00.tar.gz
```

ACTIVE IMAGES

Active images, clickable images—whatever they are called, you have certainly seen them and you would love to have them. Having an active image means that you can click your mouse on the image and have different things happen, depending on where you clicked. For example, the active image could be a city map, where clicking on different locations inside the image returns information about particular buildings, transportation routes, or historic monuments.

Active images require special features on both the client and the HTTP server. First, the client must be able to measure the coordinates of your mouse pointer when you click on the active image, and must be configured to send this information to an HTTP server gateway program for interpretation and action. Second, there must be a gateway program on the server capable of interpreting this image data. Third, there must be a database on the server relating, for this particular image, the click coordinates to the appropriate action. This means you have to sit down with your image file, mark out regions of the image, link them to particular functions, and store this information in a file that can be read by the gateway program.

ALLOWED FORMATS FOR ACTIVE IMAGES

You must use GIF format for active images. Several browsers cannot measure image coordinates in X-Bitmaps, so active images will not work with this format. If you have an X-Bitmap or X-Pixelmap image that you want to use as an active image, you must convert it into the GIF format. The various image-processing programs mentioned earlier in this chapter can all do this conversion.

THINGS TO THINK ABOUT BEFORE STARTING

Before you get carried away with active images, stop and think about your audience. First, you must recall that not everyone will be able to view your active images, either because their browser does not support that capability (rare now but still possible), or because they are using a text-only browser, such as **lynx** (quite common). Also, people geographically far away or linked by slow Internet connections often disable image loading because of the inherent slowness in accessing large image files. Consequently, you should make the images as small as possible and should try to provide a text-only way of accessing the same data. For example, your active image document can have a line of text explaining what the image does and offering a hypertext link to a document providing a text-only approach to the same information. This will involve a little extra work, but the customer satisfaction is well worth the effort.

MAKING THE IMAGE ACTIVE

In HTML, you include an image within a document using the **IMG** element. For example:

```
<IMG SRC="image.gif">
```

This image is passive and just sits there. As discussed in Chapters 1 and 2, you can turn this image into a hypertext link by putting it inside an anchor element; for example:

```
<A HREF="http://some.site.edu/linked_doc.html">
   <IMG SRC="image.gif">
</A>
```

Now, when you click on the image, you are linked to the indicated document. In a sense, this is an active image but the action is restricted to a single function.

To make an image fully active, you must do two things. First, you need to add the **ISMAP** attribute to the **IMG** element, which tells the browser that this is an active image. Second, you must surround the **IMG** element with a hypertext anchor that points to the gateway program that can process the image and coordinate data. Thus, the HTML markup for an active image is:

```
<A HREF="http://some.site.edu/cgi-bin/imagemap/my_database">
       <IMG SRC="image.gif" ISMAP>
</A>
```

This tells the browser that this is an active image and that, when a user clicks inside the image, the coordinates of the click should be sent to the gateway program *imagemap* at the given URL. The coordinate information is sent to this URL using the HTTP GET method. The HTTP request header sent to the server looks like:

```
GET /cgi-bin/imagemap/my_database?x,y HTTP/1.0
```

where x and y are the *integer pixel coordinates* of the mouse pointer measured from the *upper left-hand corner* of the image.

Note that the path *my_database* is appended to the end of this URL. As discussed in Chapter 4, URLs that point to gateway programs are treated in a special way, and any directory-like information appended to the URL after the program name (like *my_database*) is treated as *extra path* information and is passed as a parameter to the gateway program. In this example, *my_database* is additional path information used by the *imagemap* program to find the image map database for this particular image. This allows the imagemap program to be used for any number of active images, each image having its own personalized database.

Imagemap is an actual CGI program for handling active image data, and is distributed with the current NCSA HTTPD server. An older version of this program is also available and has similar, if somewhat more limited, functionality. The newer and more flexible version is available at:

```
http://hoohoo.ncsa.uiuc.edu/docs/setup/admin/imagemap.txt
```

Imagemap is a CGI-compliant C-language program and can be used on any HTTP server that supports the CGI specifications. The remainder of this discussion centers on using the newer **imagemap** program and on creating the associated databases. Additional online documentation, including interactive examples, can be found at:

```
http://hoohoo.ncsa.uiuc.edu/docs/setup/admin/NewImagemap.html
```

INSTALLING IMAGEMAP

If you are installing the **imagemap** program, or are replacing your old version, you simply take the file:

```
http://hoohoo.ncsa.uiuc.edu/docs/setup/admin/imagemap.txt
```

rename it *imagemap.c*, and compile with your C compiler. You should then install the resulting *imagemap* program in your server CGI executable directory. On NCSA servers, this is usually the *cgi-bin* directory located in the directory containing the server executable, server support directories, and configuration files. (Note that this is *not* the directory that contains the

HTML and other documents you make available via the server.) Once installed, the program is accessible through URLs, such as:

```
http://some.site.edu/cgi-bin/imagemap
```

where the *cgi-bin* directory is a *virtual* name used by the server to reference the directory containing CGI programs. Check your server configuration files to verify that this name is correct.

CREATING THE IMAGE DATABASE

This section describes the format of the image map database and explains how it is constructed. It also describes some software tools useful in building these image map databases.

The image map database file relates a region of the image to a URL to be accessed when you click inside that region. You can specify these regions as circles, rectangles, polygons, or points. You can also include comments in these map files by placing a hash character (#) as the first character in the line. For example, here is a simple map file named *blobby.map* (Figure 5.1):

```
# Imagemap file for blobby.gif
circle    /dir1/blob2/his_head.html         50,20 50,30
rect      /dir1/blob2/his_left_foot.html   25,78 40,85
poly      /dir1/blob2/his_body.html         45,38 35,50 40,72 50,75 60,72 65,50 55,38
default   /cgi-bin/nph-no_op.sh
```

Figure 5.1 The *blobby.map* image map database.

This file declares the circle centered at coordinates 50,20 (and with an edge at 50,30) to be linked to the designated URL, and makes similar declarations for a rectangle (indicated by rect) and a polygon (indicated by poly). These coordinates are measured in pixels from the upper left-hand corner of the image. The default method indicates the URL to access if the user clicks in places not falling inside the mapped regions.

The general form for map file entry is:

```
method   URL   x1,y1 x2,y2 ... xn,yn
```

where `method` specifies the manner in which the region is being specified (`circle`, `rect`, `poly`, `point`, `default`); `URL` is the URL to be accessed if the click occurs inside this region; and xn,yn are the integer coordinates of a point measured from the upper left-hand corner of the image. These coordinates are measured in pixels, so you will need some way of measuring the pixel coordinates in an image. Tools for doing this are presented later.

Note that mapped regions can overlap. The **imagemap** program accesses the map file from the top so that if a click occurs at a point lying within two mapped regions, the program takes the one nearest the top of the file.

The URLs specified in a map file can be complete URLs or partial URLs of the form:

```
/path/stuff/file
```

This references a file or gateway program relative to the HTTP server *document directory* (see Figure 1.11). With the NCSA server, you can also use the form:

```
/~user/stuff/file
```

where `user` is the name of a user on the system. This references a file or gateway program relative to the user's personal HTML area.

The following is a list of the different methods for declaring active regions and the parameters required for these methods:

`circle   URL   center edgepoint`—This maps the region inside the indicated circle to the given URL. Two coordinate pairs x,y are required: one for the circle `center`, and the other for an `edgepoint` lying on the edge of the circle.

`point   URL   x,y`—This declares a specific *point* in an image as active, and is really useful only if you have more than one active point. When you click on the image, and the click is not inside a circle, rectangle, or polygon, the **imagemap** program locates the point closest to the coordinates of the click and accesses the indicated URL.

`poly    URL    x1,y1, x2,y2, ....... xn,yn`—This maps the region inside the indicated multisided polygon to the given URL. Each coordinate pair represents a vertex of the polygon. You should make sure that the line segments do not cross one another. The polygon is automatically closed by linking the last point `xn,yn` to the first point `x1,y1`. The current NCSA program limits you to, at most, 100 corners in a given polygon.

`rect    URL    upper_left_corner lower_right_corner`—This maps the region inside a rectangle to the given URL. The `x` and `y` coordinates of the upper left and lower right corners of the rectangle are required, in that order.

`default    URL`— This URL is accessed if the click did not lie inside any other region. This is never accessed if you define a point, since a clicked location will always be *closest* to that point.

REFERENCING THE DATABASE

Now that you have a database—for example, the *blobby.map* database of Figure 5.1—where should you put it and how do you reference it? This database can go anywhere you can put regular HTML documents or data files; you indicate its location to the **imagemap** program via the URL. For example, let us suppose that the HTTP server document directory is */u/We*, and that the collection of documents and images related to blobby is found in the directory */u/Web/weird/blobby*. A reasonable choice is to put the map file in the same directory as the image so that the absolute path for the map file is */u/Web/weird/blobby/blobby.map*. You can access this map file from the *imagemap* program by writing in your HTML document:

```
<A HREF="http://some.site.edu/cgi-bin/imagemap/weird/blobby/blobby.map">
    <IMG SRC="blobby.gif" ISMAP>
</A>
```

where *some.site.edu* is the site containing all these documents. Note that the path to the *blobby.map* file, relative to the document directory of the

HTTP server (*/u/Web*), has been added to the imagemap URL. The string /weird/blobby/blobby.map is passed to the **imagemap** program, and is used by **imagemap** to locate the database *blobby.map*.

With the NCSA server, this method is not restricted to the regular document directory. If a user has created a personal HTML directory, he or she can place map files in this directory and access the map using URLs, such as:

```
<A HREF="http://some.site.edu/cgi-bin/imagemap/~user/path/blobby.map">
<IMG SRC="blobby.gif" ISMAP>
</A>
```

where user is the username of the person with personal HTML documents, and *path/blobby.map* is the path leading to the map file from the root of his or her personal document directory.

GETTING A CLICK TO DO NOTHING

Sometimes, you want a click to do nothing: For example, your image could be a map of buildings, but you don't want anything to happen when the user clicks on nonmapped objects, such as roads or trees. The ideal solution would be for the client to retain the current document on the browser window screen. You can ask the client to do this by linking the default method in your imagemap file to a server script that sends a message to the client telling it to do exactly this: Do nothing and keep displaying the same page. This is the intent of the default method in Figure 5.1. This default method references the script *nph-no_op.sh,* which contains the five simple lines:

```
#!/bin/sh
echo "HTTP/1.0 204 No response -- server CGI-script output"
echo "Content-type: text/plain"
echo "Server: $SERVER_SOFTWARE"
echo
```

Output from a script with the *nph-* prefix is sent directly to the client without being parsed by the server (see Chapter 4 for more information about *nonparsed header* gateway programs). This script sends the HTTP status code 204, which tells the client that there is no server message and that the client should retain the current document.

TOOLS FOR GENERATING IMAGEMAP FILES

Generating a map file is not difficult and requires only some concentration, a piece of paper, and an image viewing program that gives you the pixel coordinates of the mouse pointer. The generic UNIX program for this purpose is **xv** (found at many anonymous FTP sites by searching for the string xv-3.00). You load the image into **xv**, locate the coordinates, and type the numbers into a map file. A similar procedure can be followed with typical Macintosh or PC image editing programs.

Of course, this process would be much easier if you had a graphical tool for editing images and automatically generating the map files. Thomas Boutell has satisfied this need with his program **mapedit**, which allows you to read the GIF image into a resizable window; use the mouse to draw circles, rectangles, and polygons on top; and specify a URL for each of the marked regions. You can also insert comments as you go, which is important if you want to understand the contents of the map file at a later date.

Mapedit is available for both UNIX systems and PCs running Windows. Both version are found at:

```
ftp://sunsite.unc.edu/pub/packages/infosystems/WWW/tools/mapedit
```

The PC version comes as a *zip* archive containing the executable program, support files, and documentation; while the UNIX version comes as a compressed tar file (the current version is in the file *mapedit1.1.2.tar.Z*). The UNIX package must be compiled for your system. You will need an ANSI C compiler, The X-Windows libraries at level X11R5 or higher, the X11 imake utility (usually a part of the X distribution), and the X11 Athena widget set. Compilation instructions come with the installation kit. Additional information about **mapedit** can be found at:

```
http://sunsite.unc.edu/boutell/mapedit/mapedit.html
```

ICON ARCHIVE SITES

There are several sites on the World Wide Web that maintain extensive archives of image icons. These are often ideal places to find icons for use in your own document development. The following is a list of some of the more popular sites, along with pointers to more extensive lists of icon and image archives:

Icon Archives

```
http://www-ns.rutgers.edu/doc-images/

http://www.dsv.su.se/~matti-hu/archive.html

http://www.di.unipi.it/iconbrowser/icons.html

http://alice.cli.di.unipi.it/iconbrowser/icons.html

http://www.cit.gu.edu.au/~anthony/icons/index.html
```

Other Lists and Image Archives

```
http://white.nosc.mil/images.html

http://akebono.stanford.edu/yahoo/Computers/World_Wide_Web/Programming/Icons/

http://oneworld.wa.com/htmldev/devpage/dev-page3.html#doc-i

http://www.cs.yale.edu/HTML/YALE/CS/HyPlans/loosemore-sandra/clipart.html
```

CLIENT-SIDE EXECUTABLE PROGRAMS

The emphasis up to this point has been on programs that run on the server using data passed from the client. Sometimes, however, you want to execute a program on the *client*. For example, you might want the user to be able to start up a USENET newsreading program on the client by pressing a FORM button or a hypertext link. Or, you might want the user to be able to start up an interactive teleconferencing session in the same manner.

Both these situations require that the server send information to the client, requesting the execution of a program, or actually send a program to the client for execution. For example, the newsreader could be launched by sending the client a simple startup script, while the teleconferencing example would require a more complicated script that launches the teleconferencing program, and also provides the information needed to contact the other party.

Although clearly a powerful tool, client-side executable programs incur many security risks, because the program arriving from the server is an unknown quantity—the client has no way of knowing what it will actually do. For example, a vicious server administrator could create a script that deletes files on the client computer. These real possibilities warrant efforts on your part to protect your system.

The following discussion outlines how client-side program execution is allowed, and includes hints to ensuring the security of this procedure. It also discusses the packages **vsafecsh** and **w3launch,** which are useful tools for facilitating safe execution of client-side programs.

SENDING THE SCRIPT TO THE CLIENT

The first stage is to send the executable script or program from the server to the client. This is done from a CGI gateway program, using a special MIME content-type in the response headers (see Chapter 4) that tells the client that the data being sent by the gateway program is a program or script that the client should execute. As an example, you could use the header:

```
Content-type:  application/x-www-local-exec
```

Note that the type *must* be application, while the subtype name must begin with x-. The x- prefix is used for all local, experimental, or otherwise unregistered MIME-types. This example uses x-www-local-exec, but you can choose whatever you like.

Here is an example of a server-side CGI program that sends the preceding content-type header, followed by the executable script, to the client. The example is a simple UNIX Bourne-shell script:

```
#!/bin/sh
echo Content-type:  application/x-www-local-exec
echo
echo "#!/bin/sh"
#
#    Bourne shell scripts to run on the client. For example, this
#    could start up some client program, and use server environment
#    variables to control the configuration of the program
#
#    This UNIX example simply launches a local xterm window running the
#    tin Usenet newsreader program
#
echo
echo "xterm -display $DISPLAY -e  /usr/local/bin/tin"
echo
```

When a client browser accesses this CGI program, the browser receives the following message from the HTTP server:

```
HTTP/1.0 200 OK
Date: Monday, 03-Oct-94 22:19:31 GMT
Server: NCSA/1.3
MIME-version: 1.0
Content-type:  application/x-www-local-exec
Content-Length: 57

#!/bin/sh

xterm -display $DISPLAY -e  /usr/local/bin/tin
```

which includes the content-type header that was generated by the CGI program. The next step is to configure the client to know what to do with this special content-type, and with the message body.

CONFIGURING THE CLIENT

The browser must be configured to know what to do with messages of the `application/x-www-local-exec` MIME-type. To do this, you add information about this content-type to your browser's configuration files. For **Mosaic for X-Windows**, this means editing the *mailcap* file, which is the **Mosaic for X-Windows** file that matches MIME-types to helper programs. For this simple example, you could add the line:

```
application/x-www-local-exec;   /bin/sh %s
```

which tells **Mosaic for X-Windows** to pass any document of type `application/x-www-local-exec` to the program **/bin/sh** (the Bourne shell) for execution. The `%s` is the symbolic representation of the document sent to the client. Similar configurations are possible on Macintosh or PC browsers, in which case, you can often add the new MIME-types using a pull-down menu for helper applications.

The preceding example of a client-side program requires a UNIX client. This is true because of the UNIX Bourne-shell script being passed as an executable program, and because of the use of the UNIX **tin** newsreader as the client-side program. This illustrates how strongly client-side program execution can be tied to the client architecture. One way to resolve these differences is to have the server-side script use the *HTTP_SERVER_SOFTWARE* environment variable to determine the type of the host, and to then send the program or script file relevant to the client hardware and software.

SECURITY ISSUES

The preceding example program is harmless; however, scripts that contain the following lines pose greater concern:

```
#!/bin/sh

xterm -display my.home.display:0      # pop xterm somewhere else
```

This script would open an xterm window on the remote machine `my.home.display` but under the client user's account, thus giving the person at my.home.display access to the user's entire directory. Obviously, you do not want to allow scripts to do this type of thing! Fortunately, you can add client-side security features that significantly reduce or eliminate the risk of such nightmarish events.

There are essentially two approaches to improved security. The first approach is to execute all programs on a client using a *secure* local shell. You would then modify the *mailcap* (or other) file to direct execution to this safe shell. For example:

```
application/x-www-local-exec;  /usr/local/bin/secure_sh %s
```

where secure_sh is a special shell program that includes extra security features. This might run under the system's restricted shell (often called **rsh**), which restricts a program's ability to modify variables or files, or it might contain internal tests that check for dangerous commands. (The **vsafecsh** program, described in the following section, is one package that implements this type of protection; in this case, for scripts that are executed using the UNIX *csh* shell.)

The second option is to design special client-side programs, place them on every client and in a special directory, and allow the program passed from the server to access *only* these predesigned packages. For example, you could prepare small client scripts for starting up the newsreader or the teleconferencing package, and allow the script sent from the server to access these scripts only. Careful design of the small client scripts can significantly enhance the security of the local systems. This, in part, is the approach taken by **w3launch**.

The following are brief descriptions of the **vsafecsh** and **w3launch** utilities.

VSAFECSH

Vsafecsh is a C-language program that acts as a protective gateway for client-side **csh** executions on UNIX platforms. Ordinarily, you enable **csh** execution on a client with a *mailcap* entry, such as:

```
application/x-www-localc-exec; csh -f %s
```

As just described, this is not secure. Safety can be improved by replacing this entry with:

```
application/x-www-localc-exec; vsafecsh -f %s
```

which causes the **csh** script passed from the server to first be parsed by **vsafecsh**.

Vsafecsh forks and executes *only* those executable programs that are authorized by the user. Currently, the list of allowed programs is compiled into the code of **vsafecsh**, so the user or workstation administrator has to recompile **vsafecsh** for any newly allowed programs. However, this is a small price to pay in exchange for safe client-side execution.

Additional information about **vsafecsh** is found at:

```
http://www.eit.com/software/vsafecsh/vsafecsh.html
```

Vsafecsh was written by Vinay Kumar of Enterprise Integration Technologies.

W3LAUNCH

Much of the difficulty in setting up secure client-side execution is solved through a package called **w3launch**. Available for both UNIX and Windows PCs, **w3launch** allows a client site administrator to register certain special programs as *launchable* from a server script. This registration ensures that only secure programs are allowed to execute, and allows the administrator to control access to these programs. **W3launch** consists of client and server software for administering these registered programs and for creating server-side launch scripts that can access these programs.

Additional information about **w3launch** is found at:

```
http://www.leeds.ac.uk/bionet/w3launch/w3l-home.htm
```

The source codes and executables are available from this document or from the directory:

```
http://www.leeds.ac.uk/bionet/w3launch/
```

W3launch was written by Jon Maber of the University of Leeds.

SERVER-SIDE DOCUMENT INCLUDES

A recurring question by HTML authors is, Can I include a file within my HTML document in the same way I include an image? The answer is, in general, no. If you want to have documents that are created dynamically, you are supposed to use a CGI program. Needless to say, this can be annoying if all you want to do is patch a small piece of text into an otherwise stable document. Some kind of *include* HTML command would be a far easier mechanism than a full-blown CGI script.

The NCSA HTTP server allows for server-side file inclusion, using an extension to the HTML syntax that allows for *parsable* HTML. This allows you to include in your documents special HTML commands that can inline text files or other data, or even execute server programs and include the program output. This is a powerful feature but should not be abused, since every parsable file must be specially processed by the server, which significantly slows server response. You should reserve the use of parsable files to situations where it is the only realistic choice.

The server-side include feature is well documented in the NCSA HTTPD server online manuals. The following is a brief overview of this feature, and you are referred to the NCSA documentation and interactive tutorials for further details.

INCLUDE COMMAND FORMAT

The server-side include command is framed inside an HTML comment string:

```
<!-- include_command -->
```

When parsed by the NCSA HTTPD server, the entire comment string is replaced by the output of the `include_command`. Enclosing this command inside comment strings ensures that the document will not cause problems if it is served by another server. Other servers will simply deliver the document, including the comment line, and the client will treat the enclosed string as a comment and ignore it.

The general form for the include command is:

```
<!--#command arg1="value1" arg2="value2" -->
```

where `command` is the name of the command to be executed and `arg1` and `arg2` are arguments passed to the command. There must be no spaces between the hash sign (#) and the command name. The number and name of the arguments depends on the actual command; most commands take a single argument. Note that, despite this structure, this is *not* a comment statement. You *cannot* include comment descriptions inside an include command. Consequently, lines like:

```
<!--#command arg1="value1" This prints the time of day  -->
```

are invalid.

There are six possible commands: `config`, `include`, `echo`, `fsize`, `flastmod`, and `exec`. `Config` is used to configure the way the server will parse the document. `Include` is used to include another document (not a CGI program) at the indicated point, while `echo` is used to include the contents of one of the special environment variables set for parsed documents. `Fsize` and `flastmod` are similar to `echo`; `fsize` prints the size of a specified file, while `flastmod` prints the last modification date of a specified file. Finally, `exec` executes a single-line Bourne-shell command or a CGI program. For security reasons, the `exec` facility can be disabled in the server configuration files while leaving the include feature operational.

Here are the details of the six different commands, with examples.

INCLUDE

`Include` is used to include another document (or another parsed document) at the given location in the current document. `Include` can include only a document, and cannot include CGI program output. `Include` takes one argument that specifies the file to be included. The possible arguments and their values are:

`virtual="virtual/path"`—Virtual specifies the *virtual* path to the document relative to the server's document directory or a user's personal server directory. For example, user `fosdick` with his or her own public HTML area would access files in this area with the virtual path:

```
virtual="~fosdick/path/file.html"
```

`file="relative_path/file"`—File specifies the path to the document relative to the current document. You cannot use `file` to move up in the hierarchy, only down (i.e., you can't use `../stuff.html`). For example, to include the file *junk.html* from the same directory you would type: `<!--#include file="junk.html" -->`

Examples of `include`:

```
<!--#include file="templates/template2.html" -->
<!--#include virtual="/path/subpath/templates/template2.html -->
```

Echo

`Echo` includes in the document the contents of a named environment variable. The variable name you wish to include is indicated via the argument `var="variable_name"`. `Variable_name` can be any of the CGI environment variables listed in Chapter 4, and can also be one of the following environment variables valid only in parsable files:

DOCUMENT_NAME—The name of the current file.

DOCUMENT_URI—The virtual path to the document, such as `~fosdick/path/file.html` or `/path/subpath/templates/template2.html`

DATE_LOCAL—The current date, using the local time zone. The format of this date can be controlled using the `timefmt` argument of the `config` command.

DATE_GMT—Same as *DATE_LOCAL*, but in Greenwich Mean Time.

LAST_MODIFIED—The last modification date of the current document. The format is specified by `timefmt`.

These environment variables are also available to any program executed using the `exec` command.

Examples of echo:

```
The file is found at: <!--#echo var="DOCUMENT_URI"  -->
This file was accessed at the time: <!--#echo var="DATE_LOCAL"  -->
```

FSIZE

Fsize includes the sizes, in bytes, of a specified file. The file is specified using the file or virtual arguments, as described with the include command. Fsize is useful for presenting information about a file to be downloaded, allowing the document to tell the user the size of the file even if the file size varies continuously (such as a mail archive). Fsize can also be useful for presenting file indexes that include file size information. The output format can be controlled using the sizefmt argument of the config command.

Example of fsize:

```
The size of the file main.html is: <!--#fsize file="main.html"  -->
```

FLASTMOD

Flastmod includes the last modification time of a specified file. The file is specified using the file or virtual arguments, as described with the include command. Like fsize, flastmod is useful for providing additional information about files that are periodically changed. The output format can be controlled using the timefmt argument of the config command.

Example of flastmod:

```
This file was last changed on:
<!--#flastmod virtual="/path/dir1/dir2/main.html"  -->
```

EXEC

Exec executes the given command or CGI program. Exec can have one of two possible arguments:

cmd="cmd_string"—Causes the string cmd_string to be executed using the Bourne shell **/bin/sh.** Cmd_string can be a simple one-line shell program to do simple things, such as list directory contents, run a program to filter a data file for presentation, and so on.

cmd="cgi_program"—Executes the given CGI program, where the location of the program is given by the virtual path to the program. Note that the script must return a valid MIME-type. You cannot pass query strings or path information to the script using URL-type constructions. Thus, expressions like:

```
<!--#exec cmd="/cgi-bin/script.cgi/path1/path2?query" -->
```

are invalid. The only way you can access the script is with the command:

```
<!--#exec cmd="/cgi-bin/script.cgi" -->
```

However, suppose the parsable script *stuff.shtml* contained the command:

```
<!--#exec cmd="/cgi-bin/script.cgi" -->
```

and you access the file *stuff.shtml* via the URL:

```
...../stuff.shtml/extra/path?query_string
```

In this case, the query_string and /extra/path information *are* available to the script *script.cgi* called from *stuff.shtml*. This is illustrated in an example at the end of this section.

CONFIG

The config command controls aspects of the output of the parsed commands, such as the formats of the date and size output strings, or the error message string to include if parsing fails. Config can take three different arguments, one argument per command. These are:

errmsg="error_string"—Gives the error string to use if there is an error in parsing an include statement.

timefmt="format"—Timefmt sets the format for printing dates. This format is specified as with the C strftime library call (strftime is commonly found on UNIX computers).

`sizefmt="bytes","abbrev"`—`Sizefmt` sets the format for the specification of file sizes. The value `"bytes"` prints file sizes in bytes, while `"abbrev"` uses kilobytes or megabytes as abbreviated forms, where applicable.

Examples of `config`:

```
<!--#config sizefmt="abbrev"  -->
<!--#config timefmt="%m%d%y"  -->
<!--#config errmsg="Unable to parse scripts"  -->
```

EXAMPLE OF SERVER-SIDE INCLUDES

The following example (shown in Figures 5.2 and 5.3) shows the use of server-side includes. The example consists of a main document *stuff.shtml* (the suffix *.shtml* is used to indicate parsable HTML documents) that includes a second parsable document *inc_file.shtml* and that also executes the CGI program *test_script.cgi*. The listings for these examples are shown in Figure 5.2, while the browser rendering of the document *stuff.shtml* is shown in Figure 5.3.

In this example, the document *stuff.shtml* is accessed using the URL:

```
http://leonardo:8080/stuff.shtml/extra/path/info?arg1+arg2
```

Note that this passes query strings and extra path information to this document, just as if it were a gateway program (see Chapter 4 for more information about CGI programs and passed variables). This information should be contained in the environment variables *QUERY_STRING* and *PATH_INFO*. The documents are designed to print these variables. As you can see in Figure 5.2, these variables are empty inside the parsable HTML documents. However, as shown at the bottom of Figure 5.3, these variables *are* present inside the CGI program executed from within the parsable document. You can, therefore, access a parsable document and, through it, pass query information to a CGI program, just as if you were accessing the CGI program directly.

The `include` and `echo` commands are also illustrated in Figures 5.2 and 5.3. These can be used to print useful information about the current file. Remember, however, that you really want to avoid this type of include as much as possible, as every server execution slows the server response. For example, it is a waste of server resources to use the *LAST_MODIFIED* variable to display the last time you edited a simple HTML document, since you could just as easily add this information while editing it.

▰▰▰▰

stuff.shtml

```
<html>
<head>
<title> Test of NCSA Server-side Includes </title>

<body>
<h1> Test of NCSA Server-side Includes </h1>

<pre>
Stuff.shtml was last modified: <!--#flastmod virtual="/stuff.shtml"  -->.
Size of stuff.shtml is:        <!--#fsize file="stuff.shtml"  -->.
DOCUMENT_NAME =                <!--#echo var="DOCUMENT_NAME" -->
DOCUMENT_URI =                 <!--#echo var="DOCUMENT_URI" -->
DATE_LOCAL =                   <!--#echo var="DATE_LOCAL" -->
QUERY_STRING =                 <!--#echo var="QUERY_STRING" -->
PATH_LOCAL =                   <!--#echo var="QUERY_STRING" -->
DATE_GMT =                     <!--#echo var="DATE_GMT" -->
LAST_MODIFIED =                <!--#echo var="LAST_MODIFIED" -->
</pre>

<!--#config errmsg="Unable to parse scripts"  -->

<p><em>....now include inc_example.shtml....</em>

<!--#include file="inc_file.shtml" -->
```

```
<p> <em>..... now include test_script.cgi CGI program output...... </em>


<!--#exec cgi="/cgi-bin/test_script.cgi" -->

</body>

</html>
```

inc_file.shtml

```
<pre>

Inc_file.shtml last modified: <!--#flastmod virtual="/inc_file.shtml"-->.

Size of inc_file.shtml is:    <!--#fsize file="inc_file.shtml"  -->.

DOCUMENT_NAME:                <!--#echo var="DOCUMENT_NAME" -->

DOCUMENT_URI:                 <!--#echo var="DOCUMENT_URI" -->

DATE_LOCAL:                   <!--#echo var="DATE_LOCAL" -->

DATE_GMT                      <!--#echo var="DATE_GMT" -->

LAST_MODIFIED                 <!--#echo var="LAST_MODIFIED" -->


</pre>
```

test_script.cgi (in the cgi-bin directory)

```
#!/bin/sh


echo "Content-type: text/html"

echo

echo "<pre>"

echo "This is  CGI script output."

echo "QUERY_STRING is \"$QUERY_STRING\"."

echo "PATH_INFO =  \"$PATH_INFO\". "

echo ""</pre>"
```

Figure 5.2 Example of NCSA server-side includes. The main file is **stuff.shtml**, which *includes* the file **inc_file.html** and the output of the CGI program **test_script.cgi**. The resulting HTML document upon accessing the URL:

```
http://leonardo:8080/stuff.shtml/extra/path/info?arg1+arg2
```

is shown in Figure 5.3.

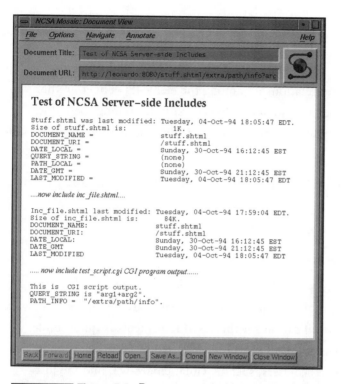

Figure 5.3 Browser rendering of the server-side executable document *stuff.shtml*, when accessed using the URL:

```
http://leonardo:8080/stuff.shtml/extra/path/info?arg1+arg2
```

For additional information about server-side includes, and particularly for information on how to configure the NCSA HTTP server to allow server-side includes, consult the NCSA online documentation at:

```
http://hoohoo.ncsa.uiuc.edu/docs/tutorials/includes.html
```

HTML UTILITY PROGRAMS

This section lists several small utility programs that are useful in managing collections of HTML documents. Most of these are small perl programs and should run on any computer that has perl, although they were mostly developed on UNIX workstations.

DTD2HTML

Dtd2html is a perl program that takes an SGML Document Type Definition (DTD) file and generates a collection of HTML documents explaining the structural relationship among the elements defined in the DTD. The resultant documents contain hypertext links among these documents. This is useful if you are interested in learning more about the HTML DTD.

Dtd2html was written by Earl Hood. More information about **dtd2html** is available at:

```
http://www.oac.uci.edu/indiv/ehood/dtd2html.doc.html
```

HTML TABLE CONVERTER

As mentioned in Chapters 1 and 2, HTML2.0 does not contain elements for creating structured tables, although such elements are defined in HTML+. In fact, the specification for the **TABLE** elements is quite stable so that actual implementation of **TABLE** elements should be just around the corner. Indeed, some browsers, such as **viola, emacs-w3**, and the just released **Mosaic for X-Windows 2.5**, already support the **TABLE** elements.

The transition from the **TABLE**-less world of today to the **TABLE**-full world of tomorrow has been made easier by a small perl package written by Brooks Cutter. This package accepts documents containing HTML+ **TABLE** elements, and formats the table portions into an appropriate plain text table, surrounding the table with `<PRE>` and `</PRE>` tags. Using this package, you can write your documents using the **TABLE** elements and then quickly convert them into a form acceptable to today's browsers. Then, when browsers mature to the point of handling tables, you will already have tables in the correct format.

The package (a UNIX shell archive) is available at:

```
ftp://sunsite.unc.edu/pub/packages/infosystems/WWW/tools/html+tables.shar
```

HYPERMAIL

Hypermail is a C-language program that takes a file of mail messages in UNIX mailbox format and generates a set of cross-referenced HTML documents. **Hypermail** converts each letter in the mailbox into a separate HTML file, with links to other related articles. It also converts e-mail addresses and hypertext anchors in the original letters into HTML hypertext links. **Hypermail** archives can be incrementally updated, which significantly eases the updating of archives on a periodic basis.

Detailed information about **Hypermail** can be found at:

```
http://www.eit.com/software/hypermail/hypermail.html
```

The program itself is available from:

```
ftp://ftp.eit.com/pub/web.software/hypermail
```

The current C-language version of **Hypermail** was written by Kevin Hughes of Enterprise Integration Technologies Inc.

MHONARC: MAIL TO HTML ARCHIVE

MHonArc is a perl package for converting Internet mail messages, both plain text and MIME-encoded, into HTML documents. This can be extremely useful, for example, if you are archiving electronic mail messages or newsgroup postings and want to make them available on the WWW. The package uses the letter's subject line for the HTML **TITLE** and as an **H1** heading in the HTML version of the letter, and converts relational headers, such as References or In Reply To, into the appropriate hypertext links if possible.

MHonArc can also sort letters according to their topical thread and connect them together with *Next* and *Previous* hypertext links. In addition, **MHonArc** creates an index of the letters or articles, and creates a link from each converted letter to this index.

The home page for **MHonArc** is:

```
http://www.oac.uci.edu/indiv/ehood/mhonarc.doc.html
```

This contains directions for obtaining the most recent version of MHonArc and pointers to extensive documentation. The author is Earl Hood.

TABLE OF CONTENTS GENERATOR

Htmltoc is a perl program that can automatically generate a Table of Contents (TOC) for a single HTML document or for a collection of related documents. **Htmltoc** uses the HTML **H1** through **H6** headings to locate sections within a single document, and uses the order of the heading (**H1**, **H2**, and so on) to determine the hierarchical relationship of the TOC. This, among many other features, can be significantly customized.

When **htmltoc** creates a Table of Contents, it creates hypertext links from the Table of Contents to the documents themselves. It does this by editing the original documents and adding the appropriate hypertext anchors. The original documents are backed up during this process so that you can easily recover the original material.

Additional documentation on **htmltoc**, including directions to the most recent version, can be found at:

```
http://www.oac.uci.edu/indiv/ehood/htmltoc.doc.html
```

Htmltoc was written by Earl Hood.

TREELINK

Treelink, written in tk and tcl, is a package that draws a hypergraph of the hypertext links, starting from a given hypertext document. **Treelink** analyzes the connections and draws a tree-like graph until it reaches a certain predefined depth (number of links). This graph often gives useful insights into the connection and arrangement of links to a particular document.

Additional information about **Treelink**, including instructions as to where to obtain the source code, can be found at:

```
http://aorta.tat.physik.uni-tuebingen.de/~gaier/treelink/
```

Treelink was written by Karsten Gaier.

CGI UTILITY FUNCTIONS

This section lists various CGI gateway programs and utilities. Some, such as the query and input parsing libraries, are of general use. Others, such as the e-mail handlers, may not be generally useful but do serve as valuable models for developing custom applications.

CGI EMAIL HANDLER

This package, due to Thomas Boutell, is a simple CGI program that allows WWW clients to send e-mail messages to a restricted set of allowed recipients. The package has three components. **Email.c** is the ANSI C program that does all the work. You also need to create FORM-based HTML documents for composing the letter: You need to create a separate FORM for each of the allowed recipients. Third, you need to create a server-side database of allowed recipients, used by **email** to verify that the user is sending mail to an authorized person.

This package is quite simple and has been used as a model for several other, more extensive implementations. Additional information about this package, including directions to the various component parts you will need, can be found at:

```
http://siva.cshl.org/email/index.html
```

CGI FEEDBACK FORM

This package of utilities by Arjan de Vet uses a FORM interface to let the client send feedback information to the server administrator. It consists of a small C-language CGI program that reads the FORM data and converts the FORM information into a mail message to the site administrator.

The package is available at:

```
ftp://ftp.win.tue.nl/pub/infosystems/www/wwwutils.tar.gz
```

DETERMINING CLIENT SOFTWARE

Sometimes, it is nice to know the type of client accessing your server CGI program. Typically, this would be to offer different documents or database interfaces, depending on the capabilities of the client—there is no point in offering a clickable image interface to someone using **lynx!**

This requires a program that can parse the *HTTP_USER_AGENT* environment variable and break it into useful fields, including the client program field. A nice perl program demonstrating this facility is found at:

```
http://www.mps.ohio-state.edu/cgi-bin/clientinfo.pl
```

This includes directions for obtaining the perl source code and additional required perl libraries. This useful script was written by Doug Stevenson.

CONVERT UNIX MAN PAGES TO HTML

There are several CGI packages for searching through UNIX online manuals and converting the manual pages into viewable HTML documents. This section briefly describes three exemplary packages. For those familiar with UNIX man pages, these are useful models of CGI programming techniques.

MAN2HTML

Man2html is a perl program by Earl Hood that can read UNIX man pages, in formatted nroff form only, and produce HTML as output. Although you can do this on a per-file basis, **man2html** is designed to be used in a CGI program: Instructions are included with the distribution on how to do this, along with an example **man.cgi** script. This gives WWW clients access to all your UNIX online documentation. You can also configure **man2html** to include hypertext links to other man pages related to the one you are reading. In addition, **man2html** supports the man -k keyword man page search facility.

Additional information about **man2html** is found at the URL:

    http://www.oac.uci.edu/indiv/ehood/man2html.doc.html

Man2html was written by Earl Hood.

Bbc_man2html

Bbc_man2html.pl is a perl program for distributing UNIX man pages via a World Wide Web server. **Bbc_man2html.pl** uses the <ISINDEX> search mechanism to prompt for a particular man page, where you enter the desired man page title in the query box. At present, man -k keyword searching is not implemented. **Bbc_man2html.pl** uses the **RosettaMan** program (discussed in the following) to format the man pages into HTML, so you also need this program.

Bbc_man2html.pl is available at:

    ftp://src.doc.ic.ac.uk/computing/information-systems/www/tools/translators

Bbc_man2html.pl was written by Brooks Cutter.

RosettaMan: UNIX Man Page to HTML

RosettaMan is a filter for UNIX-style manual pages. It takes as input man pages formatted for a variety of UNIX flavors (not just [tn]roff source) and produces as output a variety of file formats. RosettaMan is a tcl/tk script and requires the interpreters that come with the tcl/tk distribution.

The RosettaMan archive can be found at:

    ftp://ftp.cs.berkeley.edu/ucb/people/phelps/tcltk/rman.tar.Z

RosettaMan is copyrighted by T. A. Phelps.

PROCESSING QUERIES AND FORM PACKAGES

One of the most tedious aspects of writing a CGI program is parsing the environment variables, command-line arguments, or standard input data to the program: These data are encoded using the URL syntax so that a gateway program must first decode the information before it can be used. The following are some example programs and programming libraries that can help with this task.

Uncgi

Uncgi is a useful front-end package that handles this parsing for you. **Uncgi** decodes all the **FORM** fields and places them in environment variables. **Uncgi** then calls your processing program (C, perl, or whatever), passing these environment variables to it. Note that this may be a problem if the variable being passed in an environment variable becomes too large, since some systems place limits on the size of environment variables.

Additional information about **uncgi** is available at:

```
http://www.hyperion.com/~koreth/uncgi.html
```

Uncgi was written by Steven Grimm.

The EIT CGI Library

Enterprise Integration Technologies has made available a library of C functions that are extremely useful in constructing CGI programs. Included are routines for parsing input from FORM or ISINDEX queries, routines for generating MIME response headers, and much more. Details about the different available functions can be found at:

```
http://wsk.eit.com/wsk/dist/doc/libcgi/libcgi.html
```

The source code and executable libraries can be found at:

```
http://wsk.eit.com/wsk/dist/
```

in subdirectories corresponding to your operating system, and below that in the subdirectory *libcgi*. For example, if you are using the IRIX operating system, the **libcgi** material would be at:

```
http://wsk.eit.com/wsk/dist/irix/libcgi/
```

If you don't find your operating system in this list, just go to one of the other directories and get the source code.

DATABASE CGI GATEWAY PROGRAMS

Needless to say, there is great interest in using the World Wide Web as a front end to sophisticated database packages. This requires the construction of gateway programs to connect the FORM- or ISINDEX-based query input mechanisms of the WWW with the back-end SQL (or other) mechanisms used by databases, such as Sybase, Oracle, or WAIS. The following is a list of current efforts at constructing these interfaces, including instructions on how to obtain more information. All these packages will require customization to your particular database requirements. Nevertheless, they provide a powerful starting point for integrating WWW applications with your database technologies.

WAIS GATEWAYS

WAIS, for Wide Area Information Servers, is an extremely popular Internet network publishing and textual database system. **WAIS** is designed as a client-server system, with WAIS clients able to interrogate WAIS databases using a well-defined protocol. This protocol is supported by a number of WWW clients so that it is often possible to directly interrogate a WAIS server by constructing a URL (and appropriate query strings) that points to that WAIS server.

However, many clients still do not support the WAIS protocol and, in many cases, this direct method is not ideal for accessing WAIS servers. Often, it is easier to interact with a FORM interface that is designed to construct WAIS queries in a manner more convenient to the user. For these reasons, several gateway programs have been constructed that allow non-WAIS-capable clients to access a WAIS server, and that allow for sophisticated FORM interfaces to WAIS servers. The following is a list of some of the server-side CGI packages designed to accomplish these tasks.

BASIC WAIS

The NCSA HTTP server distribution comes with several small CGI programs, including *wais.pl*, a small perl program written by Tony Sanders.

Wais.pl uses the ISINDEX mechanism to obtain a query string from the user and passes this string to a local WAIS database query engine (**waisq**), and returns the results to the user as an HTML document. This is a simple and easy to understand perl script, and has served as the basis for a number of other WAIS gateway programs.

Wais.pl is available at the NCSA gateway program archive:

```
ftp://ftp.ncsa.uiuc.edu/Web/httpd/Unix/ncsa_httpd/cgi/wais.tar.Z
```

SON OF WAIS

Son-of-wais.pl is a perl script based on the original **wais.pl** package from NCSA. **Son-of-wais.pl** adds some nice formatting of the returned data and more complete instructions to the user. The perl package is available at:

```
http://dewey.lib.ncsu.edu/staff/morgan/son-of-wais.html
```

(the perl code is part of the HTML document). **Son-of-wais.pl** was written by Eric Lease Morgan of North Carolina State University Libraries. However, Eric does point out that the package **kidowais.pl** (described next) is a significant improvement over **son-of-wais.pl**.

KIDOWAIS

Kidowais.pl is another perl script WAIS gateway program based on **wais.pl**, but with significant functionality improvements over both **wais.pl** and **son-of-wais.pl**. **Kidowais.pl** also uses the **ISINDEX** query interface, but allows for pattern searches (`astro*` matches any word beginning with astro) as well as complex Boolean searches. The program returns search results complete with useful information about the resulting items, such as document type and length. In addition, when the documents are retrieved the search string is highlighted in boldface for easier identification.

Additional information is available at:

```
http://www.cso.uiuc.edu/grady.html
```

which includes pointers to the perl packages you will need (**kidowais.pl** and **print_hit_bold.pl**) and to other documents, with additional information on installing and configuring the packages. **Kidowais.pl** was written by by Michael Grady.

SF GATE

SFgate is another perl-based WAIS gateway program but is distinctly different from **wais.pl** or its derivatives. **SFgate** does not access a server-side WAIS query engine. Instead, it has WAIS client software built-in so that it can itself query any Internet-accessible WAIS database. In addition, it has a FORM query interface so that the user can select various databases (you can search more than one at the same time) and enter complex query information into text input boxes. You can also create customized FORM interfaces to make it easier for your users to access the database.

SFgate is particularly designed to work with **freeWAIS-sf** servers. **FreeWAIS-sf** is a WAIS variant modified to, among other things, allow for structured fields. Information about **freeWAIS-sf** can be found at:

```
http://ls6-www.informatik.uni-dortmund.de/freeWAIS-sf/README-sf.html
```

Additional information about **SFgate** can be found at:

```
http://ls6-www.informatik.uni-dortmund.de/SFgate/SFgate.html
```

while the perl source can be downloaded from:

```
ftp://ls6-www.informatik.uni-dortmund.de/pub/www/
```

The most recent version as of October 1994 was in the file *SFgate-3.1.tar.gz*, but this will no doubt have changed. **SFGate** was written by Ulrich Pfeifer.

WAIS GATE

WAIS Inc. is developing a WAIS to Web gateway program called WAISgate. Source code for this gateway is not available, but the gateway is accessible, for free, on the main WAIS server at *www.wais.com*. Additional information about **WAISgate** can be found at:

```
http://server.wais.com/waisgate-announce.html
```

WWWWAIS

WWWWAIS is a small ANSI C program that acts as gateway between **waisq** and **waissearch** (the WAIS programs that search WAIS indexes) and a FORM-capable World Wide Web browser. **WWWWAIS** allows for a customized FORM interface and a database access control mechanism (restricting access to certain Internet domains), and gives users the ability to search multiple databases. As with the preceding packages, **WWWWAIS** returns the search results as a hypertext document.

Additional information about **WWWWAIS** can be found at:

```
http://www.eit.com/software/wwwwais/wwwwais.html
```

The source code and support files are available from:

```
ftp://ftp.eit.com/pub/web.software/wwwwais/
```

Get the **README** file first to find out what you need. **WWWWAIS** was written by Kevin Hughes of Enterprise Integration Technologies.

GATEWAYS TO STRUCTURED QUERY LANGUAGE DATABASES

There are also several gateway packages for linking the World Wide Web to commercial database packages, such as Oracle or Sybase. The following sections list some of these efforts.

GSQL-ORACLE BACKEND

GSQL-Oracle Backend is a CGI program that can link WWW applications to an Oracle database, using both the ISINDEX and FORM interfaces. **GSQL-Oracle Backend** is written in PRO-C, the C-language development environment for ORACLE, so you need this development option to compile **GSQL-Oracle Backend**. The package comes complete with installation instructions, and should compile easily on most UNIX machines.

Additional information about **GSQL-Oracle Backend** is available at:

```
ftp://ftp.cc.gatech.edu/pub/gvu/www/pitkow/gsql-oracle/oracle-backend.html
```

while an archive of the package is available from:

```
ftp://ftp.cc.gatech.edu/pub/gvu/www/pitkow/gsql-oracle/gsql-oracle.tar
```

GSQL-Oracle Backend was written by James Pitkow of the Graphics, Visualization, and Usability Center at the Georgia Institute of Technology. For further information, see:

```
http://www.cc.gatech.edu/gvu/
```

WEB/GENERA

Web/Genera is a software toolset for the integration of Sybase databases into the World Wide Web. **Web/Genera** can be used to retrofit a Web front end (FORM or ISINDEX) to an existing **Sybase** database, or to create customized interfaces. To use **Web/Genera,** you write a specification of the Sybase database and of the desired appearance of its contents on the Web using a simple, high-level schema notation. Various **Web/Genera** programs process this description file to generate SQL commands and formatting instructions that together extract objects from your database and format them into HTML. You don't have to write a single line of code to do this, and need learn only how to describe the database using the Genera schema notation, which is reputedly easy to use.

Genera supports URLs linked to specific database objects, as well as powerful FORM-based relational query construction. You can also use **Genera** to generate full-text searches of Sybase databases via Web/WAIS and Gopher/WAIS interfaces.

Additional information about **Web/Genera,** including links to the most recent version of the package and substantial documentation, can be found at:

```
http://cgsc.biology.yale.edu/genera.html
```

Web/Genera was developed by Stanley Letovsky, under work supported by National Science Foundation grant BIR-9201652. It is freely available to the public.

WDB—A WEB INTERFACE TO SYBASE

WDB is a CGI package similar to **Web/Genera,** and is also based on perl and sybperl. Like **Web/Genera, WDB** allows you to use high-level description files to specify the structure of the database and the format of the responses so that you can construct a generic WWW-Sybase interface without writing a single line of code. Notable is the ability to turn data from the database into hypertext links so that it is possible to access any database element directly via a URL.

Additional information about **WDB**, including a list of required software and pointers to the source code archive, is found at:

```
http://arch-http.hq.eso.org/bfrasmus/wdb/wdb.html
```

WDB was written by Bo Frese Rasmussen of the European Southern Observatory.

GSQL GATEWAY

GSQL is a C program that is invoked from the HTTP server via a shell script. **GSQL** is a simple gateway to Sybase or other SQL databases. It parses an SQL-specification file (called a **PROC** file) to create an HTML FORM, and uses the user input onto this FORM to call the database back-end program to process the SQL query. Search query results are then returned to the client. The PROC file maps components of the SQL string to widgets (fields, buttons, pull-down menus, etc.) for user input or selection. Substantial documentation on GSQL and the construction of PROC files can be found at:

```
http://www.ncsa.uiuc.edu/SDG/People/jason/pub/gsql/starthere.html
```

The source code for **GSQL** can be found at:

```
http://base.ncsa.uiuc.edu:1234/gsqlsrc/gsql.tar
```

GSQL was written by Jason Ng of NCSA.

HTORACLE

HTOracle was one of the first database gateway programs developed for the WWW. **HTOracle** is a small package of programs written in Pro-C and

C that can take ISINDEX-style queries and pass them to an Oracle database as an SQL SELECT statement, and then return the results to the client as a plain text table. Documentation on the package is somewhat sketchy, but what there is can be found at:

```
http://info.cern.ch/hypertext/WWW/RDBGate/ArthurNotes.html
```

while pointers to the various source-code components are at:

```
http://info.cern.ch/hypertext/WWW/RDBGate/Implementation.html
```

The **HTOracle** code has been used as the basis for a number of other database gateways, including **OraPlex**. **HTOracle** was written by Arthur Secret of CERN.

ORAPLEX

OraPlex is an adaptation of the **HTOracle** database gateway program. Originally designed for integration with the **Plexus** HTTP server, **OraPlex** is now available as a CGI-compliant package, so it can be used with other CGI-compliant servers. To use **OraPlex,** you need a local Oracle database and **oraPerl,** a perl package written by Kevin Stock that is designed to access Oracle databases.

OraPerl can be found in the directory:

```
ftp://ftp.demon.co.uk/pub/perl/db/oraperl
```

The original Plexus-only **OraPlex** programs are found in the directory:

```
http://moulon.inra.fr/oracle/
```

under the names *oraplex_pl.html* and *oracle_search.html*, while the newer CGI-compliant package is found at:

```
ftp://moulon.inra.fr/pub/www-oracle
```

The C-language version of the database gateway package that uses the standard CGI interface and that can run under any server is discussed at:

```
http://moulon.inra.fr/oracle/www_oracle_eng.html
http://moulon.inra.fr/oracle/www_oraperl_eng.html
```

Documentation in French is available at:

```
http://moulon.inra.fr/oracle/www_oraperl.html

http://moulon.inra.fr/oracle/www_oracle.html
```

OraPlex was written by Guy Decoux of the *Institut National de la Recherche Agronomique*.

MACINTOSH SEARCH TOOLS: TR-WWW

TR-WWW is a Macintosh-based search engine that works only with the **MacHTTP** server. It provides a FORM-based interface to a search engine that dynamically searches (using Boolean searches) server document collections consisting of HTML, plain text, or Microsoft Word files. The documents do not have to be preindexed, as **TR-WWW** can index the documents in real time. **TR-WWW** is thus ideal for searching rapidly evolving collections of documents. Search results can be reviewed (as HTML documents) and sorted by keyword or by WAIS-style, relevance-ranked results.

Additional information about **TR-WWW** is found at:

```
http://informatics.med.monash.edu.au/tr-www.html
```

The latest beta version and manual updates are available by following the links at the top of the document at the preceding URL. The software itself can be found at:

```
http://informatics.med.monash.edu.au/tr-www.sit.hqx

ftp://ftp.cshl.org/transfer/tr-www.sit.hqx
```

CGI ARCHIVE SITES

The following URLs contain useful archives of CGI programs:

```
ftp://ftp.ncsa.uiuc.edu/Web/httpd/Unix/ncsa_httpd/cgi/

ftp://ftp.rz.uni-karlsruhe.de/pub/net/www/tools/cgi-src/
```

DATABASE GATEWAY REFERENCES

Additional information about setting up WAIS gateways can be found at:

```
http://wintermute.ncsa.uiuc.edu:8080/wais-tutorial/wais.html
http://wintermute.ncsa.uiuc.edu:8080/wais-tutorial/wais-and-http.html
```

Examples of useful WAIS gateway programs can be found at:

```
http://www.eit.com/software/wwwwais/wwwwais.html
http://www.cis.ohio-state.edu/hypertext/faq/usenet/wais-faq/getting-started/faq.html
```

Web Database Development Sites:

```
http://www.cs.vu.nl/~anne007/waissearch/pointers.html
http://www-rlg.stanford.edu/home/jpl/websearch.html
http://cgsc.biology.yale.edu/dbgw.html
http://oneworld.wa.com/htmldev/devpage/dev-page3.html
http://info.cern.ch/hypertext/WWW/RDBGate/Overview.html
http://www2.ncsu.edu/bae/people/faculty/walker/isindex.html
```

CHAPTER

HTML EDITORS

AND DOCUMENT

TRANSLATORS

This chapter provides an overview of the tools for creating HTML documents. This collection is constantly growing and evolving so that this list is certainly incomplete and not entirely up to date. For additional information, read the *comp.infosytems.www.users* and *comp.infosystems.www.misc* USENET newsgroups, and also the WWW Frequently Asked Questions (FAQ) list, posted regularly to these newsgroups and also found in hypertext form at:

```
http://sunsite.unc.edu/boutell/faq/www_faq.html
```

The descriptions in this chapter also include pointers to additional documentation on each package, along with directions for obtaining the software. These pointers can also be used to obtain the current status of a particular package.

This chapter is organized in three sections. The first section describes editors specifically designed for writing HTML documents. The second section looks at document translators/converters, which are programs designed to convert from one document format, such as WordPerfect, FrameMaker, or LaTeX, into HTML, and vice versa. The division is somewhat arbitrary, since the combination of a document processing system and a good HTML conversion program is often ideal for preparing HTML documents. Keep this in mind if you are looking for a tool related to a particular document processing system and do not see what you are looking for in the section on editors.

The third section lists HTML validation tools. These are programs that can check an HTML document for correct HTML syntax, and check that hypertext links reference valid URLs. These tools are very useful, as most HTML editors do not check for valid HTML syntax or the validity of the URLs. HTML syntax validation tools use the SGML *Document Type Definition (DTD)* for HTML so that you also need the HTML DTD file. This section includes suggestions of where to find these DTDs, and a description of the validation process.

HTML EDITORS

This section reviews HTML editors. Each editor is described briefly but with sufficient detail that you can see how it works and get an idea of the relative strengths and weaknesses.

At the beginning of each description, you will find the editor name and a list of supported platforms (PC, Macintosh, or UNIX). The subsequent description also notes if the product is commercial software or shareware. The bulk of the description briefly describes the overall layout and operation of the program. Also mentioned are known examples of problems with the current versions of these editors. You should regard this information as an aid in using these editors and not as a judgment on the packages, since I have not tested these packages with equal detail. No attempt is made to describe the relative ease of use, as, in general, they all seem easy to use and straightforward to learn. Each description includes a list of URLs pointing to additional information about the editor, and to actual locations of the editor if available in this way.

Some of these packages are advertised as What You See Is What You Get (*WYSIWYG*) HTML editors. In the World Wide Web, this is a misleading term, since each Web browser will display the same HTML document in a different way, varying from the graphical rendering of browsers such as **MacWeb** or **Mosaic** to the text-only rendering of **lynx**. This does not mean that WYSIWYG capabilities are bad—they can be useful to give an idea of what the document can look like. However, the actual display on real browsers may be quite different from the editor's rendition. The only effective way to verify the clarity of your document design is to preview it on a few different browsers and adjust the design to ensure that the important information is clearly presented by all of them. This may sound like a lot of work but, after going through this procedure a few times, you will quickly develop a feeling for the types of document designs that are universally successful, regardless of the browser.

SIMPLE TEXT EDITORS
(MACINTOSH, PC, UNIX)

Since writing HTML documents requires only the standard, printable ASCII characters, you can prepare and edit HTML documents using a plain text editor. For example, if you are using a PC, you can use the **EDIT** program that comes with DOS, or the **Notepad** editor that comes with Windows (note that you *cannot* use the Windows **Write** editor, as this produces documents in Microsoft's Rich Text Format (RTF), which is not standard ASCII). If you are using a Macintosh, you can use the **TeachText** text editor (limited to files smaller than 20K characters) or freeware editors, such as **BBEdit-Lite**. On UNIX machines, you can use the ever-present editor **vi** or more sophisticated editors, such as **emacs** or **epoch**.

ALPHA (MACINTOSH)

The **Alpha** text editor provides a comprehensive HTML mode for creating new HTML documents. This is complete with editing menus, automatic character entity generation, and other features. The editor can be obtained from:

```
ftp://cs.rice.edu/public/Alpha
```

BBEDIT HTML EXTENSIONS (MACINTOSH)

There are two **BBEdit** HTML extension macro packages. **BBEdit** is a popular Macintosh text editor that comes in two versions: the freeware program **BBEdit-Lite** and the full-blown commercial package **BBEdit 3.0**. Both of these text editors allow for *extension* packages for customized editing and contain useful search and replace functions and tabbing controls that can be used when editing HTML documents. The **BBEdit** editor is a product of Bare Bones Software, which can be contacted at: *Bare Bones Software*, P.O. Box 108, Bedford, MA 01730-0108 (e-mail: *bbedit@world.std.com*; phone: (508) 651-3561). The **BBEdit-lite** freeware version is available via anonymous FTP from various sites, including:

```
ftp://ftp.std.com/pub/bbedit/bbedit-lite-232.hqx
```

EXTENSIONS PACKAGE I

This macro package creates extension menus for all standard formatting commands, including FORMs. The current release of the package automatically inserts the **HTML**, **HEAD**, and **BODY** elements and can be configured to automatically insert paragraph tags at each carriage return.

More information is available at:

```
http://www.uji.es/bbedit-html-extensions.html
```

The macros themselves are found at either:

```
ftp://ftp.uji.es/pub/mac/util/bbedit-html-ext.sea.hqx
```

or:

```
ftp://sumex-aim.stanford.edu/info-mac/bbedit-html-ext-b3.hqx
```

This package was developed by Carles Bellver.

EXTENSIONS PACKAGE II

This package lacks the <HTML>, <HEAD>, and <BODY> tags, but does have
other nice utilities, such as one for previewing the HTML code—this is not
really a WYSIWYG mode but it does indent lists and enumerate list entries
where applicable. In general, this package is often easier to use. Its biggest
weakness is its lack of a FORM editing menu—all FORM tags must be
typed in by hand. Additional information about this package is found at:

```
http://ctipsych.york.ac.uk/WWW/BBEditTools.html
```

while the macros themselves are at:

```
ftp://ctipsych.york.ac.uk/CTI_FTP/pub/BBEdit/BBEdit_HTML_Tools.sea.hqx
```

This second package was written by Lindsay Davies.

You can mix together the macros from these two packages, as the macro
names are distinctly different. However, combining all the macros from
both packages produces menus so long as to be quite unwieldy. It is best to
pick and choose the macros you want and customize the editor to your
taste. This is an easy way to blend the useful features of both extension
packages.

CU_HTML.DOT (PC—WORD FOR WINDOWS)

CU_HTML.DOT is a Microsoft Word for Windows Version 2.0 and 6.0
document template that allows WYSIWYG editing and creation of HTML
documents. The **CU_HTML.DOT** template adds special HTML styles for
text processing along with a macro that takes a Word document, prepared

using these HTML styles, and converts it into the corresponding HTML file. You therefore cannot use this package to edit existing HTML documents, nor can it be easily used to convert existing Word documents into HTML. **CU_HTML.DOT** also allows you to insert inline GIF images where these images appear in the Word document so that the editor is almost WYSIWYG. You can also specify hypertext links by marking text and choosing the target file from a dialog box: Relative locations of files are converted into the correct URL notation. You can also use the normal editing features, such as spelling checking, printing, and cutting and pasting.

The documentation in HTML format is available at:

```
http://www.cuhk.hk/csc/cu_html/cu_html.htm
```

The ZIP file containing the template itself is found at:

```
ftp://ftp.cuhk.hk/pub/www/windows/util/cu_html.zip
```

This ZIP file also contains the hypertext documentation for **CU_HTML.DOT. CU_HTML.DOT** was written by Kenneth Wong and Anton Lam of The Chinese University of Hong Kong. The Computer Services Centre of The Chinese University of Hong Kong holds the copyrights of **CU_HTML.DOT** and **CU_HTML.DLL**.

EMACS (UNIX, PC)

The **emacs** editor, a product of the Free Software Foundation, is one of the most popular UNIX text editors. This is because **emacs** is available on almost any UNIX computer as well as on PCs, and because it is an extremely powerful editor that can be customized through its command language *elisp* (a version of lisp) for a variety of tasks. It is the editor of choice for many dedicated UNIX programmers, many of whom have been very active in the early development of the WWW. It is thus not a suprise that there are **emacs** elisp programs available to help with HTML editing.

The first package was written by Marc Andressen, then of NCSA. The name of this lisp program is **html-mode.el** and it is available, for example, from:

```
ftp://gatekeeper.dec.com/.3/net/infosys/Mosaic/elisp/
```

Html-helper-mode is a more recent and somewhat more full-featured **emacs** helper mode. Additional information about **html-helper-mode** is found at:

```
http://www.reed.edu/~nelson/tools/
```

while a complete tar archive of the elisp code and documentation is available at:

```
ftp://ftp.reed.ed/pub/src/html-helper-mode.tar.Z
```

Html-helper-mode was developed by Nelson Minar, based on the **html-mode.el** package.

GT_HTML.DOT (PC—WORD FOR WINDOWS)

This is another package of Microsoft Word for Windows macros developed by the Georgia Tech Research Institute (GTRI). These macros facilitate HTML document authoring by creating a template that provides a pseudo WYSIWYG authoring environment. Additional information is available at:

```
http://www.gatech.edu/word_html/release.htm
```

The authors of GT_HTML.DOT are Jeffrey L. Grover and John H. Davis III. You can contact the authors by electronic mail (*gt_html@gtri.gatch.edu*).

HOTMETAL (PC—WINDOWS, UNIX)

HoTMetaL is a shareware HTML editor from SoftQuad Inc. of Toronto, Canada. SoftQuad is a company specializing in SGML so that HoTMetaL is very careful about legal HTML markup.

HoTMetaL is context-sensitive and strongly guides you in creating new HTML documents—it absolutely refuses to let you put tags in the wrong place. HTML tags can be entered only by pull-down menus: The editor will not let you type in HTML tags, and automatically converts typed left-angle brackets and ampersands into HTML entities to block you from doing so. The editor is semi-WYSIWYG, in that lists are indented and headings are emboldened and in a larger font. Images are not displayed inline. There is also a Publish command that changes **SRC** and **HREF** attribute values from local paths to full URLs.

The editor is supposed to be useful in editing any HTML document. Unfortunately, the current version interprets the HTML markup very strictly and often refuses to edit even slightly invalid HTML files. This interpretation is built into the *compiled* DTD file *html.mtl*. SoftQuad is now distributing a second rules file, *legacy.html,* that is more lenient in this regard and is more useful in editing older files.

HoTMetaL is currently available for PC Windows machines and for Sun SPARC computers running Motif. A Macintosh version is planned. You can obtain the program from:

```
ftp://gatekeeper.dec.com//pub/net/infosys/Mosaic/contrib/SoftQuad/hotmetal
```

A **HoTMetaL Pro** commercially supported version of the editor became available in late fall of 1994. This has many additional features, including spelling checking, thesaurus tools, and utilities for editing older HTML documents and correcting markup. This version also supports the new HTML **TABLE** elements and is able to display images inline with the text.

For more information contact SoftQuad by phone (416-239-4801) or e-mail (*hotmetal@sq.com*).

HTML ASSISTANT (PC—WINDOWS)

HTML Assistant is a Windows text editor with extensions to assist in creating HTML hypertext documents. Tags are inserted by selecting text with the mouse and choosing tags from pull-down menus. A useful utility allows the user to construct HTML hypertext anchors using URLs from **WinMosaic, Cello,** and **HTML Assistant** hotlist and bookmark files. There is also a user-defined toolbox that allows the user to define special purpose tags.

Additional information about **HTML Assistant** can be found at:

    ftp://ftp.cs.dal.ca/htmlasst/htmlafaq.txt

The program is located at:

    ftp://ftp.cs.dal.ca/htmlasst/

The complete program suite is in the file *HTMLASST.ZIP*. You also need the file **VBRUN300.DLL**, which is found in the ZIP file *VBRUN300.ZIP*.

The author of HTML Assistant is Howard Harawitz.

HTMLED (PC—WINDOWS)

HTMLed is a customizable, text-mode HTML editor. As with other Windows editors, **HTMLed** allows the user to insert tags by marking sections of text and selecting the appropriate tag from pull-down menus. **HTMLed** also allows the user to save and print tag-free versions of the document; preview the document with an external viewer, such as **WinMosaic**; and insert URLs from WinMosaic hotlist files. The user can also create regular and floating toolbars to customize the behavior of the editor.

For more information about **HTMLed**, see:

    http://info.cern.ch/hypertext/WWW/Tools/HTMLed.html

HTMLed is available at either:

    ftp://pringle.mta.ca/pub/HTMLed/

or:

    ftp://pringle.mta.ca/pub/HTMLed10.zip

or:

    http://pringle.mta.ca/~peterc/

in the files *HTMED*.ZIP* (where * refers to the version number). **HTMLed** was written by Peter Crawshaw.

HTML.EDIT (MACINTOSH)

HTML.edit is a stand-alone HyperCard 2.2 application and does not require HyperCard to run. **HTML.edit** allows for standard graphical editing features: Items are marked with the mouse and the desired HTML element is selected from a pull-down menu. **HTML.edit** includes extra features such as multiple document editing and template files for automatic inclusion of headers and footers.

Additional information about HTML.edit can be found at:

```
http://nctn.oact.hq.nasa.gov/tools/HTMLedit/HTMLedit.html
```

while the program itself is available from:

```
ftp://ftp.oact.hq.nasa.gov/tools/HTMLedit/
```

HTML EDITOR (MACINTOSH)

A partially WYSIWYG editor, **HTML Editor** displays different level headings as different size boldface fonts, and shows italic, boldface, and underlined characters explicitly. Images, however, are not displayed, and lists are not explicitly formatted. There is also no tool for creating HTML FORMs, and some optional arguments are missing for certain elements (for example, there is no **ALIGN=BOTTOM** argument for the **IMG** element). However, the editor does allow you to add your own *user elements* to a user menu, so you can add many of these missing components to a customized selection list.

HTML Editor is a shareware program written by Rick Giles of Acadia University. Registered users receive free electronic updates. More information can be found at:

```
http://dragon.acadiau.ca:1667/~giles/HTML_Editor/Documentation.html
```

HTML FOR WORD 2.0
(PC—WORD FOR WINDOWS)

This is another package of Word for Windows templates that facilitates writing HTML documents. The template creates a structured HTML document environment for Word 2.0. It has a simple user interface and preserves the Word environment as much as possible. It creates document instances that conform to the SGML standard, and is available from:

```
ftp://ftp.cica.indiana.edu/pub/pc/win3/uploads/html.zip
```

This software is an extended prototype of a production version that will be based on Word 6.0. Enough SGML functions have been implemented to ensure the creation of correct HTML instances. Performance of most functions will be greatly enhanced in the production version.

For additional information, contact: Eric van Herwijnen, NICE technologies, Chemin des Hutins, Veraz, 01170 Gex, France (phone (33)-50424940).

HTMLTEXT (UNIX)

Htmltext is a UNIX HTML text editor that supports a WYSIWYG editing environment and includes such useful features as spelling checking and automatic Table of Contents generation. Various menus are available for assigning attributes to different elements, inserting elements, and so on. It is X-Windows-based, but, more importantly, it is based on the graphical **Andrew Toolkit,** an object-oriented model for developing multimedia applications. Thus, to compile and install **Htmltext,** you will also need the **Andrew Toolkit.** Information on the Andrew Toolkit is found in the **Htmltext** documentation at:

```
http://web.cs.city.ac.uk/homes/njw/htmltext/htmltext.html
```

NEXTSTEP HTML-EDITOR (NEXT)

NextStep HTML-Editor is a graphical HTML editor for NeXT workstations. Information about the editor can be found at:

```
http://scholar.lib.vt.edu/jpowell.html
```

while the program itself is available at:

```
ftp://borg.lib.vt.edu/pub/next/HTML-Editor0.5.FAT.app.compressed
```

NextStep HTML-Editor was written by James Powell.

S.H.E. (MACINTOSH)

S.H.E., for Simple HTML Editor, is a text-mode editor written as a HyperCard stack, so you need HyperCard to run this program. S.H.E. allows you to create new HTML documents and edit old ones, and it has a palette for marking sections of text as bold, italic, list items, headings, and so on. It explicitly includes the **HTML, HEAD,** and **BODY** elements. However, it does not support some of the newer elements, such as **PRE** or **CODE,** and uses some obsolete elements, such as **PLAINTEXT.**

S.H.E. supports the **FORM** elements with a special **FORM** pull-down menu. S.H.E. also allows you to cut and paste between the S.H.E. window and other windows. S.H.E. does not have spelling checking and, because it is a HyperCard stack, it is limited to files smaller than around 30,000 characters (including the HTML markup).

Additional information about S.H.E. is found at:

```
http://dewey.lib.ncsu.edu/staff/morgan/simple.html
```

while the HyperCard stack can be obtained at either of:

```
ftp://ericmorgan.lib.ncsu.edu/Public/simple-http-editor.hqx
ftp://dewey.lib.ncsu.edu/pub/software/mac/simple-http-editor.hqx
```

S.H.E. was written by Eric Lease Morgan.

TKHTML (UNIX)

The **tkHTML** editor is actually a tk/tcl script and requires the interpretive shell **wwwish. TkHTML** is a graphical editor: Editing is accomplished by marking text and selecting markup tags from the pull-down menus. The editor is not WYSIWYG but comes with a preview mode that can preview most types of formatting.

Some elements are missing from the menus, such as the <TITLE> element and FORM support. The editor also does not include the <HTML>,<HEAD>, or <BODY> elements, so you have to insert these by hand.

Additional information about **tkHTML** is found at:

```
http://alfred1.u.washington.edu:8080/~roland/tkHTML/tkHTML.html
```

The program itself is available from:

```
ftp://ftp.u.washington.edu/public/roland/tkHTML
```

You should download the latest **tkHTML** tar archive and the latest **wwwish** tar archive. TkHTML was written by Liem Bahneman.

TKWWW (UNIX)

TkWWW is actually a UNIX WWW *browser* that allows the user to edit the retrieved document. Like **tkHTML**, **tkWWW** is based on the tk language, and the package also requires the interpretive shell **wwwish**. TkWWW allows you to edit active HTML documents in a manner similar to **tkHTML**, although with less able editing tools. An important difference is that the documents are *live*, so the hypertext links are real hypertext links and not just editable objects. You have to edit carefully, or else you will activate the links. **TkWWW** is discussed in more detail in Chapter 7.

DOCUMENT TRANSLATORS AND CONVERTERS

Often, you have a number of preexisting files that you would like to convert to HTML format. Alternatively, you may already be using a document preparation program, such as LaTeX, Scribe, or FrameMaker, and would like to be able to continue using these tools and convert the resulting documents into HTML. These are jobs for a document translator or converter: a program that can take your document in its original format and convert it to a close equivalent in HTML.

There are several packages that have been written to accomplish this task, including some powerful commercial products. As mentioned earlier, these conversions may not be ideal, since there is often no direct match between print markup languages and HTML. Consequently, you may have to edit the resulting HTML documents to add elements that could not be translated. Nevertheless, editing a largely correct document is a much easier task than typing the whole thing in from scratch.

There are also several packages that can convert from HTML to another markup language more appropriate for printing. This is very useful for preparing printed versions of HTML documents for reading away from a computer. Some packages (such as **latex2html** and **WebMaker**) allow you to prepare parent manuscripts containing alternative blocks of markup: one block for printing and another for HTML. This is very useful for preparing documents that read well in either presentation format.

Many of these packages are script programs, often written in perl. Thus, these programs require that you have perl or another appropriate interpreter on your machine.

The programs are listed in the following section in alphabetical order. You are most likely interested in matching a document format or program name to a particular tool. Table 6.1 matches conversion programs to standard word-processor names and document formats.

■■■■■■ **Table 6.1** Conversion Programs for Different Document Formats

Format	Program
FrameMaker	Cyberleaf, FasTag, frame2html, mif2html, miftran, Webmaker
Interleaf	Cyberleaf, FasTag, TagWrite
LaTeX/tex	hyperlatex, latex2html, tex2rtf
Microsoft Word	FasTag, TagWrite, Cyberleaf
nroff/troff	mm2html, ms2html
Plain text	striphtml, asc2html, charconv
PostScript	ps2html

Continued

▰▰▰ **Table 6.1** Continued

Format	Program
Rich Text Format (RTF)	HLPDK, rtfohtml, RTFTOHTM, tex2rtf
Scribe	scribe2html
SGML (other than HTML)	TagWrite
Texinfo	texi2html
UNIX Man Pages	RosettaMan
Ventura Publisher (Corel)	TagWrite
WordPerfect	Cyberleaf, FasTag, TagWrite, wptohtml, wp2x

ASC2HTML

Asc2html.pl is a perl script for converting plain ASCII files into HTML. This script adds a `<TITLE>` element containing the name of the file that has been converted, and places the body of the document inside a `<PRE>`.... `</PRE>` element so that it reproduces the formatting of the typed text. However, the script also locates URLs embedded in the text and converts them to hypertext links.

Asc2html can be found at:

```
ftp://src.doc.ic.ac.uk/computing/information-systems/www/tools/translators
```

Asc2html was written by Oscar Nierstrasz of the University of Geneva, Switzerland.

CHARCONV

Charconv is a program filter (written in ANSI-C) that can transform one encoding of an extended character set into another; for example, transforming ISO-Latin I into MS-DOS or Macintosh encoding. This is important for conversion of text containing special characters, such as umlauts, diphthongs, and so on, since the ISO Latin-1 encodings of these characters used by Windows and UNIX machines are different from the encodings used by MS-DOS or the Macintosh operating system.

This program can also handle special character codes found in TeX or HTML documents, and the filtering process removes the HTML or TeX macros. The result is a plain text document.

Charconv is available at:

```
ftp://src.doc.ic.ac.uk/computing/information-systems/www/tools/
```

Charconv was written by Burkhard Kirste.

CYBERLEAF

Cyberleaf is a commercial document-conversion package from Interleaf Inc. planned for release in early 1995 on UNIX and Windows platforms. **Cyberleaf** is a stand-alone product (it does not require Interleaf) for converting documents authored in Interleaf, FrameMaker, Microsoft Word, and WordPerfect into HTML. In the conversion, **Cyberleaf** preserves hypertext links present in the original documents and converts native-format graphics into GIF images. For more information, contact your local Interleaf representative.

FASTAG

FasTag is an add-on package for HTML authoring packages, such as **HoTMetaL Pro**. **FasTag** is a conversion filter that can read documents in various formats (for example, Word, WordPerfect, formatted ASCII) and convert them into SGML encodings, including HTML. You can use **FasTag** to read a large WordPerfect document into **HoTMetaL Pro**, and then use the HoTMetaL editor to further process the HTML code to include those features that are not present in the original format. **FasTag** can handle formatted tables, and converts equations into inlined graphics. Optional add-on packages for other document formats, such as Interleaf and FrameMaker, are also available.

FasTag is a commercial product of Avalanche Development. For more information, contact Avalanche Development (phone: 303-449-5032). If you are interested in purchasing the package as an add-on to **HoTMetaL Pro,** you can also contact SoftQuad (phone: 416-239-4801; e-mail: *hot-metal@sq.com.*).

FRAME2HTML

Frame2html is a collection of programs to facilitate the conversion of FrameMaker documents and books to HTML, primarily on UNIX platforms. It consists of several programs, some as perl scripts, and some as C-language programs that must be compiled.

The frame2html package is available at:

```
ftp://bang.nta.no/pub/
```

Frame2html also requires several other packages to work properly, including **gs** (**GhostScript**), **yacc, flex,** and **pbmplus** (**pnm** and **ppm** filters). Guides to obtaining these additional packages are included with the **frame2html** documentation.

Frame2html was written by Jon Stephenson von Tetzchner of Norwegian Telecom Research.

HLPDK

HLPDK is a Windows software package for developing online hypertext help documentation. **HLPDK** uses a native document format (HDF) that is then converted to the target format—HTML is one target format supported by HLPDK. The user front end is a Windows graphical editor comparable to some of the HTML editors discussed previously.

A shareware version of HLPDK is available at:

```
ftp://garbo.uwasa.fi/pc/programming
```

in the files *hdk115a.zip, hdk115b.zip,* and *hdk115l.zip.* There is also a professional supported version. For additional information, contact Ron Loewy (*rloewy@panix.com*).

HYPERLATEX

Hyperlatex is a package that allows you to use a subset of the LaTeX language to prepare documents in HTML and, at the same time, define a document that will be nicely typeset on paper. It consists of a lisp macro for the **emacs** editor and a LaTeX style file for printing the specially marked-up latex documents. **Hyperlatex** is a much simpler package than **latex2html** and lacks some of the **latex2html** features, such as the ability to display equations.

Additional information about **hyperlatex** can be found at:

    http://www.cs.ruu.nl/people/otfried/html/hyperlatex.html

while the source for the program is available at:

    ftp://ftp.cs.ruu.nl/pub/SGI/IPE/Hyperlatex-1.0.tar.gz

Hyperlatex was written by Otfried Schwarzkopf.

LATEX2HTML

Latex2html is a powerful perl package that can translate LaTeX documents into corresponding HTML documents. It has many controls for inlining equations (converting equations to GIF images and including them inline with the text); converting LaTeX cross-references into hypertext links; creating hypertext Tables of Contents and Lists of Figures; and breaking up large LaTeX files into smaller, more manageable HTML documents. It also allows for special LaTeX modes so that text can be marked for display in only the HTML version or only the printed version.

Latex2html requires several additional packages to function properly, as explained in the **latex2html** documentation.

The source archive for **latex2html** can be found at:

    ftp://ftp.tex.ac.uk/pub/archive/support/latex2html

Latex2html was written by Nikos Drakos of the Computer Based Learning Unit, University of Leeds.

MIF2HTML

Mif2html is a commercial product of Quadralay Corporation. **Mif2html** provides users with an interface for converting existing FrameMaker documents to HTML documents suitable for use with the World Wide Web and with GWHIS, Quadralay's online, context-sensitive help system. It allows developers to create documentation within FrameMaker's Maker application, and to convert those files into HTML. This allows the user to maintain a single set of documentation for both printed and hypertext use.

For more information, contact Quadralay Corporation (*support@quadralay.com*).

MIFTRAN

Miftran is a general purpose MIF (FrameMaker's Maker Interchange Format) translation program. **Miftran** was designed primarily to translate to HTML, but is flexible enough that it could be used for other translations. It is a C-language program (along with some UNIX Bourne-shell scripts) with a single configuration file. It converts cross-references into HTML hypertext references, and special characters into the proper character or entity encodings, and can also generate Tables of Contents and Indexes. However, it cannot handle embedded image files or conditional blocks of text.

Miftran can be found at:

```
ftp://ftp.alumni.caltech.edu/pub/mcbeath/web/miftran/
```

Miftran compiles successfully on most UNIX workstations. Unfortunately, there isn't a version for PCs or Macintoshes. The author of **Miftran** is Jim McBeath.

MM2HTML

Mm2html is a perl script that converts nroff documents, written using the "mm" macros, into HTML. Its design is based heavily on the perl scripts

ms2html and **fm2html**. To properly display picture, equation, and table environments, you also need the **psroff** and the **pbmplus** packages.

Mm2html can be found at:

```
ftp://bells.cs.ucl.ac.uk/darpa
```

Mm2html was written by J. Crowcroft.

MS2HTML.PL

Ms2html.pl is a perl script that converts an annotated text file (annotations based on the troff "ms" macros) into the corresponding HTML markup. For **Ms2html.pl** to function properly, each ms macro command must be on its own line.

Ms2html.pl can be found at either of the following:

```
http://cui_www.unige.ch/ftp/PUBLIC/oscar/scripts/
ftp://cui.unige.ch/PUBLIC/oscar/scripts
```

You need the three files *ms2html.pl*, *button.pl*, and *url.pl*.

Ms2html.pl was written by Oscar Nierstrasz.

PS2HTML

Ps2html is a perl package that converts arbitrary PostScript text to HTML. It is written for UNIX platforms, but should be adaptable to other systems. Because PostScript is a nontrivial language, there can be considerable variability in converting PostScript to HTML. This package provides a *types* specification file that allows you to control this conversion and make allowances for the underlying format of your PostScript documents. Additional information about **ps2html** can be found at:

```
http://stasi.bradley.edu/ftp/pub/ps2html/ps2html-v2.html
```

while the package itself can be obtained from:

```
ftp://stasi.bradley.edu/ftp/pub/ps2html/v2/ps2html-v2.tar
```

Ps2html was written by Jerry Whelan.

ROSETTAMAN

RosettaMan is a filter for UNIX-style manual pages. It takes as input manual pages formatted for a variety of UNIX flavors (not just troff or nroff source), and produces as output a variety of file formats. Currently, **RosettaMan** accepts manual pages formatted by the following flavors of UNIX: Hewlett-Packard HP-UX, AT&T System V, SunOS, Sun Solaris, OSF/1, DEC Ultrix, SGI IRIX, and Linux; and produces output for the following formats: printable ASCII only, headers only, TkMan, [tn]roff, Ensemble, (not now but soon) SGML, HTML, LaTeX, and RTF. **RosettaMan** is a tcl/tk script and requires the interpreters that come with the tcl/tk distribution.

The **RosettaMan** archive can be found at:

```
ftp://ftp.cs.berkeley.edu/ucb/people/phelps/tcltk/rman.tar.Z
```

RosettaMan is copyrighted by T. A. Phelps.

RTFTOHTML

Rtftohtml is a program that converts Microsoft Rich Text Format (RTF) documents into their HTML equivalents, and produces HTML containing graphics, tables, and equations along with the regular text. It supports RTF 1.2 and is compatible with Word 6.0 RTF output, as well as RTF output from WordPerfect, FrameMaker, and Interleaf.

Additional information about **rtftohtml** can be found at:

```
ftp://ftp.cray.com/src/WWWstuff/RTF/
```

Executable versions are available for Sun and Macintosh platforms. These are found at:

```
ftp://ftp.cray.com/src/WWWstuff/RTF/latest/binaries/
```

while the source code is found at:

```
ftp://ftp.cray.com/src/WWWstuff/RTF/latest/src/unix.tar
```

Rtftohtml was written by Chris Hector.

RTFTOHTM

RTFTOHTM is a Word 2.0 for Windows extension package that allows conversion of RTF documents to HTML, and also allows you to save edited files in an HTML format. **RTFTOHTM** can be found at:

```
ftp://oak.oakland.edu/SimTel/msdos/windows3/htmtl060.zip
```

(or higher numbers for more recent revisions). **RTFTOHTM** was written by Jorma Hartikka.

SCRIBE2HTML

Scribe is a document markup and production system similar to markup languages such as [tn]roff or LaTeX. The **Scribe2html** package allows you to use Scribe to generate HTML documents from a Scribe manuscript. This requires special markup codes in the Scribe manuscript, so you cannot simply convert a preexisting Scribe document to HTML. However, smaller manuscripts can be converted quite easily.

Scribe2html consists of Scribe macros for introducing special HTML commands, and a small **awk** program that breaks up the large HTML file produced by **Scribe** into several smaller files linked together by hypertext links. The package is free and is available at:

```
ftp://gatekeeper.dec.com/pub/DEC/NSL/www/
```

The package comes with documentation, as a collection of HTML documents.

STRIPHTML

Striphtml is a small perl program that strips HTML markup from a text document to create a plain text version. It also converts the entity references <, >, and & into the correct printable characters.

Striphtml was written by Earl Hood and is available at:

```
http://www.oac.uci.edu/indiv/ehood/perl/striphtml
```

TAGWRITE

TagWrite is a commercial document-conversion tool produced by Zandar Corp. **TagWrite** is a Windows package that can read Microsoft RTF, WordPerfect, ASCII files, and other formats to produce tagged output in various markup formats, including HTML. Untagging is also possible so that you can convert in either direction. **TagWrite** is also able to convert into other markup languages, such as Ventura Publisher, Quark, Interleaf, and troff. The package can also convert from HTML to these other formats. Indeed, Corel has licensed **TagWrite 3.1 for Windows** and includes it as a document-conversion tool with its new release of the Ventura line of document-processing tools. For more information (including pricing), contact Zandar Corp. (phone: 802-365-9393; FAX: 802-365-4974).

TEX2RTF

Tex2rtf is a utility for converting from a simple LaTeX subset to HTML, RTF, and Windows Help RTF formats. The input document is a LaTeX subset combined with some additional hypertext macros. LaTeX equations are not supported, and there is minimal support for tables.

Compiled versions of **tex2rtf** are available for Windows and for Sun SPARC stations, or you can obtain the source code. All these different versions can be found at:

```
ftp://skye.aiai.ed.ac.uk/pub/tex2rtf
```

Tex2rtf was written by Julian Smart.

TEXI2HTML

Texi2html is a perl script that converts texinfo files to HTML. The quality of the HTML documents is close to that of the printed output. The program understands most Texinfo Version 2 commands, and runs without problem on big texinfo files, such as the GNU Emacs manual.

Texi2html can be obtained at:

```
ftp://src.doc.ic.ac.uk/computing/information-systems/www/tools/translators
```

Texi2html was written by Lionel Cons.

WPTOHTML

This is a WordPerfect macro package for converting WordPerfect 5.1 for
DOS and WordPerfect 6.0 for DOS files into HTML. The macro packages
are available at:

```
ftp://oak.oakland.edu/SimTel/msdos/wordperf/
```

in the files **wpt60d10.zip** (for WordPerfect 6.0) and **wpt50d10.zip** (for
WordPerfect 5.1).

WPTOHTML was written by Hunter Monroe.

WP2X

Wp2x is a C-language program for converting WordPerfect 5.1 files into
other formats, including HTML. This is a UNIX package but should compile on a PC, provided you have a standard ANSI-C compiler. Additional
information can be found at:

```
http://journal.biology.carleton.ca/pub/software/
```

This includes pointers to the up-to-date archive for the package. **Wp2x** was
written to convert WordPerfect documents into a form suitable for a local
Conservation Ecology online journal and, consequently, does some rather
specific things to the document.

Wp2x was originally created by Raymond Chen.

WEBMAKER

WebMaker is a package for creating FrameMaker documents and converting them to HTML. **WebMaker** includes special FrameMaker macro definitions to facilitate writing HTML documents, and programs for converting

the resulting MIF files into a hypertext network of HTML files. **WebMaker** is an actively supported product of the Programming Techniques Group at CERN and currently runs only under UNIX.

Additional information about **WebMaker,** including information about how to obtain the package, can be found at:

```
http://www.cern.ch/WebMaker/
```

or by writing (*webmaker@cern.ch*.).

HTML VERIFIERS

There are two simple tools for checking the validity of HTML elements in a document. These both use the HTML Document Type Definition (DTD) file as the definition of the HTML syntax, so you will need this file to use these tools. The HTML DTD can be obtained from:

```
http://www.hal.com/%7Econnolly/html-spec/html.dtd
http://www.hal.com/%7Econnolly/html-spec/html.decl
```

(the second file is the SGML *declaration* for HTML and should be appended to your *html.dtd* file). New DTD files will appear with each revision of the language. To test your documents' compatibility with this new standard, you need only download the revised DTD and plug it into your verification program.

SGMLS

Sgmls is an SGML syntax-checking program. This program takes as input an SGML file and checks the document structure against the relevant document type definition (DTD). URLs pointing to the current HTML DTD are listed in the foregoing and in the References section at the end of Chapter 2. As output, the program prints a list of syntax errors and the line number at which the errors occurred.

As an example, consider the file ***test.html*** shown in Figure 6.1, which shows the output of **sgmls** after *testing* this file against the HTML DTD.

```
<HTML>
<HEAD>
<TITLE> <em> Instructional </em>and Research Computing Home Page</TITLE>
</HEAD>
<BODY>


<h1> Instructional and Research Computing </H1>


<hr>


This is the Instructional and Research Computing Group <B>(IRC)</B>
World Wide Web home page. If you get lost try the
<a href="big%20dog.html"> big dog help </a> or
<a href="http://www.university.ca/</a>home.html"> right here </a>


<hr>


<oL>
<LI> consulting services in <A HREF="InsT/intro.html"> instructional
technology and applications</A>
applications</A>.<P>


</ol>
<HR>


</BODY>
</HTML>
```

■■■■■■ **Figure 6.1** Example HTML document ***test.html***.

The following command on a UNIX computer will validate the file
test.html:

```
sgmls -s html.dtd test.html
```

On a PC running DOS, the command is:

```
sgmls.exe -s html.dtd test.html
```

The output lists the errors and the line numbers at which they occurred.
Figure 6.2 shows the **sgmls** output for the preceding file.

```
sgmls:SGML error at test.html, line 3 at ">":

      EM end-tag ignored: doesn't end any open element (current is TITLE)
sgmls:SGML error at test.html, line 3 at ">":

      Bad end-tag in R/CDATA element; treated as short (no GI) end-tag
sgmls:SGML error at test.html, line 3 at "d":

      HEAD end-tag implied by data; not minimizable
sgmls:SGML error at test.html, line 3 at ">":

      TITLE end-tag ignored: doesn't end any open element (current is HTML)
sgmls:SGML error at test.html, line 4 at ">":

      HEAD end-tag ignored: doesn't end any open element (current is HTML)
sgmls:SGML error at test.html, line 21 at ">":

      A end-tag ignored: doesn't end any open element (current is OL)
```

■■■■■■ **Figure 6.2 Sgmls** error output, after parsing *test.html* (shown in
Figure 6.1).

The errors at line 3 are due to the illegal character markup inside the
TITLE element. The subsequent errors at lines 3 and 4 are a result of this
same mistake. The error at line 21 is a very typical error: The file has a
duplicate </A> ending tag.

Where do you find **sgmls**? It is a public-domain package, available from
many anonymous FTP sites. An example location is:

```
ftp://jclark.com/pub/sgmls/
```

The source code archive is in the files *sgmls*.tar.Z*, while the PC executables are in the files *sgmls*.zip* (where * is a version number). **Sgmls** was written by James Clark (*jjc@jclark.com*).

HTML VALIDATION SITE

If you want to check your files but do not feel comfortable downloading the **sgmls** package, you can use it remotely instead. Dan Connolly has developed a FORM-based HTML validation service accessible from anywhere on the World Wide Web. The URL for this useful resource is:

```
http://www.hal.com/%7Econnolly/html-test/service/validation-form.html
```

The FORM interface contains an HTML **TEXTBOX** into which you *paste* (or type if you do not have cut-and-paste editing) your entire HTML document. When you submit the form, the submitted HTML file is checked by **sgmls** and the results are returned in a subsequent document.

LINK VERIFIERS

Sgmls verifies that your HTML tags are correctly placed, but cannot ensure that the hypertext links go to valid locations. To check hypertext links you need a *link verifier*, which is a program that reads your document, extracts the hypertext links, and tests the validity of the URL.

LINKCHECK

Linkcheck is a perl program written by David Sibley of Pennsylvania State University. It is designed to run on UNIX machines but may run on other platforms, given some effort.

Linkcheck is a program for checking **gopher, ftp,** and **http** URLs in a document. It cannot check other URLs, such as **mailto, wais, telnet, rlogin,** or **tn3270. Linkcheck** tests **gopher** URLs by fully accessing the indicated URL, which can be slow if the URL links to a large file. It tests **ftp** URLs by listing directory contents rather than fetching the document, which is a lot nicer. **Http** URLs are checked by using the HTTP HEAD method, which is just as nice. If the HEAD method access fails, **linkcheck** tries the GET method (some servers do not understand the HTTP HEAD method).

Linkcheck does have difficulties with relative URLs. You must specify the URL of the directory *containing* the file to allow checking of relative URLs, so the document must be in an HTTP server-accessible directory. This makes it impossible to check the file prior to placing it on the server. In addition, **linkcheck** cannot validate partial URLs containing relative paths: Any URL starting with the string ../ is labeled as invalid.

Linkcheck is available from:

```
ftp://ftp.math.psu.edu/pub/sibley/
```

You need the files *linkcheck*, *about.linkcheck* (documentation for the package), *ftpcheck* (for checking FTP links), and *mconnect.pl*.

Linkcheck also requires a program called **mconnect**, which allows an interactive connection with a remote mailer program. If your system does not have **mconnect**, you can use the **mconnect.pl** perl program indicated in the preceding list.

If you use **mconnect.pl**, you also need the two additional perl packages **sock.pl** and **telnet.pl**. These are found in the files:

```
ftp://anubis.ac.hmc.edu/pub/perl/scripts/netstuff/sock.pl.gz
ftp://ftp.cis.ufl.edu/pub/perl/scripts/telnet.shar.gz
```

If you use **ftpcheck**, you need the auxiliary **ftplib.pl** library. This can be found at:

```
ftp://ftp.cis.ufl.edu/pub/perl/scripts/ftplib.pl
```

VERIFY_LINKS

Verify_links is a FORM-based CGI program for validating hypertext links in an HTML document. **Verify_links** is limited to verifying **http** URLs and cannot check FTP, Gopher, telnet, and other links. In this respect, it is not as useful as **linkcheck**. However, it is more reliable than **linkcheck** in validating **http** URLs and particularly local or relative URLs. It also can check POST actions to a limited degree, and will *push the buttons* in a FORM to verify the existence of the attached CGI program. Like **linkcheck**, **verify_links** attempts to use network-friendly requests, such as the HTTP HEAD request, to minimize the load on the network, and falls back to full file retrieval only if this fails.

Additional information about **verify_links** can be found at:

```
http://wsk.eit.com/wsk/dist/doc/admin/webtest/verify_links.html
```

Verify_links is available in executable program. Instructions for obtaining and installing **verify_links** is found at:

```
ftp://eit.com/pub/wsk/doc/README.verify_links
```

Verify_links is a product of Enterprise Integration Technologies Corporation.

CHAPTER

WEB BROWSERS AND

HELPER APPLICATIONS

This chapter reviews the WWW browsers available for UNIX VAX/VMS and NeXT workstations; PCs running DOS, Windows, or OS/2; Macintoshes; and Amigas. Almost all of these browsers have documentation available on the WWW, and corresponding URLs are given when applicable. Monitoring these URLs and reading the various WWW newsgroups are the best ways of keeping up to date with the changes and improvements to a particular package. These tools are evolving quickly, and it is impossible for any book to be completely current.

The reader will also find some helper applications that can be used to decompress, unzip, or unstuff files; play movies or sound files; or view images. I also suggest sites on the Internet where these programs can be obtained.

ACCESSING SOFTWARE

Most browsers are freely available on the Internet; a number of URLs for
the executable versions or source code have been included in this chapter.
These are not exclusive locations, and you may find that a program is no
longer available at the site indicated here. In this case, use **archie** to locate
an alternative site. The **archie** client program is available for almost all
computer platforms and is available for downloading from many anonymous FTP sites. A detailed description on using **archie** to search for programs is given in Appendix C, along with instructions for obtaining an
archie client.

PC PLATFORM BROWSERS

Running any browser requires an Internet connection, either an ethernet
(or other) card connecting your computer to a local network or a telephone
dial-up SLIP or PPP network link. In both cases, you also need software
that allows your computer to *talk* to the connection using TCP/IP, which
means you must install TCP/IP networking software. Some free TCP/IP
software is available on the Internet, but you must really understand what
you are doing to set this up properly. There are also a number of commercial packages that provide TCP/IP functionality at modest cost. Consult
your local computer shop if you are uncomfortable with installing these
packages.

PCs running DOS or Windows can obtain essentially free TCP/IP software
by installing the **trumpet winsock** package. This is found at many FTP
sites; for example:

```
ftp://ftp.utas.edu.au:/pc/trumpet/wintrump/
ftp://ftp.csn.net/pub/dos/trumpet/
```

A word of warning: There is also a USENET newsreader program named
trumpet, so be careful not to get the two mixed up.

ftp.trumpet.com.au

If you are running a Windows application, you may also need the Windows *WINSOCK.DLL* program library. This is a package of routines that act as an interface between your Windows application (such as **Mosaic**) and the actual TCP/IP software. This library is free and comes as part of the **trumpet winsock** distribution. Many browser distributions also include this library with the browser.

Finally, your Windows application may be a 32-bit application and require the *win32s* package, which allows you to run proper 32-bit applications under Windows. *Win32s* is currently a Beta release package and is undergoing constant changes, so you may have to download the most recent version to get your browser to work (this is true for **Mosaic 2.0A7** and later, and perhaps for others). The most recent release, *win32s1.15*, can be found at the URLs:

```
ftp://ftp.ncsa.uiuc.edu/Mosaic/Windows/win32s.zip
ftp://ftp.microsoft.com/developr/win32dk/sdk-public/
```

If you are running OS/2 Version 2.1, you will need to purchase TCP/IP networking software from IBM. OS/2 Version 3.0, on the other hand, has TCP/IP software built into the operating system.

MSDOS BROWSER: DOSLYNX

DosLynx is a DOS-based version of the full-screen text browser **lynx**. It is a full-screen text-mode browser, so inlined images are not displayed; however, images can be displayed by separate helper graphics programs if you have them on your machine. **Lynx** is a useful browser, and ideal for users who are running systems that are unable to run Windows. **DosLynx** can even run on old 8086-based computers.

Additional information about **DosLynx** can be found at:

```
ftp://ftp2.cc.ukans.edu/pub/WWW/DosLynx/readme.htm
```

The program itself is found at the URL:

```
ftp://ftp2.cc.ukans.edu/pub/WWW/DosLynx/
```

The current package is found in the archive *DLX0_8A.EXE.* You may find a more recent version in this directory, with a later (i.e., larger) version number.

WINDOWS AND OS/2 BROWSERS

Almost any 16-bit Windows application will run under OS/2, including browser software. The situation is more problematic with 32-bit Windows applications, since Microsoft keeps changing its special *win32s* 32-bit library package. IBM can't keep up, so newer 32-bit Windows applications, written for the newer *win32s* libraries, will not work on OS/2. This means that newer versions of **WinMosaic** and possibly the 32-bit version of **Air Mosaic** will not run under OS/2 Version 2.1. This has hopefully changed with the release of Version 3.0. But then, Version 3.0 comes with a WWW browser built in!

AIR MOSAIC

Air Mosaic from Spry is a commercially supported version of **Mosaic** that has all the features of the NCSA program, plus several enhancements. Spry currently produces 16- and 32-bit versions of **Air Mosaic**. The 16-bit version runs easily under Windows and OS/2, while the 32-bit version requires an up-to-date *win32s* library and may have problems running under OS/2.

Air Mosaic understands all URLs, including **wais** and **mailto**. It also has support for proxy servers, and a kiosk mode that hides the navigation and control buttons and menus. There are also well-organized pull-down menus for editing helper application lists, for adding new MIME-types, and for editing hotlists. **Air Mosaic** also allows for secure online financial transactions using the company's *Secure Encryption Transaction* (SET) architecture, but you will, of course, also need appropriate server software.

You can obtain a fully functional demonstration copy of the 16-bit version from:

```
ftp://ftp.spry.com/AirMosaicDemo/
```

Spry can be contacted at 1-800-SPRYNET (1-800-777-9638), valid in the U.S. and Canada only, or via e-mail (*info@spry.com*). You can also find out more information at:

```
http://www.spry.com/
```

CELLO

Cello is an elegant Windows 3.1 graphical interface to the WWW. Cello also runs under the most recent release of OS/2; a patch is needed to the TCP/IP software for earlier OS/2 releases. IBM has a patch for this, so if you find that **Cello** does not work, you can contact IBM Service and ask for the fix (for APAR #PN52335). This should not be a problem with the current TCP/IP package, or with OS/2 Version 3.0.

Cello is easy to use and simple to configure, and can use external viewers to display noninlined images and movies, and to play audio files. It can access HTTP, Gopher, FTP, telnet, CSO/ph/qi, and USENET (NNTP) servers directly, and requires a gateway to access WAIS.

Cello has a flexible bookmark utility, and you can easily reconfigure the interface colors and fonts. **Cello** does not support proxy servers or SOCKS, so it is of limited use inside a firewall-protected local network. It also does not support the HTML **FORM** elements, although an upcoming release will do so.

Additional information about **Cello** can be found at:

```
ftp://fatty.law.cornell.edu/pub/LII/Cello/default.htm
http://www.law.cornell.edu/cello/cellofaq.html
```

You can find the archive for the **Cello** program at the URL:

```
ftp://fatty.law.cornell.edu/pub/LII/Cello/
```

in the file *cello.zip*. The additional files *cellofaq.zip* (or *cellofaq.tar.gz*) contain useful notes about **Cello**. This directory also contains the helper programs *lview31.zip* (for images), *wham131.zip* (for audio), and *gswin.zip* (for PostScript files).

Cello was written by Thomas R. Bruce.

SPYGLASS

Spyglass produces commercial versions of **Mosaic** but sells its product to Original Equipment Manufacturers (OEMs) only. Spyglass also distributes the commercial licenses to **Mosaic**: NCSA ceded these Licensing Rights to Spyglass in the fall of 1994. Currently the **Mosaic** software is licensed to IBM, FTP Software, Digital Equipment Corp., O'Reilly, and Firefox. Spyglass is located in Illinois, at:

> Spyglass, Inc., 1800 Woodfield Drive Savoy, IL 61874 (phone: 217-355-6000).

WINMOSAIC: NCSA MOSAIC FOR WINDOWS

WinMosaic was one of the first Windows World Wide Web browsers and spurred the development of several others. The current Version 2.0A7 does not run under OS/2, as it requires up-to-date *win32s* support. **WinMosaic** Version 2.0A2 is a 16-bit application and does run under OS/2.

WinMosaic is a well-designed WWW browser for Windows PCs, with support for **http, gopher, file, news** (USENET), and **telnet** URLs, as well as support for WAIS access via a gateway. The **mailto** URL is not supported. There is also a bookmark/hotlist facility; a *stop* button to stop file downloads; and pull-down menus for configuring the display. Unfortunately, configuring the helper applications requires you to edit, by hand, the *MOSAIC.INI* file. This is complicated but is explained in the documentation that comes with the program. **WinMosaic** also comes with built-in proxy support. There are also several commercially available derivatives of **WinMosaic**, which are described next.

Additional information about **WinMosaic** is found at:

```
http://www.ncsa.uiuc.edu/SDG/Software/WinMosaic/HomePage.html
http://www.ncsa.uiuc.edu/SDG/Software/WinMosaic/Bugs.html
```

Instructions for obtaining **WinMosaic** executables are found at:

```
http://www.ncsa.uiuc.edu/SDG/Software/WinMosaic/General.html
```

Versions are available for Intel processors running Windows and Windows NT, as well as for DEC ALPHA and MIPS machines running Windows NT.

WINWEB

WinWeb is a graphical Windows WWW browser for PCs currently at release Version 1.0Alpha2; this version runs well under OS/2.

The current version (1.0A2) of **WinWeb** has some important limitations. It currently supports only **http, file, ftp,** and **gopher** URLs—all other URLs are ignored. It does, however, have proxy support for access through a firewall, and includes useful features, such as bookmarks and easy configuration of fonts and background screen colors. It also has a *stop* button for interrupting document retrieval.

WinWeb is under rapid development—Up-to-date information is found at:

```
http://galaxy.einet.net/EINet/Winweb/DeveloperNotes.html
http://galaxy.einet.net/EINet/Winweb/Winweb Home.html
```

while the most recent **WinWeb** program release can be found in:

```
ftp://ftp.einet.net/einet/pc/Winweb/Winweb.zip
```

WinWeb uses the *VBRUN.DLL* library to access helper programs (for playing movies, sounds, and so on), so you will also need the *vbrun300.zip* package. This is found in the same directory as *winweb.zip*.

WinWeb is being developed at the Microelectronics and Computer Technology Corporation (MCC) by the Enterprise Integration Network (EINet) Group. EINet is a trademark of the Microelectronics and Computer Technology Corporation (MCC).

HELPER APPLICATIONS

The following is a list of some typical shareware or freeware packages for viewing alternative image formats, playing audio and movie files, decompressing downloaded files, and so on, on PCs. There are many other packages that can do these things, so you should not feel restricted to this collection. The **Cello** program archive site (noted earlier) has several of these helper applications. Here is a list of the most common helper applications and the names to look for when doing **archie** searches.

Audio Files (*.au, wav, .aiff, .iff*):   **archie** search string: wham

This can be found at:

    ftp://ftp.ncsa.uiuc.edu/Web/Mosaic/Windows/viewers/

The most recent version number is 1.3, found in the file. **Wham** works with most standard audio cards, including Soundblaster.

Gnu Zip File (*.gz*):   **archie** search string: gzip

Note that **gzip** is also common on UNIX computers, so make sure you are accessing a DOS/Windows version. You can find many different PC-archiving and -unarchiving programs, including **gzip**, at:

    ftp://ftp.std.com/src/pc/archivers/

Image Files (*.gif, .jpeg, .jpg, .tif, .tiff*): **archie** search string: lview

Lview can display JPEG, JFIF, GIF, Truevision Targa, Windows, and OS/2 BMP image files, among others. A registered version of the shareware package *WECJLIB.DLL* from Express Compression Laboratories is also recommended for fast JPEG image file decompression. These can both be found at:

    ftp://akiu.gw.tohoku.ac.jp/pub/network/www/Web/Windows/viewers/

Lview will run without *WECJLIB.DLL*; it will just be slower.

MPEG Video (*.mpeg, .mpg*):   **archie** search string: mpegw

This is a shareware **mpeg** movie player that can be found at:

    ftp://alfred.ccs.carleton.ca/pub/civeng/viewers/

Look for files *mpegw32e.zip* and *mpegw32e.txt* (installation instructions).

PostScript Files (*.ps, .eps*):   archie search strings: `gsview` and
`gs261exe` (you need both)

The Ghostscript/Ghostview PostScript previewer can be found at:

`ftp://ftp.ncsa.uiuc.edu/Web/Mosaic/Windows/viewers/`

QuickTime Video (*.mov*) :   archie search string: `qtw`

Qtw stands for QuickTime for Windows. This can be found at:

`ftp://winftp.cica.indiana.edu/pub/pc/win3/desktop/qtw111.zip`

MACINTOSH PLATFORM BROWSERS

Similar to the PCs, you must have appropriate SLIP, PPP, and TCP/IP software on your Macintosh to run these browsers. All Macintosh browsers
require at least System 7, and you will also need MacTCP 2.0.2 (and
preferably 2.0.4) to provide the TCP/IP software. There is also a MacPPP
package for PPP support. Contact your local Macintosh software outlet to
obtain these packages.

MacMosaic: Mosaic for Macintosh

MacMosaic is a Macintosh version of the Mosaic program developed by
the NCSA development team. The last stable and fully supported release is
Version 1.0.3. This is a good browser, but cannot interpret the **FORM** elements, which severely limits its usefulness. It also cannot communicate
with proxy servers, so it is of limited use inside a firewall. The latest release
is **MacMosaic** 2.0A8; this version supports the FORM elements as well as
proxy servers and SOCKS firewall access. Therefore, if you need these
facilities, you will need this (or a later) version. **MacMosaic** 2.0A8 tends to
be slow and takes up a lot of memory (3.0 MB minimum). **MacWeb**,
another Macintosh browser, is generally smaller and faster.

Both versions of **MacMosaic** support all URLs, except for **mailto**, and support WAIS access only through a WAIS gateway. **Telnet, rlogin,** and **tn3270**

URLs are enabled using telnet/rlogin tools already present on your
Macintosh, so you also need a telnet/rlogin package. **MacMosaic** has an
extensive hotlist interface and built-in lists of useful Web starting points,
including pointers to **MacMosaic** information pages. **MacMosaic** also has
a *stop* button to interrupt file downloads. Menus are available for configuring helper applications.

NCSA documentation on **MacMosaic** is found at:

```
http://www.ncsa.uiuc.edu/SDG/Software/MacMosaic/MacMosaicHome.html
```

and the online **MacMosaic** users guide is at:

```
http://www.ncsa.uiuc.edu/SDG/Software/MacMosaic/Docs/MacMosa.0.html
```

The Mosaic executables (in binhexed files) are found at:

```
ftp://ftp.ncsa.uiuc.edu/Mosaic/Mac/
```

Several versions are available; the version number is part of the filename.
The current 2.0A8 versions are found in the files *NCSAMosaic A8.68k.hqx*
(for Macintoshes with 680x0 processors) and *NCSAMosaic A8.PPC.hqx*
(for PowerPC machines). Another site containing **MacMosaic** executables
is:

```
ftp://sunsite.unc.edu/pub/packages/infosystems/WWW/clients/MacMosaic/
```

MACWEB

MacWeb is a fine Web browser with features both similar and complemen-
tary to **MacMosaic**. It supports most URLs, but does not support **rlogin,
mailto,** or **wais.** Telnet and tn3270 connections are provided through
external programs. Helper application configuration is easily done using
editable pull-down menus. There is a very convenient hotlist editor for
storing and sorting hotlists, as well as a history mechanism for switching
randomly between previously visited pages. **MacWeb** supports the CERN
Proxy protocol, but you cannot configure this from the pull-down menus:
You must use the Macintosh **ResEdit** resource editor to edit the proxy
information.

A nice feature is the ability to access hypertext link information: If you place the mouse over a hypertext anchor and hold down the mouse button, you are presented with a menu of choices for what to do with the linked item (get information about the link, retrieve and save to disk, etc.).

Unfortunately, **MacWeb** does not have a *stop* button—once a transfer is started there is no way of interrupting it. This is an unfortunate weakness in an otherwise fine program.

Additional information about **MacWeb** is found at the URLs:

```
http://galaxy.einet.net/EINet/MacWeb/MacWebHome.html
http://galaxy.einet.net/EINet/MacWeb/DeveloperNotes.html
```

while the latest version of the program executable is found at:

```
ftp://ftp.einet.net/einet/mac/macweb/macweb.latest.sea.hqx
```

The EINet MacWeb software was developed at the Microelectronics and Computer Technology Corporation (MCC) by the Enterprise Integration Network (EINet) Group. EINet is a trademark of the Microelectronics and Computer Technology Corporation (MCC). For additional information, you can write to EINet (*macweb@einet.net*).

MACINTOSH HELPER APPLICATIONS

Helper applications display image formats that cannot be displayed inline; play movies or sound files; unpack binhexed files; and so on. Here is a list of the most common helper applications and the names to look for when doing **archie** searches. Several of these applications can be found at:

```
ftp://boombox.micro.umn.edu/pub/gopher/Macintosh-TurboGopher/helper-applications/
ftp://ftp.ncsa.uiuc.edu/Mosaic/Mac/Helpers/
```

Basic Audio (*.au, .aiff, .aifc*):   **archie** search string: `soundmachine`

This is found at the preceding URLs, in the file *SoundMachine.sit.hqx*.

Expander Enhancer (*.sit, .zip* ...):   **archie** search string: `enhanc`

This add-on package enables **StuffIt Expander** to expand files compressed with virtually all compression formats used on Macintosh, UNIX, or PC systems, including ZIP (*.zip*), ARC (*.arc*), AppleLink (*.pkg*), gzip (*.gz*), UNIX compress (*.Z*), and UUencode (*.uu*), not to forget StuffIt archive (*.sit, .sea*).

Image Files (*.gif, .jpeg, .jpg,* ...):　　archie search string: `jpegview`

This is found at the preceding URLs, in the file *JPEGView-3.1.sea.hqx* (or a newer version).

MPEG Video (*.mpeg, .mpg*):　　archie search string: `sparkle`

This is found at the preceding URL, in the file *Sparkle16.sit.hqx*.

PostScript Files (*.ps, .eps*):　　archie search string: `mac-ghost`

This can be found, for example, at:

```
ftp://sumex-aim.stanford.edu/infor-mac/grf/util/
```

QuickTime Video (*.mov*) :　　archie search string: `simpleplayer`, or `simple_player`

This is found at the preceding URL, in the file *Simple_Player.hqx* (you also need *QuickTime1.5.hqx* if you don't already have it).

StuffIt Archives (*.sit.hqx, .cpt.hqx*): archie search string: `sit-expand`

There are many packages that can expand StuffIt archives: **StuffIt Expander** is one popular version.

Zip Files (*.zip*):　　archie search string: `mac-unzip`

This can be found, for example, at:

```
ftp://sumex-aim.stanford.edu/infor-mac/cmp/
```

Many of these packages may be available as shareware at your local Macintosh software store.

UNIX AND VAX/VMS PLATFORM BROWSERS

UNIX and VAX/VMS computers come with TCP/IP software as part of the operating system, which is a nice improvement over the PC and Macintosh platforms. Unfortunately, you will often have to compile the browsers for your platforms, as executable versions are often not available. This is usually not difficult, and most programs include compilation and installation instructions. You will need to be a system administrator to complete the installation.

BATCH MODE BROWSER (UNIX)

Url_get is a perl program that operates like a batch-mode browser. It allows you to retrieve a document via any of the WWW protocols simply by specifying the document URL. This is useful for downloading WWW documents, or for use in automated processing, such as UNIX cron jobs.

Additional information can be found at:

    http://wwwhost.cc.utexas.edu/test/zippy/url_get.html

A tar archive of the package is found at:

    http://wwwhost.cc.utexas.edu/test/zippy/perl/url_get/url_get.tar.Z

Url_get was written by Jack Lund.

CHIMERA (UNIX)

Chimera is a UNIX X-Windows-based WWW browser. Most UNIX browsers user the Motif X-Windows widget set, which is not available on some systems. **Chimera** uses the public-domain Xaw Athena widget set, so it can be compiled almost anywhere. You will need, at a minimum, a C compiler and the standard X11 libraries. This is not a task for the timid, as **chimera** does not always compile without prodding. Still, an experienced systems manager should be able to get the package running in a couple of hours.

Chimera has a look and feel similar to **Mosaic**, but with a different arrangement of buttons and menus. **Chimera** is fast and, on slow workstations, can be significantly faster than **Mosaic for X-Windows**. This may be important if you are using an older, underpowered workstation. **Chimera** supports most URLs, but not **wais**, **mailto**, **news**, or **rlogin**. **Chimera** requires the **pbmplus** library to display inlined images. If you don't have **pbmplus** on your system, images are replaced by a default *image not available* bitmap.

The distributed **chimera** package does not support proxy servers or SOCKS. You can patch **chimera** to use SOCKS firewall access by following the instructions in the **chimera** distribution documentation.

The **chimera** home page is:

```
http://www.unlv.edu/chimera/
```

This gives a brief description of the program and some pointers to anonymous FTP sites housing the **chimera** source code. The original home of the **chimera** source code is:

```
ftp://ftp.cs.unlv.edu/pub/chimera/
```

EMACS-W3 MODE (UNIX, VMS, OTHERS)

Emacs-w3 is a WWW browser mode for the **emacs** text editor. If you are using the **emacs** variants **lemacs** or **epoch**, **emacs-w3** will display HTML documents using multiple fonts for the headings, titles, and so on, and can also display inlined graphics. **Emacs-w3** mode supports all URL forms and implements many of the HTML+ features. If you are familiar with **emacs**, you should give this package a try.

The **emacs-w3** package is available at the URL:

```
ftp://moose.cs.indiana.edu/pub/elisp/w3/
```

You will need the three files: *w3.tar.gz, extras.tar.gz*, and *icons.tar.gz*. You should also read the *README* file for the latest details and installation instructions.

Emacs-w3 mode was written by William Perry, with help from a large and supportive cast.

LINEMODE BROWSER (UNIX, VMS)

This program, developed at CERN, was one of the first WWW browsers. The **LineMode browser** allows anyone with a dumb terminal to view WWW documents, but is not as flexible as such programs as **lynx**. It can also be run as a background process to download documents.

Up-to-date information is found at:

```
http://info.cern.ch/hypertext/WWW/LineMode/Defaults/CommandLine.html
```

Executables (for various platforms) are found at:

```
ftp://info.cern.ch/pub/www/bin
```

in the subdirectory appropriate to your computer type, and in files with names *www*.tar.Z* (where * is a version number). The source code is located at:

```
ftp://info.cern.ch/pub/www/src/WWWLineMode.tar.Z
```

LYNX (UNIX, VMS)

Lynx is a full-screen hypertext browser that can run on any dumb terminal. It uses the arrow and tab keys and single letter keycodes to navigate around the document and for executing program commands. It is the best character-based browser and should definitely be part of your browser collection. Recent versions support proxy access, which means that if you are inside a secure local network, you can use **lynx** to access external documents via a *proxy* hypertext server that you must install on your own network (the CERN HTTPD server can do this). When you request a URL, your client passes the URL on to the proxy server inside your network, which makes the request of the machine outside your network on your behalf, and then passes you the returned result. Proxy service is discussed in more detail in Chapter 3.

Lynx was written by Lou Montulli (*montulli@ukanaix.cc.ukans.edu*) of the University of Kansas. Sources and precompiled binaries for several machines are available at:

```
ftp://ftp2.cc.ukans.edu/pub/lynx/
```

Lynx online documentation is available from:

```
http://www.cc.ukans.edu/lynx_help/Lynx_users_guide.html
```

This set of documents comes with the **lynx** distribution.

MIDASWWW (UNIX, VMS)

The **Midas WWW** browser is based on the Midas hypertext library. The browser has undergone substantial revisions in its short life and is currently at Version 2.1. It still has a few bugs, but appears generally stable.

MidasWWW is an elegant graphical browser supporting inlined images and clear marking of hypertext links. In addition, visited links are marked differently from unvisited ones to help you navigate an unfamiliar collection of documents. This list is lost when you quit the program. **MidasWWW** supports all the standard HTML markup, including the **FORM** elements. **MidasWWW** supports all URLs except **tn3270, login,** and **mailto. MidasWWW** comes with a built-in default configuration that can be changed by creating an *app-default* file. **MidasWWW** does not appear to support proxy server or the SOCKS package, and is, consequently, of limited use inside a firewall.

MidasWWW has extensive online help, but this is downloaded from the home site in Stanford, California, which can be slow. There is a Cancel Download pop-up menu that appears when downloading a new document. However, on my system, this menu does not always appear, which is annoying, given there is no other way of canceling a file download. On one workstation (Sgi Indigo2), the program occasionally locks up the X terminal when downloading files. The X terminal or workstation eventually recovers, but it is not a pleasant experience.

Additional information about **Midas WWW** can be found at:

```
http://www-midas.slac.stanford.edu:80/midasv21/overview.html
http://www-midas.slac.stanford.edu:80/midasv21/about.html
```

Executables and the source code are found at:

```
ftp://freehep.scri.fsu.edu/freehep/networking_email_news/midaswww/
```

Binaries are recommended, as compiling this program is nontrivial. Precompiled programs for DEC Alpha, AIX, HPUX, SGI, and Sun SPARC systems are available in the *binaries/* subdirectory. There is also a Vax VMS binary, found in *binaries/vms*.

MidasWWW was created by Tony Johnson and Chung Huynh of the Stanford Linear Accelerator Laboratory.

MOSAIC FOR X-WINDOWS (UNIX)

Mosaic for X-Windows is a full-featured WWW browser distributed by NCSA. This browser supports all URLs except **mailto,** and has many nice features, including hotlists, document source viewing and printing, FORMs support, hypertext help, and document annotation. Hypertext links are also specially marked when accessed so that you can keep track of previously explored links. There is also a tool for making local HTML annotations to documents and a text search tool for searching for words in the displayed document.

Mosaic for X-Windows does not have proxy server or SOCKS support. If you can obtain the Mosaic source code and the SOCKS library, you can recompile **Mosaic** to support SOCKS firewall access, but this is not supported by NCSA. For more information on this option, contact Ying-Da Lee (*ylee@syl.dl.nec.com*). In some cases, the precompiled binaries distributed by NCSA do not have native WAIS support. If you obtain the **Mosaic** source code, you can recompile it to include WAIS support, provided you also obtain the **freeWAIS** software.

Precompiled binaries of **Mosaic for X-Windows** Version 2.4 (the current supported version) are available at many sites, including:

```
ftp://ftp.ncsa.uiuc.edu/Mosaic/Unix/binaries/2.4/
```

In mid-October 1994, NCSA announced the release of NCSA **Mosaic 2.5b2 Beta.** This is an enhanced program that includes support for **TABLE,**

SUP, and SUB HTML elements; nested hotlists; and a kiosk mode. This
new release still has some bugs and is available as an executable only at:

```
ftp://ftp.ncsa.uiuc.edu in/Mosaic/Unix/binaries/2.5/
```

MOSAIC (TUEV) 2.4.2

The Computing Center (ZDV) of the University of Tuebingen in Germany
has developed an extensively modified version of **Mosaic,** known as
Mosaic (TueV) 2.4.2. This is a multilingual update to NCSA **Mosaic 2.4
for X-Windows;** it supports a multilingual user interface and **mailto** URLs,
and incorporates many other patches and improvements. The source code
is available at either:

```
ftp://ftp.uni-tuebingen.de/pub/WWW/Mosaic-TueV/source
http://ftp.uni-tuebingen.de/pub/WWW/Mosaic-TueV/source
```

while precompiled binaries are found at the following URLs:

```
ftp://ftp.uni-tuebingen.de/pub/WWW/Mosaic-TueV/binaries
http://ftp.uni-tuebingen.de/pub/WWW/Mosaic-TueV/binaries
```

QUADRALAY GWHIS BROWSER (UNIX)

Quadralay markets a *Global Wide Help & Information System (GWHIS)*
that allows application developers to add online documentation to applications via a WWW hypertext system. The browser portion of this package is
derived from NCSA **Mosaic.** The **GWHIS** package combines this browser
with hypertext servers, database search engines, a **GWHIS** API, and auxiliary tools for converting existing documents into HTML format.

GWHIS is currently available for several different UNIX platforms, but not
for Macintoshes or PCs (Macintosh and PC platform support is planned).
Additional information can be found at:

```
http://www.quadralay.com/www/ProductInfo/gwhis/pr05.html
```

RASHTY VMS CLIENT (VMS)

This text-based browser is based on the VMS SMG screen management
routines, and has an interface similar to a Gopher client.

The **Rashty VMS client** was written by Dudu Rashty and is available at:

```
ftp://vms.huji.ac.il/www.dir/vms_client.dir/
```

TKWWW (UNIX)

Tkwww is a WWW browser based on the tk and tcl toolkits. **Tkwww** compiles easily on many UNIX systems, but you must first install the tk and tcl libraries.

Tkwww's most interesting use is as an HTML editor. **Tkwww** contains many editing commands for marking emphasized text, creating lists, and so on, which allow you to edit and dynamically create HTML documents. You can even create hypertext links and immediately test that they work.

Tkwww is somewhat weak as a browser. It can display inline images (only in a separate window); does not support **mailto, rlogin,** or **wais** URLs; and does not understand the **FORM** elements. There also is no *stop* button to interrupt transfers that have gone bad, or that are simply taking too much time. **Tkwww** does have the native ability to display almost any image format, and has built-in hooks for playing movies and sounds.

There is a useful if somewhat out-of-date collection of **tkwww** documentation at:

```
http://tk-www.mit.edu:8001/tk-www/help/
```

The current version of **tkwww**, 0.12 Beta, can be found at:

```
ftp://nntp.cs.ubc.ca/mirror1/x-contrib/misdirected
```

Tkwww was written by Joseph Wang (*joe@athena.mit.edu*).

VIOLAWWW (UNIX)

ViolaWWW is an X-Windows-based browser based on the Viola *interactive media* scripting language/toolkit. Once again, this is a package you will likely have to compile yourself; there is an executable available only for Sun SPARC platforms. Compilation is a difficult task, as **ViolaWWW** is a complex package. This should not be attempted by the timid!

Viola can be compiled with or without Motif—Motif compilation is recommended. **Viola** supports most standard URLs except **wais** and **mailto**.

Viola has several nice features—notably, its high level of HTML+ support: **Viola** supports **TABLES**, paragraph formatting control, and **FORMs**, and also experimental equation formatting elements.

Additional and up-to-date information on **Viola** is found at:

```
http://xcf.berkeley.edu/ht/projects/Viola/docs/Viola/about.html
http://xcf.berkeley.edu/ht/projects/Viola/README
```

Source code for **Viola** is available at:

```
ftp://ora.com/pub/www/Viola
```

while binaries for Sun SPARC systems are found at:

```
ftp://ora.com/pub/www/Viola/old/
```

Viola was developed by Pei Y. Wei.

UNIX HELPER PACKAGES

Most of the following helper packages will have to be compiled and installed, as was the case for the browsers. In some cases, you will find executable program files, which is a bonus.

If you are using a UNIX system, you are encouraged to obtain the help of a systems manager when installing these tools.

Audio Files (*.au, .aiff,* etc.): **Showaudio** (found inside the **metamail** package—see the following)

> **Metamail** contains the script **showaudio**, which can be used on several UNIX computers to play audio information.

Control Panel (for Movie Players): **Archie** search string: xplaygizmo

> The xplaygizmo is found, for example, at:

```
ftp://ftp.ncsa.uiuc.edu/Mosaic/Unix/viewers/xplaygizmo
```

General Video (*.mpeg, .mov*):   Archie search string: `xanim`

The **xanim** program is found, for example, at:

`ftp://crl.dec.com/pub/X11/contrib/applications`

Image Files (*.gif, .jpeg, .tiff*, etc.):   Archie search string: `xv-`

The **xv** program is found, for example, at:

`ftp://ftp.cis.upenn.edu/pub/xv`

Metamail (MIME Mail Viewer):   Archie search string: `mm`

Metamail, a multimedia mail package, contains the **showaudio** audio player script. **Metamail** is found, for example, at:

`ftp://thumper.bellcore.com/pub/nsb`

MPEG Video (*.mpeg, .mpg*):   Archie search string: `mpeg_play`

The **mpeg_play** program is found, for example, at:

`ftp://tr-ftp.cs.berkeley.edu/pub/multimedia/mpeg`

PostScript Files (*.ps, .eps*):   Archie search string: `ghost`

You need the three components *ghostview*, *ghostscript*, and the ghost-script *fonts*. These can be found at:

`ftp://ftp.cs.wisc.edu/pub/ghost/gnu/`

in the files *ghostscript-2.6.1.tar.gz*, *ghostscript-fonts-2.6.1.tar.gz*, and *ghostview-1.5.tar.gz*.

TeX .dvi Files (Display *.dvi* Files): Archie search string: `xdvi`

The **xdvi** *.dvi* file previewer is found, for example, at:

`ftp://export.lcs.mit.edu/contrib/applications`

NEXT PLATFORM BROWSERS

The NeXT platform comes with TCP/IP software as part of the standard operating system. Browsers also come as ready-to-install packages so that compilation is not necessary.

THE CERN NEXT BROWSER

CERN has developed a NeXT browser that is also a WYSIWYG HTML editor. The current Version 2.02 is relatively stable, although not bug-free. Additional information about CERN can be found at:

```
http://info.cern.ch/hypertext/WWW/NextStep/Status.html
http://info.cern.ch/hypertext/WWW/NextStep/Menus.html
```

The executable file is found at:

```
ftp://info.cern.ch/pub/www/bin/next-fat/
```

in the archive file *WWW.app_n.nn.tar*, where *n.nn* is the version number.

The program has a rich collection of commands for editing HTML documents. You can, for example, create links within the document and then immediately test that they work. This browser supports most URL protocols and can support proxy servers. It does not support the FORM elements.

OMNIWEB

Omniweb gets good reviews from NeXT users, who describe it as "pretty cool." It can handle most URLs, including **mailto**. However, it does not support the **FORM** elements and does not have proxy support.

By default, **Omniweb** can display only *.tiff* or *.eps* image formats inline (these are the native image formats for the NeXT windowing system). For the standard WWW formats, you need a helper application. Omni provides an image filter that allows **Omniweb** to view inline GIF and other image formats. This **OmniImageFilter** package is found at:

```
http://www.omnigroup.com/Software/OmniImageFilter/OmniImageFilter.pkg.tar
```

You need this to view most HTML documents, since the default Web image formats are GIF or X-Bitmap.

Additional information about **Omniweb** can be found at:

```
http://www.omnigroup.com/Software/Omniweb/
```

The executable program is available at:

```
http://www.omnigroup.com/Software/Omniweb/Omniweb.app.tar.gz
```

AMIGA BROWSER: AMOSAIC

AMosaic is an Amiga browser based on the NCSA **Mosaic** package. The browser requires Amiga OS 2.0 or greater, and preferably 3.0. You also need TCP/IP software.

The home page for additional information about **AMosaic** is:

```
http://insti.physics.sunysb.edu/AMosaic/home.html
```

the installation page, at:

```
http://insti.physics.sunysb.edu/AMosaic/Installation.html
```

which also explains how to obtain Amiga TCP/IP software.

COMING ATTRACTIONS

Various companies are preparing or have just announced new WWW browser products. This is a brief list of these companies and their plans.

IBM OS/2 BROWSER: WEB EXPLORER

IBM intends to bundle a browser with the release of OS/2 Version 3.0, sometime in early 1995. This browser will be based on the Mosaic program. Early reviews of the beta release compare this product favorably with **Netscape** (see following).

MICROMIND SLIPKNOT

This is a Windows 3.1 WWW browser that can function via a telephone dial-up connection to a UNIX account, without requiring SLIP or PPP access. It provides background document loading (over the phone connection), multiple document windows, and other features. It is currently available as a shareware package.

NETSCAPE COMMUNICATIONS CORP.

Netscape Communications Corp. was founded in part by Marc Andressen, the primary developer of the original NCSA **Mosaic**. Netscape

Communications has designed an all-new WWW browser, **Netscape**, that has significant enhancements over the original Mosaic program. The beta version of **Netscape** was released in mid-October 1994, to much acclaim and controversy. Acclaim over its elegant design and new features, such as the ability to view documents while they are loading, its elegant USENET news interface, and a common look and feel across PC Macintosh and UNIX platforms. Controversy over some new and **Netscape**-specific HTML extensions that include flowing text around images, changing font sizes inside regular text, and the centering of text. The controversy comes about because several of the HTML extensions are not compatible with the SGML model for HTML. Whatever comes of the controversy, it is clear that Netscape Communications has jumped to the front with some exciting new ideas, and will certainly spur the development of WWW browsers and the HTML language.

You can obtain executable **Netscape** binaries for PC, Macintosh, and various UNIX platforms from:

```
ftp://ftp.mcom.com/pub/netscape/
```

or from other sites listed at:

```
http://Mosaic.mcom.com/info/how-to-get-it.html
```

General information about **Netscape** can be found at:

```
http://home.mcom.com/welcome.html
```

You can also send inquiries by e-mail (*info@mcom.com*) or by old-fashioned mail to:

Mosaic Communications Corporation, 650 Castro Street, Suite 500, Mountain View, CA 94041 (phone: 415 254-1900).

HTTP SERVERS AND SERVER UTILITIES

So, you are thinking of setting up your own server. You have a connection to the Internet (hopefully, a fast one!) and perhaps a computer. Now, you want to get some server software and get things running. At this stage, a little advance planning can help you avoid much future grief. The following guidelines, followed by brief descriptions of the different servers available, should help you make your decision. The chapter concludes with a list of small applications that can help you analyze the server log file output to determine average usage and other diagnostic information.

BASIC SERVER ISSUES

The assumption is that you want to set up a reliable server and that you are not doing this just for fun (although fun should be a component in this process). You then need a server that is fast, easy to maintain, and reliable (the machine does not crash), since you want it to run 24 hours a day (your server can be accessed at any hour, day or night). Given these criteria, there are a number of options available. In order of decreasing desirability, these are: UNIX servers, Windows NT or OS/2 servers, and other platform servers.

UNIX SERVERS

The consensus among WWW administrators is that a UNIX machine, combined with either the CERN or the NCSA HTTP servers, is the ideal package for distributing hypertext materials. There are several reasons for this choice. First, the UNIX operating system is designed to run many simultaneous processes (multitasking) so that a well-designed UNIX server can almost effortlessly respond to many simultaneous HTTP service requests. Also, UNIX is designed to isolate the server and user processes from the management level of the operating system, which ensures reliable operation even under heavy loads. Last, the powerful HTTP servers from CERN and NCSA were originally written for UNIX machines and are generally the most full-featured servers available. They are also freely available with precompiled executable versions available for UNIX computers from *Sun*, *Hewlett-Packard*, *Silicon Graphics*, and others. The source code is also publicly available, so you can download and compile it yourself.

If you use a UNIX server but have other machines, such as Macintoshes or PCs, you can make the server filesystems accessible to these users by remote mounting of the HTTP server directories on the PCs or Macintoshes. For example, **PC-NFS** allows PCs to mount UNIX filesystems, while **CAP** (Columbia Appletalk Protocol) allows similar access for a Macintosh. Setting up a development environment such as this requires some thought, as you must take into account the peculiarities of each system (for example, PCs allow only 8-character filenames and 3-character filename extensions); but, in general, this networked approach is useful in integrating a WWW development environment into a heterogeneous collection of computers.

Setting up a UNIX server need not be expensive. Although buying a machine from a vendor such as *Sun* or *Hewlett-Packard* is one option, you can also purchase a standard PC clone and install the freeware UNIX clone **linux**. The NCSA server has been successfully ported to **linux**, so you can set up a **linux**-based HTTP server for little more than the cost of a PC.

The downside of the UNIX approach is complexity. UNIX is a sophisticated operating system and can be difficult to learn and manage. If you do not have someone in your organization familiar with UNIX, you should consider hiring someone who is; learning UNIX and installing an HTTP server are not things you want to be doing at the same time.

VMS SERVERS

The VMS operating system, which runs on VAX and some DEC ALPHA machines, is a multitasking operating system that, like UNIX, can also efficiently support server software, such as an HTTP server. There are currently two HTTP server packages for VMS. The CERN server, ported to VMS from UNIX, retains the features of the UNIX package but is reputedly slow. The **DECthreads** HTTP server is faster but does not have all the capabilities of the CERN package.

WINDOWS NT OR OS/2

Windows NT and OS/2 are the next best choice for hosting an HTTP server. Both Microsoft's Windows NT and IBM's OS/2 efficiently run simultaneous processes, and also carefully separate user processes (such as an HTTP server) from the management level of the operating system. These systems are also generally easier to configure than a UNIX system, particularly for those coming from a PC background (this may be more perspective than fact!). It is certainly true, though, that both OS/2 and Windows NT are easily integrated into PC networks, since this was a major goal of their system designs.

There are two servers available for these systems. **OS2HTTPD** is a port of the NCSA HTTPD Version 1.3 server to OS/2. **HTTPS** is a similarly powerful server written expressly for Windows NT.

WINDOWS OR MACINTOSH

There are a number of packages available for PCs running Windows, and for Macintoshes. Several of these are quite full-featured. The Windows or Macintosh option is at the bottom of the list because of the limitations of the operating systems. DOS, Windows, and the Macintosh System-7 operating systems are not designed for multitasking, nor are they designed to safely separate the management level of the operating system from user processes. The first limitation means that it is difficult to write an efficient HTTP server—in general, they quickly bog down when the number of HTTP requests grows large. The second limitation is the reason PC and Macintosh computers often crash while running innocuous programs, such as spreadsheets or word processing programs (or HTTP servers!). For a Macintosh or PC user, this is an irritation. For World Wide Web users trying to access your now *dead* server, this is a major annoyance.

If you are going to use a Windows or Macintosh HTTP server for serious dissemination of material on the Web, you should dedicate a machine specifically to that task. This means not letting anyone use it to do other tasks, since extra user programs significantly increase the risk of a system crash. In addition, you will want to regularly test that the system is *alive*. This is true of any server but even more so for platforms for which crashes are more likely. Nothing will impress prospective clients or customers less than a fancy service that does not work properly or is unavailable.

BEHIND A FIREWALL?

Finally, just a reminder that if you are behind a firewall and want to both run a server and access the outside world, then you need the CERN HTTP server. This is the only server providing the *proxy support* you need.

LIST OF SERVER SOFTWARE

The following is a list of the different server packages available for different platforms and operating systems. This includes URLs pointing to additional documentation and to places where you can obtain the actual programs.

CERN HTTP SERVER (UNIX, VMS)

The CERN HTTP server is a publicly available, full-featured server developed by Ari Luotonen, Henrik Frystyk, and Tim Berners-Lee of CERN. It supports the HEAD, GET, POST, and PUT methods, is fully CGI/1.1-compliant, and comes with several useful CGI applications, including a program for handling active images. It also supports file and directory access control and encrypted user-authentication. The CERN server can also act as a *caching* proxy server, which is ideal if you want to both run a server and also access other servers through an Internet firewall. There is both printable and online documentation. By reputation, it is somewhat more complicated to install and configure than the NCSA server.

Information about the current version can be found at:

    http://info.cern.ch/hypertext/WWW/Daemon/Status.html

The current release is Version 3.0, which was made publicly available in late September 1994. Precompiled executables can be found at:

    ftp://info.cern.ch/pub/www/bin/

in subdirectories corresponding to the name of your operating system. You will want the files *cern_http_x.x.tar.Z* and *cern_httpd_utils_x.x.tar.Z*, where *x.x* is the version number (currently 3.0). VMS software is located in the *vms* subdirectory. Information on installing the VMS version is found at:

    http://delonline.cern.ch/disk$user/duns/doc/vms/www_run_httpd.html

The source code for the CERN HTTP server can be found at:

    ftp://info.cern.ch/pub/www/src/cern_httpd.tar.Z

A VMS source code archive is found in the file *cern_httpd_vms.zip*. This directory also contains the online documentation in the archive file *cern_httpd_docs.tar.Z*. A PostScript version of the documentation is found in *cern_httpd_guide.ps.Z*.

CL-HTTP (SYMBOLICS LISP MACHINES)

CL-HTTP is an HTTP server written using the Common Lisp Object System (CLOS). It runs on Symbolics LISP Machines under Genera 8.3, although ports of the package to Common LISP running on other machines and operating systems are expected in the near future (most notably, Mac Common Lisp).

CL-HTTP supports the HEAD, GET, and POST methods. Gateway programs are possible but do not use the CGI mechanism, because, with lisp, an arbitrary lisp function can generate returned HTML for a given URL. This has two advantages: First, lisp is a much more powerful language for writing response functions than the typical scripting languages used with the CGI interface. Second, all these run as compiled and dynamically linked objects.

CL-HTTP uses a sophisticated object-oriented approach to pass information between the server and query engines. As a result, high-level abstractions are available for automatic form processing and other gateway applications. Access control through domain name or IP addresses is also possible at the level of the entire server or of any specific URL.

Additional documentation on the **CL-HTTP** server can be found at:

```
http://www.ai.mit.edu/projects/iiip/doc/cl-http/server.html
```

The source code for the package is available at:

```
ftp://ftp.ai.mit.edu/pub/users/jcma/cl-http/sources.tar.Z
```

while the most recent revisions are always available at:

```
http://research.ai.mit.edu/code/server/
```

A Lisp Machine distribution file is available at:

```
ftp://ftp.ai.mit.edu/pub/users/jcma/cl-http/lispm.reel-1
```

CL-HTTP was written by John C. Mallery of the Artificial Intelligence Laboratory, Massachusetts Institute of Technology. Support for the MIT Artificial Intelligence Laboratory's artificial-intelligence research is provided, in part, by the Advanced Research Projects Agency of the Department of Defense under contract number MDA972-93-1-003N7.

CMS HTTPD (VM/CMS)

There are still a lot of IBM mainframes about, and a lot of organizations are still built around the services provided by these machines. **CMS HTTPD** is ideal for these communities and allows them to implement a WWW server with a minimum of fuss.

CMS HTTPD supports the GET and HEAD methods and is fully CGI-compliant. At present, there are a limited number of CGI programs written for the CMS system—the **CMS HTTPD** server author is currently writing a program to handle active images.

Additional information about **CMS HTTPD** is available at:

```
http://ua1vm.ua.edu/~troth/rickvmsw/rickvmsw.html
```

The source code is available in both VMARC and tar archive formats at the URLs:

```
http://ua1vm.ua.edu/~troth/rickvmsw/cmshttpd.vmarc
http://ua1vm.ua.edu/~troth/rickvmsw/cmshttpd.tar
```

CMS HTTPD was created by Rick Troth and is written entirely in **REXX**.

DECTHREAD HTTP SERVER (VAX/VMS)

The **DECthread HTTP** server is a native VAX/VMS HTTP server that uses the DECthreads model for multithreaded processing. As a result, this server should be significantly faster than the straightforward port of a UNIX server (such as the CERN HTTP server port), which is forced to run under the `inetd` to service more than one request at a time.

The **DECthread HTTP** server fully implements the HEAD and GET methods and supports CGI-compliant gateway scripts. The server comes equipped with example CGI scripts, including one to handle active images. There is also a facility to restrict file access based on the domain name of the client making the request; more sophisticated authentication schemes are also possible.

Additional information can be found at :

```
http://kcgl1.eng.ohio-state.edu/www/doc/serverinfo.html
```

which provides pointers to the server source code.

GN GOPHER/HTTP SERVER (UNIX)

GN is a single server supporting both the Gopher and HTTP protocols. It allows both protocols to access the same data so that GN is extremely useful for Information Services managers making a transition from a Gopher-based system to an HTTP-based one. **GN** is a freeware program, subject to the GNU general-public license.

GN fully implements the HEAD, GET, and POST methods, and supports CGI-compliant gateway programs. Access control is possible on a directory basis only, and is implemented by restricting access to particular Internet domain names or IP addresses. User authentication is not supported. The distributed package comes with installation instructions written from the point of view of Gopher service, so installation should be easy for those with this background.

The home page for **GN** information is:

    http://hopf.math.nwu.edu/

This includes links for accessing the most current version of the source code. At present, the source code for **GN** and its support programs is found at:

    ftp://ftp.acns.nwu.edu/pub/gn/gn.tar.Z

A **GN** server FAQ list is available at:

    http://gopher.cwru.edu:70/0/about.gopher/gn.faq

GWHIS HTTP SERVER (UNIX)

The **GWHIS HTTP** server is a commercial server package distributed by Quadralay Inc. It supports the GET, HEAD, and POST methods, and is CGI-compliant. It also includes special components for data encryption, user authentication, and gateways to special Quadralay database software. Additional information is found at:

    http://www.quadralay.com/

HTTPS (WINDOWS NT)

HTTPS is the only server that runs under native Windows NT. HTTPS supports the GET, HEAD, and POST methods, and is fully CGI-compliant. The server does not support access control or user authentication. These features are expected to be added to a planned commercial version.

HTTPS comes with extensive installation instructions and has convenient window-driven configuration menus. Additional information about **HTTPS** can be found at:

    http://emwac.ed.ac.uk/html/internet_toolchest/https/contents.htm

The executable program, in zipped format, is found in the directory:

    ftp://emwac.ec.ac.uk/pub/emwac/

There are three **.zip** files for the three different Windows NT hardware architectures. These are *hsalpha.zip* (DEC ALPHA), *hsi386.zip* (Intel 80386 or higher), and *hsmips.zip* (MIPS R4000 or higher).

HTTPS was written at the European Microsoft Windows NT Academic Centre (EMWAC) of Edinburgh University.

JUNGLE (UNIX)

Jungle is an HTTP server written in tk and tcl. This server supports the GET and POST methods. Additional information is available at:

    http://catless.ncl.ac.uk/Programs/Jungle/

Jungle is under continuous development by the program author, Lindsay Marshall. **Jungle** will be of interest to those familiar with the tk/tcl languages who might be interested in participating in the development of a tk/tcl server. The author intends to implement all the features of the CERN HTTP server.

MACHTTP (MACINTOSH)

MacHTTP is the only Macintosh HTTP server. **MacHTTP** supports the GET and POST methods, and is CGI-compliant. Instead of invoking UNIX-shell scripts, MacHTTP can invoke and pass arguments to **AppleScript, MacPerl, HyperCard,** or any custom application written to support MacHTTP's custom suite of AppleEvents. Sample code is available.

MacHTTP also has an interface to **AppleSearch** that allows the server to present searchable indexes. This interface is provided by the companion application **AppleWebSearch**, which makes any **AppleSearch** source-accessible on the World Wide Web.

MacHTTP supports access control on a per-machine or per-domain basis by denying (or allowing) access to machines or groups of machines with specific IP addresses. **MacHTTP** also supports the Basic authentication scheme that allows access to be controlled document by document.

Additional information about **MacHTTP** is found at:

```
http://www.uth.tmc.edu/mac_info/machttp_info.html.
```

which includes pointers to useful **AppleScript** and other support programs. Another useful site is:

```
http://www.uwtc.washington.edu/Computing/Internet/MacintoshWebDevelop.html
```

The **MacHTTP** package is available from:

```
ftp://oac.hsc.uth.tmc.edu/public/mac/MacHTTP/machttp.sit.hqx
```

This executable will run on all Macintoshes, including those using the PowerPC chip. The archive includes hypertext documentation and installation instructions. **MacHTTP** was written (and is being continually improved) by Chuck Shotton.

NCSA HTTPD (UNIX)

The NCSA public-domain HTTP server implements the HEAD, GET, and POST methods, is fully CGI-compliant, and supports access control through encrypted user-authentication (although you must supply the authentication routines separately) and domain-name restrictions (restricting access to users connecting from registered Internet domains). The distribution package comes with several useful gateway programs, including a program for handling active images (*imagemap*).

The NCSA server also permits executable HTML documents, which allows you to create parsable HTML documents that *include* other documents on-the-fly. This is often called the *server-side include* feature. The server can also be configured to allow users to have executable CGI programs in their own home directories.

The NCSA server comes with online documentation and installation instructions. Printed documentation is also available. The NCSA server is easy to install and configure, and is an ideal choice if you don't require proxy server capabilities.

Additional information is found at:

```
http://hoohoo.ncsa.uiuc.edu/docs/Overview.html
http://hoohoo.ncsa.uiuc.edu/docs/FAQ.html
```

while a PostScript version, can be found at:

    http://hoohoo.ncsa.uiuc.edu/docs/postscript-docs/Overview.html

The current release of the source code is available at:

    ftp://ftp.ncsa.uiuc.edu/Web/httpd/Unix/ncsa_httpd/current/httpd_source.tar.Z

while executables for various platforms are found at:

    ftp://ftp.ncsa.uiuc.edu/Web/httpd/Unix/ncsa_httpd/current/

OS2HTTPD (OS/2)

OS2HTTPD is a port of the **NCSA HTTPD** Version 1.3 server to OS/2.
OS2HTTPD supports virtually all the features of NCSA HTTP Version
1.3, including the HEAD, GET, and POST methods; CGI gateway programs; file and directory access control; and server-side includes.

Additional information can be found at:

    ftp://ftp.netcom.com/pub/kfan/overview.html

and the executable is found in the same directory:

    ftp://ftp.netcom.com/pub/kfan/

The current release is found in the file *web2-101.zip*, but this release number will change with updates and improvements.

The author, Frankie Fan, has released **OS2HTTPD** to the public as a freeware package for noncommercial use only.

PLEXUS (UNIX)

Plexus is an HTTP server written in the perl language. It is a public-
domain server designed to be fast, extensible (for prototyping custom
servers with new protocols and interfaces), and easy to use. **Plexus** requires
perl 4.0 patchlevel 36 or later, and runs on almost any UNIX platform.
Plexus fully implements the HEAD and GET methods, and is CGI-compliant. **Plexus** has a limited facility for user authentication and access control.

Gateway programs are possible using the CGI specification and also using
the **Plexus** native gateway interface (which is around ten times faster than
the CGI, since the **Plexus** interface does not require an exec()). Native gateway programs are treated as additional perl modules to the server. An
explanation of how this works, along with example gateway programs, are
included with the online documentation.

Additional information about **Plexus** can be found at:

    http://www.bsdi.com/server/doc/plexus.html

The source code is available at:

    ftp://ftp.earth.com/plexus/3.0-beta/prerelease/Plexus-3.0m.tar.Z

Plexus was written by Tony Sanders, a member of the technical staff at
Berkeley Software Design, Inc.

SERWEB (WINDOWS 3.1)

SerWeb is a simple, easy-to-use HTTP server that supports the GET
method only. It does not support gateway programs or access control.
However, it is easy to install and run, and comes with source code (in C++)
for those interested in developing their own server software.

SerWeb can be found at:

    ftp://128.83.218.12/pub/windows/winsock/serweb03.zip

and a version for Windows NT is available at:

    ftp://emwac.ed.ac.uk/pub/serweb/serweb_i.zip

SerWeb was written by Gustavo Estrella.

WEB4HAM (WINDOWS 3.1)

Web4Ham is a Windows 3.1 server that supports the GET and HEAD
methods only. The most recent version (0.17) does have some support for
gateway programs, but the documentation is limited. However, the package
has been improving rapidly since its debut (March 1994).

Additional information is available at:

    ftp://ftp.informatik.uni-hamburg.de/pub/net/winsock/

The server software is found in the file *web4ham.zip*, while documentation
is found in *web4doc.zip*. **Web4Ham** was written by Gunter Hille.

WINHTTPD: NCSA HTTPD
FOR WINDOWS (WINDOWS 3.1)

WinHTTPD (also called **WHTTPD**) is a port of the NCSA UNIX server
to Windows. It retains most of the features of the UNIX version: It supports the GET, HEAD, and POST methods, and is fully CGI-compliant.

The distribution archive comes with several example gateway applications, including programs for handling active images. **WinHTTPD** also supports file and directory access control, and allows for sophisticated user-authentication—you have to provide the authentication programs separately.

Additional information about **WinHTTPD** can be found at:

```
http://www.alisa.com/win-httpd/
```

while the program archive is found at:

```
ftp://ftp.ncsa.uiuc.edu/Web/httpd/Unix/ncsa_httpd/contrib/winhttpd/
```

in the file *whtp13p1.zip* (Version 1.3 Prelease 1). Note that the revision numbers change rapidly. The NCSA FTP server is often busy: If you are having trouble accessing it, use **archie** to find another location.

COMING ATTRACTIONS

The following servers are announced packages that will be available in the near future.

BASIS WEBSERVER

The BASIS WEBserver, a product of Information Dimensions Inc., will be an HTTP server with added BASISplus capabilities. BASISplus is a relational database system proprietary to Information Dimensions. The BASIS WEBserver will be equipped with gateway programs to allow clients to interact with the BASICplus system and databases.

MDMA: MULTITHREADED DAEMON FOR MULTIMEDIA ACCESS

MDMA is a new HTTP server written explicitly for the Sun Solaris operating system. This server contains several exciting new features, including multithreading for speed and dynamic extensibility, to allow for dynamic inclusion of gateway-like functionality directly into the server.

MDMA is currently available as a Solaris executable and as source code, but is still a bug-filled alpha release. Additional information is available at:

```
http://elanor.oit.unc.edu/mdma.html
```

NETSCAPE NETSITE

Netscape Communications Corp. is designing new WWW servers that will have significant enhancements over current first-generation servers. The first product, **Netscape Netsite,** was introduced in late 1994, and is designed to be significantly faster than the NCSA server. The commercial version implements RSA Data Security, Inc. cryptographic technology to allow for secure commercial transactions over the Internet. For additional information, you can send e-mail (*info@mcom.com*), or look at:

```
http://mosaic.mcom.com/
```

SERVER SUPPORT PROGRAMS

Most server packages produce log files that record information about each server request. Server support programs are designed to read these log files and to convert the raw log file data into useful summaries of server usage. Not all HTTP servers use the same log format, so some of the support programs are specific to particular servers. The more recent CERN and NCSA servers (and the various ports of these packages) use a *common log file format*, and most newer support programs are designed around this standard.

GETSTATS

Getstats is a C-language program that can produce log summaries for the CERN and **NCSA HTTP** servers, **GN, Plexus, MacHTTP,** and UNIX **Gopher** servers. The **getstats** package is exceptionally well documented at:

```
http://www.eit.com/software/getstats/getstats.html
```

while the source code can be found at:

```
http://www.eit.com/cgi-bin/viewsource/software/getstats/getstats.c
```

There is an HTML **FORM** interface that allows users to access server statistics using **getstats**. Information about this interface is found at:

```
http://www.eit.com/software/getstats/getstats.html#form
```

Getstats was written by Kevin Hughes of Enterprise Information Technologies, Inc.

GWSTAT

Gwstat is a UNIX package of programs and scripts that can convert HTML output from the program **wwwstat** into GIF format graphs of server statistics. These can be inserted inline in HTML documents. **Gwstat** does not do all this itself, and requires the packages **Xmgr** (a data plotting package), **ImageMagick** (an image format conversion package), and **ghostscript** (a PostScript interpreter).

Additional information on **gwstat** can be found at:

```
http://dis.cs.umass.edu/stats/gwstat.html
```

This includes general information about **gwstat,** as well as directions for finding the applications **xmgr, ImageMagick,** and **ghostscript. Gwstat** itself can be found at:

```
ftp://dis.cs.umass.edu/pub/gwstat.tar.gz
```

Gwstat was written by Qiegang Long.

WEBSTAT

Webstat can read common format log files (NCSA HTTP Version 1.2 (or later) and the CERN server), and return statistical information about server usage. The main features of **webstat** are:

- Generation of usage report aggregated per service and requesting domain
- Generation of usage report per connecting country
- Generation of usage report per document
- Generation of reports on usage per year, month, week, or day
- Automatic generation of summaries as HTML documents

Additional information about **webstat** can be found at:

```
http://www.pegasus.esprit.ec.org/people/sijben/statistics/advertisment.html
```

while the program itself (written in **python**) is available at:

```
ftp://ftp.pegasus.esprit.ec.org/pub/misc/webstat.tar.gz
```

You will also need the **python** program by Guido van Rossum. This is found at:

```
http://www.cwi.nl/ftp/python/index.html
```

Webstat was written by Paul Sijben of the University of Twente.

WUSAGE

Wusage is a C program that generates simple weekly-usage reports in the form of HTML documents, including inline image graphs displaying server usage and the distribution of accesses by continent. A particularly nice feature is the ability to exclude irrelevant document retrievals (of inline images, from local machines, etc.) from the analysis. **Wusage** is able to read log files in the new, common log format, as well as older log files produced by the NCSA Version 1.1 server.

Additional information about **wusage** can be found at the **wusage** home page:

```
http://siva.cshl.org/wusage.html
```

The source code for **wusage** can be found at:

```
ftp://isis.cshl.org/pub/wusage/
```

The current release is Version 3.2, found in the file *wusage3.2.tar.Z*.

Wusage was written by Thomas Boutell. **Wusage** 3.2 is copyrighted by the Quest Protein Database Center, Cold Spring Harbor Labs.

WWWSTAT

Wwwstat is a **perl** program that can read common log file formats (NCSA Version 1.2 or newer, CERN HTTP servers, and others) and produce a log summary file as an HTML document suitable for publishing on your server. The package is available at:

```
ftp://liege.ics.uci.edu/pub/arcadia/wwwstat/wwwstat-1.01.tar.Z
http://www.ics.uci.edu/WebSoft/wwwstat/wwwstat-1.01.tar.gz
http://www.ics.uci.edu/WebSoft/wwwstat/wwwstat-1.01.tar.Z
```

The distribution consists of several components, including installation instructions. It also contains the perl program **oldwwwstat**, which can be used to analyze log files produced by the NCSA Version 1.1 server.

Wwwstat was written by Roy Fielding of the University of California at Irvine.

CHAPTER

9

REAL-WORLD

EXAMPLES

Chapter 9 is a change from the rest of the book. This chapter contains some examples of World Wide Web sites that illustrate the types of things that can be accomplished on the Web, and that also illustrate aspects of the document design process. These examples cover areas ranging from scientific research to comic strips. I asked the authors of these collections to write a brief description of their site and of the design issues they found important in developing these materials. I encourage you to read these brief descriptions and then to visit their sites—I can guarantee that you will find the exercise enjoyable and educational.

ELECTRONIC E-PRINT SERVERS

`http://xxx.lanl.gov/`

Paul Ginsparg
Los Alamos National Laboratories
`http://xxx.lanl.gov/pg.html`

The Los Alamos National Laboratory *e-print* server is an automated archive for electronic communication of research information. In many fields of physics, e-print servers have become the primary means of communicating ongoing research work, since they are inexpensive, democratic (anyone with Internet access can access the work), and fast. There are currently eight different physics e-print databases, archiving several tens of thousands of electronic articles. These articles are all written in TeX or LaTeX, which have become the text formatting languages of choice in the physics community.

E-print articles are submitted by electronic mail to an archive site, using a special electronic letter format containing both the article itself and an abstract. An automatic program running at the archive site (rather like a LISTSERV program) automatically unpacks the letter and archives the abstract and the full article, and adds both to a searchable database.

Originally, this archive was accessible only by e-mail so that accessing the archive required sending an e-mail letter containing search and command strings (such as "find all papers by Jones written this year"). The results of the search were then mailed back to the person who sent the request. This access method still works, but has been largely supplanted by a more efficient World Wide Web search interface. Submission of articles, however, still must be done by electronic mail.

Figure 9.1 shows the home page for the Los Alamos e-print server. Note that this allows for both FORM and non-FORM access to the database. When the project started, the FORM element didn't exist. While everyone should, in principle, now have access to a FORM-compliant client, the lower-end clients are frequently painful to use (the more sophisticated the use of a graphical interface, the harder it is to duplicate in a terminal mode). Therefore, it is deliberate that everything possible from the FORM page is also possible via ordinary pages. Note that the button that leads to the FORM interface is itself a FORM, so it functions only for clients that understand FORMs.

The home page design is designed to put near the top the things people access most frequently so that you need only to scroll down for secondary

▮▮▮▮▮▮ **Figure 9.1** The home page for the Los Alamos e-print server.

information. Since this was an overlay to a preexisting database, already divided into separate *archives* corresponding to different subfields of physics, it was natural to branch from the home page to a separate page for each of the archives. On the other hand, it was important to avoid the common error of slavishly reproducing exactly the functionality familiar from the previous interface.

In particular, I wanted the *new* link to daily abstract listings to be immediately accessible in order to convey the ease with which these listings could be obtained, and to eventually help people move away from the less efficient e-mail interface.

The home page is one of the few static HTML documents in the entire interface—the rest of the pages are generated by CGI scripts, and all the HTML is added dynamically at request time to the preexisting plain text files used by the e-mail interface. This has two advantages: Only a single set of files has to be maintained for both formats; and any change in the interface (e.g., a new link on an abstract page) can be made globally by changing a single script. In the next revision, even this front page will be generated by a gateway to make it easier to maintain and update.

The skull icon was originally put in as a joke during testing (it was grabbed from the *kill process* button on the processes panel from NextStep—a 2-bit monochrome image, colorized using **xv**). It was originally there to evoke the skull that appears together with *xxx* on bottles of poison, but later came to symbolize the death-defying survival of the system in the absence of funding support.

Figure 9.2 shows a typical FORM page. The FORM page is generated by a script that knows where you came from (the default selectors are *hep-th* from the front page, but if you come from the *cond-mat* page, they would be *cond-mat*). This page contains four different archive selectors in the four different FORMs. It is unfortunate that I had to use separate archive selectors, due to the limitations of the original NCSA FORMs implementation—a FORM could have only a single submit button, so different actions from different FORM submit buttons were not possible. I chose not to use horizontal line <hr> elements between the separate **FORMs**, since that stretched things out vertically and sometimes required users to scroll to see the full **FORM**.

Mosaic for X-Windows Version 2.5 does allow multiple submit buttons supporting different actions from within a single **FORM,** but it will be some time before all browsers upgrade to this feature.

The basic methods of obtaining information from the e-mail interface—find, list, get, and help—are also the basic functionalities in the FORM interface, except that *get* is restricted to *get abstract*. This allows the user to read the abstract and then decide if he or she wants to download the full article, and ensures that large file downloads are not made inadvertently.

The Find and Listings commands use the same output as the e-mail interface, except that the document is piped through **sed** (the UNIX stream editor) to automatically reformat the text, and to pattern-match appearances of the form "arch-ive/9401001" and convert them to hypertext anchors in the displayed document. The result of a Find search is shown in Figure 9.3, searched from the past year's articles containing the name "graham."

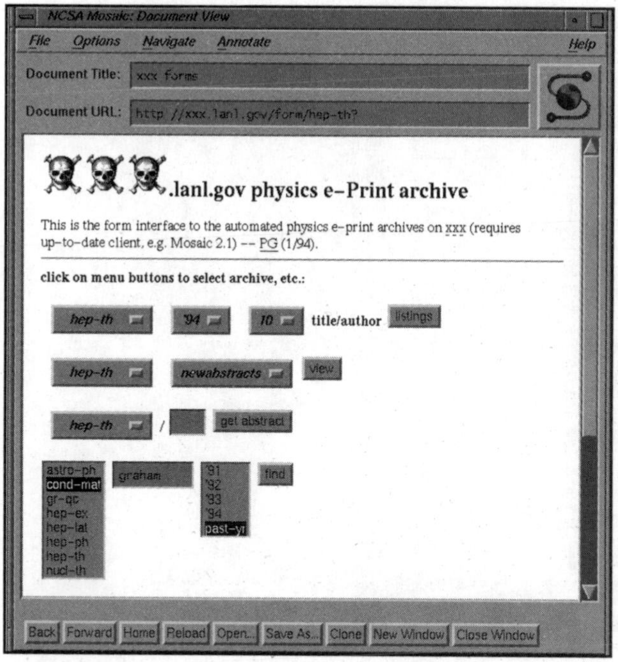

Figure 9.2 The HTML **FORM** database interface.

Clicking on the *abs* anchor downloads the article abstract. This is shown in Figure 9.4

The abs script just pipes the conventional e-mail abstract (in this case, ***cond-mat/papers/9404/9404016.abs***) through **sed** to reformat the document, maintaining the basic feel of the plain text abstract but changing the title to a header, and, of course, adding the hypertext link to the source.

The document source interface is similar to the e-mail interface, but takes advantage of HTTP's ability to transmit binary data files. Thus, the returned articles are sent in compressed formats when possible, significantly reducing the sizes of the transmitted data—most clients read the HTTP content-encoding MIME header and automatically decompress the data upon receipt. In contrast, the e-mail interface requires decompressed and specially coded data to ensure safe communication of the document.

One overall design choice was to keep the URL names as simple and logical as possible, using the NCSA HTTP ScriptAlias feature. For example, articles,

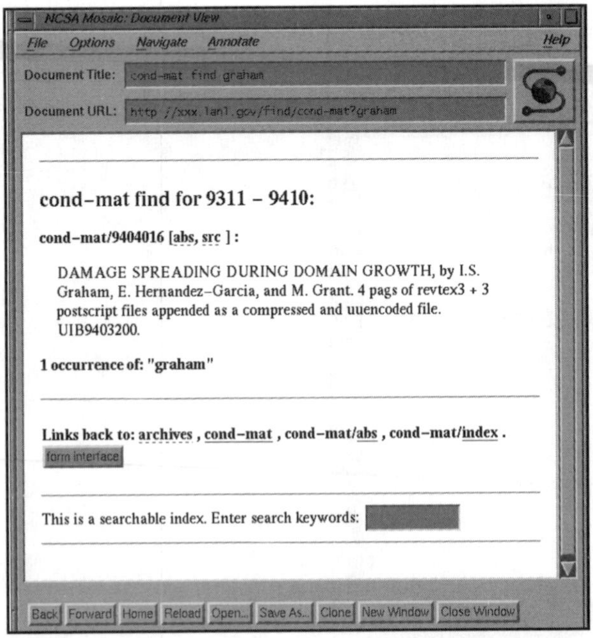

■■■■■■■■ **Figure 9.3** Result of searching with the bottom form from Figure 9.2 for the name "graham."

abstracts, and gateway programs are referenced via directory and filenames, such as */list/hep-th/9401*, */abs/hep-th/9401001*, */find/hep-th?*, */e-print/hep-th/9401001*, and so on. Since the entire package is generated by scripts, the leading field is *aliased* to the appropriate script, which parses the rest of the URL to determine archive and other information on which to operate.

ONCOLINK

http://cancer.med.upenn.edu:/

E. Loren Buhle, Jr., Ph.D.
University of Pennsylvania School of Medicine
P.O. Box 7806, Philadelphia, PA 19101
(E-mail: *BUHLE@XRT.UPENN.EDU*)
Phone: 215-662-3084
Fax: 215-349-5978

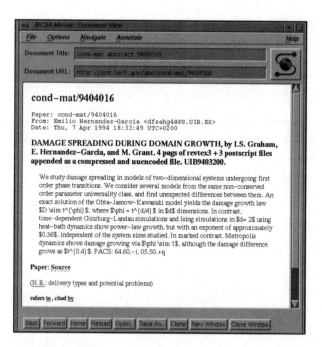

Figure 9.4 Abstract for the article found in Figure 9.3.

INTRODUCTION

OncoLink was launched on the Internet on March 7, 1994 to provide comprehensive and timely information regarding cancer to patients, physicians, health care workers, and other interested parties via either Gopher or World Wide Web clients. The type of information on this server ranges from methods of diagnosis and treatment of cancer, to the many psychosocial elements a patient and his/her family may experience throughout the cancer experience.

The material on OncoLink must be traversed with ease, regardless of topic or educational background of the user. OncoLink users range from those with no prior knowledge of biology to practicing clinical oncologists. The material on OncoLink must be both comprehensive and easy to navigate. Thus, many of the documents have extensive hypertext links to allow inexperienced users to learn as they go, while not encumbering the more experienced users. Some of the material on OncoLink is explicit, such as the stereotactic radiosurgical approach to brain tumors. Other material deals with more amorphous issues, such as quality of life, and death and dying.

THE ONCOLINK IMPLEMENTATION

The World Wide Web server **GN** (discussed in Chapter 8) was implemented
on a DEC 3000-800 computer running the OSF/1 operating system. The GN
server allows rapid dissemination of both hypertext and plain text information to both World Wide Web and Gopher clients, respectively. The GN
server software was selected on the basis of its simplicity of design; effi-
ciency of serving documents to both the World Wide Web and Gopher
clients; and the security it afforded the server. The GN server software was
felt to be the most secure WWW server in that the resources served to the
client must be defined within the server in a predetermined menu file. While
this menu file is cached to provide speedy service, no externally suggested
documents or actions are supported if they are not explicitly stated in this
menu. This arrangement tightly controls the behavior of the WWW server
and appears to preserve the integrity of the computer and its resources. The
GN software is quite portable, making the transfer of OncoLink to an HP
9000/735 computer, running HPUX for purposes of experimental mirroring,
a trivial exercise.

The OncoLink home page (Figures 9.5 and 9.6) is accessed by Wide World
Web clients at the URL:

```
http://cancer.med.upenn.edu/
```

It can also be accessed from a Gopher client via the command:

```
gopher cancer.med.upenn.edu 80
```

since the server runs on port 80 rather than the usual default port of 70.

The actual name `cancer.med.upenn.edu` is an alias for an actual numerical Internet (IP) address of a machine on the Internet. Should OncoLink
move to another machine, the name `cancer.med.upenn.edu` would
remain the same, and the alias would be changed in the Internet nameserver
tables to reflect the transition.

To track usage patterns, GN generates a detailed log of all access transactions. This log is a very important and powerful aspect of information publishing via the Internet, providing valuable feedback to OncoLink's main-
tainer. In addition to providing an insight to OncoLink's most popular

resources, the time between hypertext key requests and the path between the selection of one key and the next hypertext key gives an insight to the information sought; the portions of the document read; and the time the requester spent on each section of the document. Studying this log also revealed how many requests were from graphical WWW clients, text-based hypertext-capable WWW clients, and Gopher clients.

USE OF ONCOLINK

OncoLink was released on the Internet as a WWW and Gopher server on the evening of March 7, 1994. In the first eight months of operation, OncoLink has logged a half million transactions from more than 80 countries throughout the world. Approximately 80 percent of these accesses were from WWW clients. OncoLink access grows on an average of 10 percent per month, though a growth of 30 percent has occasionally been observed. The average weekday access rate is generally three times heavier than weekend use. Within a given day, OncoLink is accessed most heavily between 8 A.M. and 11 P.M. EST, though use between 1 and 6 A.M. EST is typically heaviest from Australia, New Zealand, and Japan, reflecting their working hours.

From the Internet domain names, we have determined the scope of OncoLink users to be international, with accesses from essentially all settled continents, even if English is not the primary language of the country (e.g., Japan, Germany, Poland, Israel, Brazil, etc.). OncoLink has been advertised only in the electronic environment, with minimal conventional print-media announcements.

```
<HTML>
<HEAD>
<TITLE>Welcome to OncoLink</TITLE>
<LINK REV="MADE" HREF="mailto:buhle@xrt.upenn.edu">
</HEAD>
<BODY>
<H2>Welcome to OncoLink</H2>
<H1><img alt="Oncolink logo" src="/I/docs/images/oncolnk2.gif">
<A HREF="/s/sounds/welcome.au">
<img alt="" src="/I/docs/images/www/sound.xbm"></A></H1>
```

```
<p>
<H2>The University of Pennsylvania Multimedia Oncology Resource</H2>
<HR>
<A HREF="/0h/stuff/upmc">
<img alt="Info about Penn" src="/I/docs/images/penn1.gif"></A>
<A HREF="/I/docs/images/child.gif">
<img alt="Children's artwork" src="/I/docs/images/child_sm.gif"></A>
This artwork was donated by a pediatric cancer patient and <b>will change
</b>at frequent intervals!
<i>(Click here to see the gallery of children's artwork)</i>
<A HREF="/0h/docs/images/child/gallery1">
<i>in Part 1</I></A> or <A HREF="/0h/docs/images/child/gallery2"><i>Part
2</i></A><p>
<HR>
<img src="/I/docs/images/light_bulb.gif">
<A HREF="/1s/stuff/latest_stuff">
What's <i>NEW </i> on OncoLink?</A><p>
<img src="/I/docs/images/question.gif">
<A HREF="/7wc/stuff/search_wais/OncoLink.inv">
<b>WAIS Search</b> of OncoLink</A> or a <A
HREF="/7g/stuff/search_dir1"><b>single-word SEARCH</b></A> of OncoLink.<p>
<img alt="" src="/I/docs/images/news1.gif">
<A HREF="/1s/buhle/cancer_news">
CANCER news, warnings, etc.</A>
<P>
<HR><img alt="" src="/I/docs/images/menat.gif">
<i>This cancer information resource is under continuous development.
OncoLink is best used with a World-Wide Web client (e.g. Mosaic, lynx,
etc.), but can also be reached via a gopher server, using
port 80.</i><BR><b>October has been designated as Breast Cancer
Month in the United States of America and Canada.</b><p>
<HR>
.
.

.
<b>OncoLink</b> was awarded the International
<b>Best of the Web '94
Award</b> for <b>Best Professional Service</b>. To see the other award
winners, please
<A HREF="http://wings.buffalo.edu/contest/awards/index.html">click
here</A>.
 Thank you for your support and we look forward
to making this resource even more valuable!
</BODY>
</HTML>
```

■■■■■■ **Figure 9.5** HTML document of OncoLink home page (this file has been truncated to save space).

Gopher access could be discerned by the selection of the non-HTML files. In the early days of OncoLink, the cancer resources served by Gopher and WWW were essentially identical, the Gopher resources lacking only the multi-

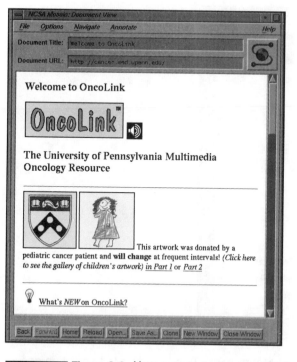

Figure 9.6 Home page to the OncoLink resource site.

media and the hypertext. As OncoLink developed, the Gopher menus were extended to allow access to contents formerly available only within the hypertext keys of HTML documents. Documents such as the *Pediatric Oncology Case of the Month* progressed in a more nonlinear direction, requiring access to hypertext keys to access the treatment given. While still represented in the classical linear or sequential fashion of printed literature (i.e., the entire document is laid out in a chronological sequence), the hypertext documents such as the *Case of the Month* remains the most popularly requested document. An example of a *Case of the Month* is shown in Figure 9.7.

A critical element to disseminating information on the Internet is to listen to the user and generate a flexible and intuitive interface that accommodates the user's needs. OncoLink began with discrete menus defining specialties within the practice of oncology (cancer) treatment. Thus, there were menus pertaining to Pediatric Oncology and Gynecologic Oncology, as well as Medical Oncology, Surgical Oncology, and Radiation Oncology. Our users

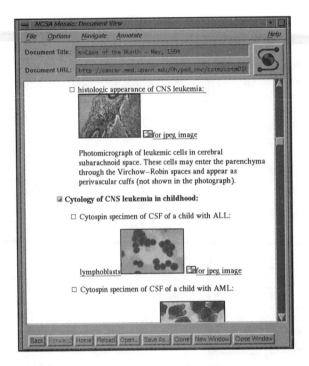

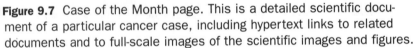

Figure 9.7 Case of the Month page. This is a detailed scientific document of a particular cancer case, including hypertext links to related documents and to full-scale images of the scientific images and figures.

quickly requested a disease-oriented selection of menus, as a breast cancer patient would not necessarily know which menu item to select first. We rapidly discovered that a certain class of OncoLink users rarely used the menus at all, preferring to move from document to document via the hypertext links, reading very small portions of the documents they accessed. When we looked at what portions of the documents the users read, we realized there was a tight focus on information sought. Thus, some users browsed the many items on OncoLink, while others focused their attention very sharply for certain pieces of information.

World Wide Web documents that used icons of images for hypertext keys were more apt to be selected than merely hypertext documents. Using several pediatric oncology *Case of the Month* presentations, where the user is led through the initial presentation of the patient to the patient's treatment, we recorded the sequence of hypertext selections as a given user (tracked by following an IP address in a contiguous block of time). While physicians usually selected the hypertext keys in the order of their presentation, the completeness of the selection was higher when the hypertext anchors were miniaturized icons of the full-size figure. In documents targeting patients, iconic hypertext keys for procedures were often selected over text-based hypertext keys.

OncoLink must also allow inexperienced users, who are not exactly sure what their questions are, to make use of the many navigational aids to find what they are looking for in the OncoLink resources. One of the design criteria behind OncoLink is to allow users to find something relevant to their queries within five minutes of their first interaction with OncoLink. By using the search mode (Figure 9.8), a user can rapidly examine pertinent articles contained anywhere on OncoLink. When OncoLink numbered just a few hundred documents, an internal searching function (using a fast *grep*) was used. While fast, this search procedure returned an unweighted list of OncoLink documents containing a case-insensitive match. This was useful for examining potential hypertext links from the perspective of generating new hypertext links, but was hardly useful for users unfamiliar with the contents of OncoLink. When OncoLink grew to over 1,500 documents, this type of search became quite slow.

OncoLink now employs WAIS and a similar *glimpse* search to give the user a prioritized list of likely resources. The interface to these tools is shown in Figure 9.8, while the results of a typical search (for *Tamoxifen* and *breast*) is shown in Figure 9.9. Soundex and phonix algorithms were employed to help users who could not spell the medical terminology. In the case of exact matches, if users could not spell the search word (e.g., rhabdomyosarcoma), they had great difficulty finding relevant material. The search facility also allows Boolean query syntax (e.g., red and green, not blue), as well as partial search requests (hum* locks the search on any word starting with hum).

The ability to use search tools was codified into previously *static* links to provide *dynamic* links. An example of a simple dynamic link would be to

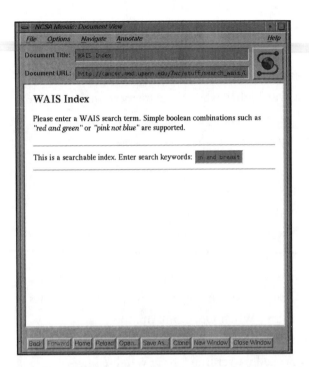

Figure 9.8 OncoLink WAIS search page. The documents at OncoLink are indexed by a WAIS database. These can be searched to find useful documents. In this case, the search is for *"Tamoxifen"* and *"breast."*

request "All the recent papers on breast cancer" from the National Institute of Cancer. The result of this hypertext selected query would be different from month to month. A more complicated example is the selection of the hypertext link *taxol*. OncoLink has dozens of different articles discussing taxol. Is the user interested in the isolation of taxol from the Yew tree; the patient side effects of taxol; clinical protocols using taxol; the molecular action of taxol; or the organic synthesis of taxol? A static link to only the side effects of taxol addresses only some of the issues. If the server tracks the type of documents requested on OncoLink, the server may be able to steer patient-oriented articles to the patient, clinical articles to the oncologist, and so on.

OncoLink strives to present *one-stop shopping* for people involved with cancer. Clearly, all the knowledge of cancer will never be stored on OncoLink. Much of the information on cancer will be shared elsewhere on the Internet.

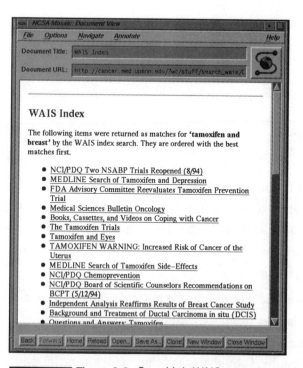

Figure 9.9 OncoLink WAIS search results. The documents listed contain information related to *"Tamoxifen"* and *"breast."* Clicking on the highlighted text downloads the document for viewing. This list is created by a gateway program that sorts the search results and inserts the hypertext links.

The ability to reproducibly find this information, as well as monitor the issues of concern of OncoLink's users and the Internet cancer population, is an area for future work using active and passive computer agents. Active agents, also called KnowBots and World Wide Web Worms (WWWW), are useful for indexing the contents of other information services on the Internet. Passive agents, also called sentries, can monitor the USENET newsgroups, Internet LISTSERVers, and other forums of electronic cancer information (e.g., CompuServe's CANCER forum).

OncoLink is developing interactive sessions much like the multithreaded bulletin board services found on CompuServe. The developers see their goal as an interactive television service.

VIEWS OF THE SOLAR SYSTEM

http://www.c3.lanl.gov/~cjhamil/SolarSystem/homepage.html

Calvin J. Hamilton
Los Alamos National Laboratory
Mail Stop 3265
Los Alamos, New Mexico 87545

BACKGROUND

While browsing the Internet during the fall of 1993, I ran across some images of planets in our solar system, which sparked in me a latent interest in astronomy. I subscribed to *sci.astro* and related astronomy USENET newsgroups and, after a short time, found the major Internet repositories of deep space and solar system images.

I found many nice images, but the selection was not very complete. In particular, there were very few images of Pluto, Uranus, Mercury, and of the satellites of the planets. Some of the images were well done; others were only sloppy scans of photographs. I could also tell that many of the images had been subsampled or reduced in size from the original data that was available.

It is understandable why larger images were not provided on the Internet. Large images require a lot of disk space, and individuals who want to download them to their personal computers may not have the ability to handle or view such large files. However, I considered the selection and resolution of images unacceptable. I had seen very high-quality photographs in books about astronomy and I wanted those images, in high-quality formats, to be available to the public via the Internet.

I located the raw image data taken by the Voyager and Viking spacecraft at the anonymous FTP site *explorer.arc.nasa.gov*, but, without a lot of image processing, these images displayed poorly on a computer. Using my image-processing background, I began filtering and enhancing the raw data and produced some high-resolution image mosaics and image files. When I created inline images, I tried to make them display well on 8-bit color computer monitors (recall that an 8-bit monitor can display only 256 different colors at the same time).

At about this same time, I was introduced to NCSA **Mosaic** and the World Wide Web. I could see that this would be an ideal way to make my images available to the public. Although I did not know it, this was the beginning of Views of the Solar System (Figure 9.10). I started by making an HTML document for each planet, with links to my images and the Jet Propulsion Laboratory/NASA (JPL/NASA) images. Then, I decided that it would be nice to have some statistical information about each planet. I went to the library, located some books on astronomy, and added a few selected statistics to each of the planetary pages. By this time, I had become fascinated with the solar system and with astronomy. Every couple of weeks, I checked out a stack of astronomy-related books. From these books, I got the idea of including a short description for each of the planets. I also found that there was a lot of information from JPL/NASA available on the Internet, which I also incorporated into the tour.

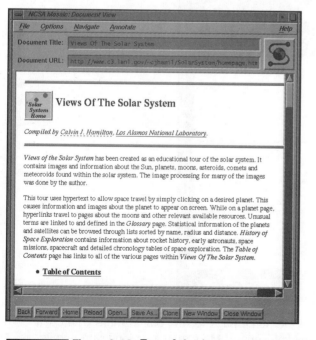

▪▪▪▪▪ **Figure 9.10** Top of the home page for Views of the Solar System.

As time went on, I decided to add separate WWW pages for each planetary satellite for which I had an image. In my free time, I would process new images and add them to my pages. Often, I would look through the astronomy books I had checked out from the library and, when I found an image I liked, I would locate the raw Voyager/Viking data and process it to give computer images of quality comparable to those found in the book (Figure 9.11). I subsequently added sections on asteroids, comets, and the history of space exploration.

At the present time, Views of the Solar System has the greatest variety of planetary images available on the Internet. It is being used by several schools in New Mexico and elsewhere. There is a German publisher writing a book on the Internet who is publishing a CD-ROM with examples of WWW pages. This project will include the entire tour on the CD-ROM. In addition, the University of Southwestern Louisiana is using information from the tour for a NASA contract to develop multimedia courseware for high-school students.

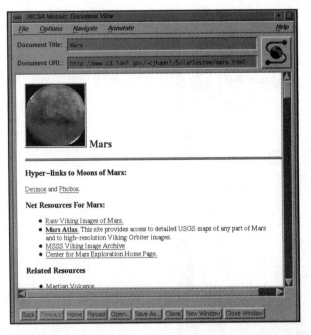

Figure 9.11 Top of the home page for the planet Mars. The document contains several icons of Mars images, along with details about the martian surface, atmosphere, and so on.

HTML ISSUES

When I started writing HTML pages, my biggest obstacle was finding proper documentation. I eventually found that the best way to learn the HTML syntax was to look at examples on the Internet. One problem I found was that my **Mosaic** browser overlooked certain errors that other browsers did not. I found out about these problems only when someone on the Internet was kind enough to point them out.

Since Views of the Solar System uses a lot of inline images, I found that certain pages used up all of the available colors on my 8-bit color monitor and that, as a result, some of the images didn't look good at all. I resolved this problem by using image color compression software developed at Los Alamos National Laboratories. Whenever I found an HTML page that used too many colors, I compressed the colors in the images so that they used far fewer colors, typically 128. This greatly improved the appearance of the pages when displaying on 8-bit color monitors.

Another important issue was the size of the inline images. On my home page, I used 68×68-pixel images, and, on my other pages, I chose a maximum width and height of 150 pixels. This tends to be a bit larger than many sites on the Internet. The advantage of the larger inline image is that the details are much clearer. The disadvantage is that it takes longer to transfer these large images across the Internet. A 150×150-pixel GIF image is approximately 12,000 bytes, whereas a 68×68-pixel image is only about 2,700 bytes.

I also had to decide what types of image files and formats to use when transferring noninlined images across the Internet. Should a small representative image be returned, or the best image available? I chose the latter option. In certain cases, I have very large mosaics, in which case, I provide both a small and a large version of the same image (Figure 9.12). I also avoid lossy compression methods, such as JPEG, unless I receive the raw image in that format. The JPEG lossy image-compression technique tends to leave the image with unsightly blocks scattered throughout the image. Once lossy compression is used, further image processing or enhancement is useless. I

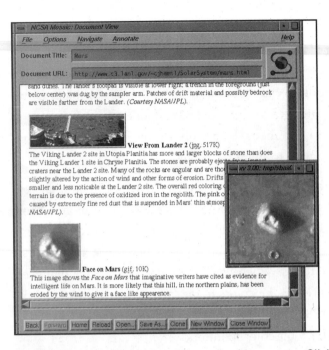

The following text appears within the browser window image:

NCSA Mosaic: Document View

File   Options   Navigate   Annotate   Help

Document Title: Mars

Document URL: http://www.c3.lanl.gov/~cjhamil/SolarSystem/mars.html

sand dunes. The lander's footpad is visible at lower right; a trench in the foreground (just below center) was dug by the sampler arm. Patches of drift material and possibly bedrock are visible farther from the Lander. (*Courtesy NASA/JPL*).

View From Lander 2 (jpg, 517K)

The Viking Lander 2 site in Utopia Planitia has more and larger blocks of stone than does the Viking Lander 1 site in Chryse Planitia. The stones are probably ejected from impact craters near the Lander 2 site. Many of the rocks are angular and are thought slightly altered by the action of wind and other forms of erosion. Drifts smaller and less noticable at the Lander 2 site. The overall red coloring terrain is due to the presence of oxidized iron in the regolith. The pink c caused by extremely fine red dust that is suspended in Mars' thin atmosp *NASA/JPL*).

Face on Mars (gif, 10K)

This image shows the *Face on Mars* that imaginative writers have cited as evidence for intelligent life on Mars. It is more likely that this hill, in the northern plains, has been eroded by the wind to give it a face like appearence.

Back   Forward   Home   Reload   Open...   Save As...   Clone   New Window   Close Window

Figure 9.12 Detail from the Mars page. Clicking on the Face of Mars downloads the larger GIF image of the same feature.

save all of my images in GIF format if I need 8 bits of color, or in TIFF format if I need 24 bits.

Until recently, I used the HTML <HR> tag for separator bars dividing document sections. I now use a three-dimensional-looking bar (a GIF image) as a separator. This bar uses three colors and takes up 579 bytes. I tried separators with a rainbow appearance but they required too many colors: I needed these colors for the actual images instead.

I organized Views of the Solar System somewhat like a book. The home page is like an introduction, with links to the major portions of the tour. The home page also contains links to educational and other space-related resources. Organizationally, the home page links to a cover page; a Table of Contents; a solar system introduction; each planet in our solar system; asteroids; comets; meteoroids; and the history of space exploration. The planet pages have further links to each of their satellites and to other related

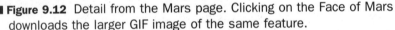

resources. Many of the terms used in Views of the Solar System are linked to an extensive glossary page. There is also a section on people who have made a contribution to the understanding of the world and universe we live in.

SUMMARY

I am not an astronomy professional but, during the last year, I have read many books and have learned much about our solar system. Perhaps this demonstrates that you don't have to be an expert in a particular field to make a significant contribution. If time and money permit, I would enjoy making continual improvements to this tour. Views of the Solar System has been an evolving and somewhat experimental project that I hope will continue to be educational and beneficial for others.

NETBOY—CHOICE OF AN ONLINE GENERATION

http://www.interaccess.com/netboy.html

Stafford Huyler

E-mail: *netboy@interaccess.com*

I had been looking for a way to publish a comic years before I came into contact with the Web. I spent all my time in school drawing cars and spaceships, while my teachers sneered that my work wasn't *real art*. I knew that the standard was to get a little strip going in a free edition of some college rag, and nurture it for years while praying that it would be noticed. This wasn't the way for me; it was just not dynamic enough.

In my job as the marketing director for InterAccess, a Chicago-based Internet provider, I thought a lot about the possibilities of self-publishing on the Net. There was a tremendously intelligent audience out there, hungry for good entertainment. I knew that I should approach them. At the time, however, there was no way to distribute a comic effectively.

When I discovered the Web, I realized that it was a very promising forum. I felt that it was the up-and-coming interface with the Net—yet, there was so little of interest on it! I wanted to read a comic that was cool enough to joke about the standard knowledge that all onliners have. It didn't exist, so I decided to create it. NetBoy is the first Internet-topical comic.

Between my own experiences online and behind the scenes at InterAccess, I observed a lot of funny stuff. I also had the resources to produce a comic—a scanner, technical help, and a company willing to give my comic a chance. If I were producing this alone, it could get quite expensive because of the amount of traffic moving through the site. However, I have worked out a reciprocal arrangement with InterAccess. They feel that the publicity that they get from NetBoy's success is a good reward for assisting me in getting the comic out.

I played with different styles and felt that a black-and-white stick figure column would serve several purposes. It would play with the fact that the delivery medium was colorful. It would be easy to download. It would be simple for me to draw, so I could keep my day job. It seemed pleasingly goofy to me that my technological heroes were mere stick figures. Finally, the medium meant that I could choose any size and format.

I draw the comic by hand, as it gives the best control. Once it is scanned in, all the touch-ups and lettering are done in Photoshop with a custom font. For file formats, I chose GIF over JPEG because of the inline capability. Format is very important; you must plan your readers' traffic well in advance.

I created a beta in May 1994 to get a feel for my capabilities and audience. I experimented for a couple of months, and the current version of NetBoy debuted on July 1, 1994. The home page for NetBoy is shown in Figure 9.13.

The goal of NetBoy is really to create a hip place to be online. There is the comic, but there are also back issues, feedback, N-Mart, contests, and links to other comic pages (Figure 9.14). It's paying off; NetBoy has been growing with the Web. In just the first three months, readership went from 500 per month to over 90,000. Over a million people have read it now, and the audience is growing by 20 percent a month. This is thanks to enthusiastic word of mouth, comics being tacked up in computer labs, links from many pages, and media coverage.

Of course, I do all this for free, but I have been thinking of ways to make money from my project. For a time, I flirted with the idea of offering a paid

Figure 9.13 Home page for NetBoy. Clicking on Today's Comic down-loaded the displayed GIF image; this image is new every day.

daily subscription to NetBoy via e-mail as a MIME-encoded document, but I realized that this move would greatly restrict my readership (even though I had planned to keep the large Saturday editions free). I am now taking the Microsoft approach—making NetBoy the standard against which all others are judged (and copied). I know that I can build up a loyal readership by giving them a strong product for free.

With this readership growing every day, I feel the future is in merchandising. Because so many people are reading NetBoy, there is a growing market for NetBoy books, mugs, and so on. I have already done a good business selling NetBoy t-shirts.

My advice to anyone else starting out would be to learn good HTML and provide a solid service. If you do a weekly or daily, keep it up religiously. If

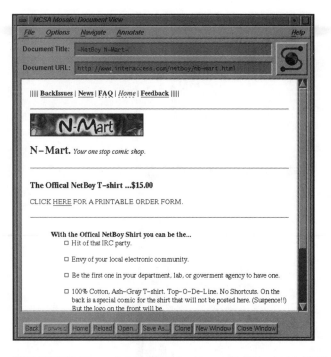

the competition is 100-percent reliable in their new pages, and you're not, then you may lose.

With strong perl programming skills, you can create forms to monitor reader feedback, which is most helpful. You can see what's working and what's not—everything from a certain vein of humor to the layout of the page.

Another pointer is that you should give your feature a consistent name each day it is released. For example, I call each new comic "today-netboy.gif." This way, readers can link the GIF image into their home page. People want their reading delivered with a minimum of fuss.

The Web is the most effective publishing medium that I have ever encountered. I am very pleased with it, and if I had to do it again, I would only have started sooner.

SAN FRANCISCO RESERVATIONS' WORLD WIDE WEB PAGE

`http://www.hotelres.com/`

Eric J. Fraser
Programmer/Analyst
University of California
Computer Science Division
e-mail: *fraser@CS.Berkeley.EDU*

INTRODUCTION

San Francisco Reservations (SFR) is a central hotel reservations agency serving the San Francisco Bay area. SFR agents reserve hotel rooms at volume discount rates, and monitor seasonal specials and promotions, passing on the savings to the public. Before the WWW page was set up, business was handled by a toll-free telephone number and by fax. While much of the business infrastructure was done on computers (a UNIX network), there was no previous need for an Internet connection.

In June of 1994, at an informal dinner party, a discussion began on ways to improve the computing environment at SFR. On that day's front page of the Business section of *The New York Times*, there was an article of a florist that had set up a WWW page:

```
http://florist.com:1080/flowers/bf1006.html
```

We decided that the Net had definitely "gone commercial" and that if a florist shop could make it on the Internet, then surely SFR should have a place as well.

In the following month, the details were worked out on how much it would cost to get an Internet connection, on which local service provider to use, whether to get a dedicated SLIP-type connection or to get a dedicated digital line, and what additional hardware might be needed. After much boring deliberation, it was decided that SFR would get a dedicated frame-relay (56kbps) connection to a small co-op style Internet provider, and to use one of the already owned 486 machines running **linux**.

SFR's WWW server was up and operational in the beginning of September 1994. Even before we announced the page to the relevant newsgroups, users were accessing the documents. As it went, first someone logged in from Stanford, then from Japan, and then from Australia, all within an hour. It was very exciting to see that quick a response. Since that day, the number of people accessing the page has grown quite rapidly. On average, there are around 150 users per day, more than we expected in our first month.

WHY ON THE WORLD WIDE WEB?

Designing a system using HTML/HTTP seemed like the natural choice for SFR. In fact, it was decided that it was the only way to go in connecting to the Internet. Some of the deciding factors were:

- HTML/HTTP was quickly becoming the standard of information servers
- Ease of programming
- Several easy-to-use browsers, including Mosaic, lynx, tkwww, and so on
- Nonintrusive nature
- Support for graphics, sounds, and MPEG movies
- CGI and FORMs capabilities

The foremost appeal of WWW is its widespread use. WWW is rapidly becoming the standard for information servers around the world, replacing the text-only Gopher servers. SFR's hope was to allow access to the greatest number of people. WWW seemed to be the most popular.

Another advantage is that the WWW offers a way that people can do business in a nonintrusive manner on the Internet. Unlike mailing lists and postings to USENET newsgroups—which take up disk space and network bandwidth on computers, where it is unwanted—the WWW gives users the ability to browse only those remote servers that they choose. SFR is generally perceived as a service-oriented business, since clients are not charged for making reservations. The notion of invasive business is not as relevant to SFR as it may be to someone selling life insurance, for instance, but it is still in any company's best interest to play by the rules of the Internet.

The most desirable quality about HTML and the World Wide Web, for someone creating pages, is the ability to copy something and use it as a model. Browsers such as **Mosaic** allow users to view the source code of the document they are presently looking at. By piecing together ideas from several different pages, you can quickly get something presentable up and running. In the creation of SFR's pages, many ideas were found in other documents.

Mosaic has become the WWW viewer of choice. There are, however, several others that are available, giving users the ability to view the same information in several different ways. **Lynx** allows users to get a text-only view of WWW. This is quite useful to those who do not have a fast connection, or for those who do not have an IP address (or TIA).

In addition, the glory of sight and sound is available to those who have a fast connection. HTML offers an easy way to include graphics, sounds, and MPEG movies with the documents. As you will see in the following, the ability to display images was a key design element in SFR's WWW pages.

Finally, HTML includes CGI and HTML FORMs capability (although not all viewers support this). These give HTML the flexibility and power to handle almost any task. If a script can be written that sends output to the standard output, then it can be incorporated into an HTTP server and be accessed from your HTML documents. There are several cases where SFR's WWW page requires this sort of flexibility, including the ability to check availability of all hotels for any given day, the ability to search hotel lists for those that match specific criteria, and the ability to process reservation requests.

DESIGNING THE WWW PAGE

The overall design goal for San Francisco Reservations' World Wide Web page (Figure 9.15) was to create an easy-to-use system that would give users the ability to virtually browse through hotels before making a reservation: Trying to describe, in words, the way a hotel lobby looks or feels is difficult. Given this desire, there were other important considerations.

First of all, information should be clear and concise. The most important place for this is the home page. Here, it should be clear to the user what exists on the server. For the design of SFR's page, we asked ourselves the following two questions: "What do users know when they get here?" and "What do they want to find out now that they are here?" This helped shape the notion of having several search paths for finding hotels: by hotel location, price, type, and keyword (if the user has a specific hotel in mind). To maintain conciseness, depth was always chosen before breadth whenever possible. By this, I mean it is better to have a single link to a page listing other WWW pages than to list all the pages on the front page (which I have seen done on several pages). Also, we included a Help button in as many places as possible, allowing us to keep many details off of the main pages (see, for example, Figure 9.16).

One of SFR's key design constraints was to give users the ability to get partial lists of hotels based on certain criteria. Originally, we had thought we would build static lists of hotels for these criteria: After all, hotels do not change their location, name, type, or prices very often. For the sake of longevity and robustness, however, we decided to build a single database of hotel data and write perl scripts to extract the desired information from this database.

Similarly, we needed to have a standardized reservation request form for users to complete, plus the ability to get up-to-the-hour hotel availability information. Perl scripts were written to handle these situations, although in an imperfect manner. Availability of San Francisco hotels can change suddenly, especially in high tourist season. We had hoped that when users completed their search of hotels, a list would be provided that matched their criteria, along with the availability information for each hotel. Users would then be restricted from submitting a reservation request for any hotel that was not available. We determined, empirically, that this method could be ineffective, since hotels could quickly become *unavailable* during the time the user was browsing the *available* hotels list. We maneuvered around this problem by checking availability only at the time a user is ready to make a reservation. However, it is rather inconvenient to find a few hotels that you like only to discover, one by one, that they are sold out. To handle this, we allow the user to view all hotel availability for an entire month when a hotel is deemed sold out (we also have a link to this information on the home page, for those who know exactly what days they are to be in San Francisco).

Inline images in HTML pages should be small, should have a minimal number of colors, and should be used sparingly. While it was important for SFR to have a flashy WWW server, it was realized early on that there is a beauty versus usability trade-off, and that usability is far more important. Sending large pictures over busy networks will test the patience of any user. After all, there are thousands of other pages they could be looking at instead of waiting for your GIF image to arrive. In SFR's case, the details about each hotel include pictures of sample hotel rooms, exterior photographs, hotel lobbies, and local area maps that the user might wish to view. We made these available without sacrificing usability by making a small-size copy of the image (an *icon*), and linking the small images to the full-size versions. By doing so, users can get an idea of what the picture is like from the small version, and if they are interested in seeing the details, they can click on the image (see, for example, Figures 9.17 and 9.18). Here is some example HTML code of this:

```
<A HREF="majes_l.gif">
<IMG ALIGN=middle SRC="majes_l_small.gif">
lobby photo</A>
```

If users like the look of a hotel they will most likely want to book a room or check room availability. This information can be accessed directly from the Hotel page (Figure 9.18) by pressing the *Submit Reservation Request* button. This returns the document shown in Figures 9.19 and 9.20, which allows you to book and confirm a reservation or check room availability.

A final constraint was to make our server both **Mosaic**- and **lynx**-friendly. Many WWW servers cater to only one or the other. **Mosaic** users love all kinds of graphical buttons, big pictures, and clickable imagemaps. **lynx** users, however, cannot see the pictures and are sometimes left helpless on what to do. An example of this is the use of graphical buttons. SFR's home page uses clickable buttons for the different search paths, with descriptions of the button on the button itself. **Mosaic** users will see the nice descriptive button (e.g., Hotel Location), while, if you are not careful, **lynx** users will see only the text string "[IMAGE]". To solve this problem, the **ALT** attribute should be used. Here is an example:

```
<A HREF="/srchloc.html">
<IMG SRC="srchloc.gif" ALT="[Hotel Location]">
</A>
```

With the ALT command, **lynx** users will see "[Hotel Location]" in place of the image, providing a useful and aesthetically pleasing page to view. In general, it is good practice to view each page in several formats before you are done. You should also realize that there are many people using **Mosaic** who have the inline image loading turned off. Try this out. SFR is still working on how to make this look nice.

```
<title> San Francisco Reservations</title>

<img src="sfrheader.gif" ALT="SAN FRANCISCO RESERVATIONS">
<hr>

Welcome to <b>San Francisco Reservations</b>' (SFR) World-Wide Web
page! This service provides hotel reservations in the San Francisco
area at no cost to the user. SFR rates are, in most cases, the lowest
rates available. Feel free to browse around and send us
<A href="/feedback.html">
  <img align=top src="icons/email.gif" ALT="[e-mail]">
</a>
if you have any questions or concerns.

<h2>Search San Francisco Hotel List by:</h2>

<A href="/srchloc.html">
<img src="icons/srchloc.gif" ALT="[Hotel Location]"></a>
<A href="/srchprice.html">
<img src="icons/srchprice.gif" ALT="[Hotel Price]"></a>
<A href="/srchtype.html">
<img src="icons/srchtype.gif" ALT="[Hotel Type]"></a>
<A href="/srchkey.html">
<img src="icons/srchkey.gif" ALT="[Key Word]"></a>

<h2>Other Information</h2>

<A href="/sfrinfo.html">
<img align=middle src="icons/sfrinfo.gif" ALT="[Help]"></a>
For more information about San Francisco Reservations. <br>
<A href="/availability.html">
<img align=middle src="icons/availability.gif" ALT="[Availability]"></a>
Examine hotel availability.<br>
<A href="/otherwww.html">
<img align=middle src="icons/otherwww.gif" ALT="[Elsewhere]"></a>
Other points of interest on the World Wide Web.<br>

<hr>

<b>San Francisco Reservations</b><br>
22 Second Street, 4th Floor<br>
San Francisco, California 94105<br>
<img src="icons/phone_num.gif" ALT="(800) 677-1550 or (415) 227-1500">
<address>sfr@hotelres.com</address>
```

Figure 9.15 HTML document for the San Francisco Reservations' home page.

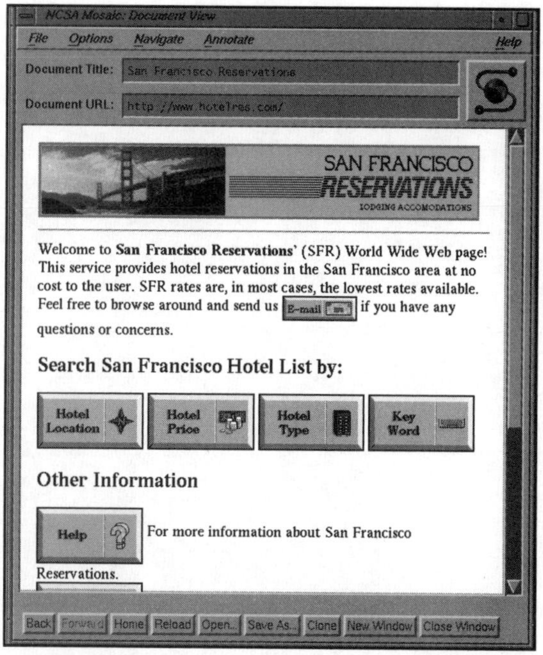

Figure 9.16 Home Page for San Francisco Reservations.

```
<title>Cartwright Hotel</title>

<h1>Cartwright Hotel</h1>
524 Sutter Street /Powell<br>
San Francisco, CA 94102
<br>
    <FORM METHOD="POST" ACTION="/cgi-bin/hoteldates.pl">
    <input type="hidden" name="H_code" value="`CARTWRIGHT HOTEL'">
    <input TYPE="submit" value="Submit Reservation Request"><p>

  <A href="cartw_l.gif">
  <img align=middle src="cartw_l_small.gif">
  lobby photo</a>

  <A href="cartw_r.gif">
  <img align=middle src="cartw_r_small.gif">
  sample room photo</a>

  <A href="cartw_m.gif">
  <img align=middle src="cartw_m_small.gif">
  local area map</a><br>

<hr>
<pre>     1994 Published Rates |  SFR Value Rates (based
                          |on availability)
```

```
==================================================================
                          | (4/1-10/31/94)      (11/1-12/31/94)
Dbl. 1-2 Pers.  $119/$129 | 1-2 Pers.    $79  1-2 Pers.       $69
Queen 1-2 Pers. $119/$129 | 1-2 Pers.    $79  1-2 Pers.       $69
2 Twin 1-2 Pers. $119/$129 | 1-2 Pers.   $79  1-2 Pers.       $69
Extra Pers.     $ 12/$ 12 |              $12                  $12

   Children 12 yrs. & under Free</pre>
<hr>

  <img align=middle src="../icons/question.gif">
  What are<A href="../sfrvaluerates.html"> SFR Value Rates</a>?<p>

<b>Check In</b>: [Open] <b>Check Out</b>: [1:00pm]<br>
<b>Accepted Credit Cards</b>: [AX, MC, Visa,
                Diners, Discover, JCB].<p>

<em>            Credit Card Required to Guarantee
                Arrival. To Change or Cancel a
                Reservation, Notify Us 48 hrs Prior to
                Date of Arrival to Avoid a Charge.
</em>
<pre> [N] Airport Shuttle
 [Y] Parking [$12 self-parking nearby]
 [Y] Restaurant [Teddy's 7am-11am Bkfst]
 [N] Room Service
 [Y] Continental Bkfst [$5]
 [N] In-Room Movies
 [N] VCR
 [N] View
 [N] Fireplace
 [N] Air Conditioning
 [Y] Roll Away/Crib [$10/Free]
 [Y] Suites [1 Bedroom]
 [N] Kitchen
 [N] Handicap
 [N] Business Center
 [N] Pool
 [N] Fitness Center
 [N] Pets</pre>

<b>Neighborhood</b>: Comfortable downtown location. 1 1/2 blocks from Union
Square, 1/2 block to Cable Car.<br>

<b>Lobby</b>: Light, bright lobby with overstuffed sofas and chairs.
Reading room/library adjacent. Traditional style decor. <br>

<b>Guest Rooms</b>: 114 small homey rooms and suites, fresh flowers, reading
pillows, clock radios.<br>

<b>Suites</b>: 1 bedrooms done with antiques.<br>

<b>Services</b>: Personalized service, meeting facilities available.
Turndown service.<br>
```

Figure 9.17 HTML document for the Cartwright Hotel page.

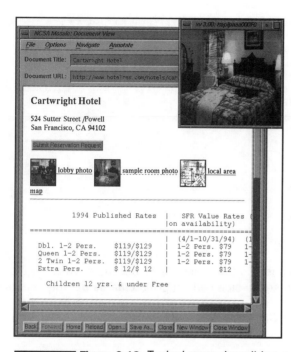

Figure 9.18 Typical page describing a San Francisco hotel. Clicking on the image icons yields larger, more detailed images of the hotel or of the rooms, as shown in the inset. Note the use of the FORMs "hidden" INPUT element.

FINAL NOTES ON SFR

The creation of SFR's WWW page was completed in about a month. It was decided that it should be *finished* before it was officially announced so that it could be thoroughly tested. We have found, however, that it is a continually changing project. By allowing users to send us feedback, we have received several suggestions that have shaped the way the pages look. The helpful and supportive atmosphere on the Internet is a vital resource that is invaluable.

```
<html><head>
<title>Travel Dates</title>
</head>
<body>
<h1><img src="../icons/box.gif" ALT="">Travel Dates
<img src="../icons/box.gif" ALT=""></h1>
<b>Hotel:</b> 'CARTWRIGHT HOTEL'
<p>In order for us to determine the availability of this hotel, please
fill out the following information. If you are making a reservation for
```

```
tonight, please call us at (800) 677-1550 or (415) 227-1500 so that we
can be sure that your request is processed in time. Our hours are 7am
to 11pm Pacific Standard Time, seven days a week.
<FORM METHOD="POST" ACTION="/cgi-bin/grind.pl">
<hr>Enter Dates in the form: MM/DD/YY
<p>Arrival Date:    <input NAME="Arrdate" SIZE="8">
<p>Number of Nights: <input NAME="Night_stay" SIZE="2">
<p><hr>
<input TYPE="submit" value="check availability">
<input TYPE="reset" value="clear">
<p><pre>

</pre>
<input type="hidden" name="H_code" value="'CARTWRIGHT HOTEL'">
</FORM>
<p> Generated by: <var>/home/http/cgi-bin/hoteldates.pl</var><br>
Date: 8:51:49 PST on Wed 19 Oct 94.<p>
</body>
</html>
```

Figure 9.19 Reservations and availability HTML document. This page was generated by the server-side perl script *hoteldates.pl*. Note the use of the FORMs `<input type="hidden"...>` element to store the name of the hotel. This is how the server-side script knows what hotel is being considered.

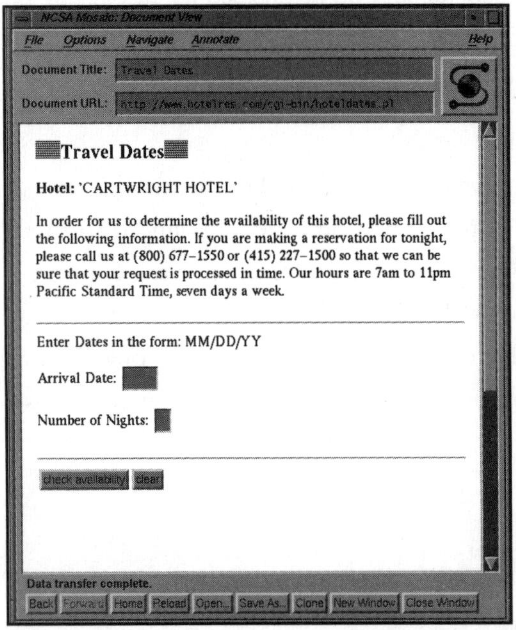

Figure 9.20 Reservations and availability query page for the Cartwright Hotel. This is accessed by clicking on the Submit Reservation Request page shown in Figure 9.18.

THE ISO LATIN-1
CHARACTER SET

A computer character set is simply an agreed-upon relationship between computer binary codes and a set of letters or graphical characters. Since almost all computers use 8-bit bytes as the basic storage unit, standard character sets are designed to use a single 8-bit byte to store a single character. Since there are 8 bits in a byte, each byte can represent 256 possible characters ($256=2^8$).

Character sets for international use are specified by the International Standards Organization (ISO). The ISO has specified several different character sets that can fit inside 8-bit characters. The default set for World Wide Web applications is the ISO Latin-1 character set, shown in Table A.1. The first 128 characters of the ISO Latin-1 character set are equivalent to the 128 characters of the US-ASCII (also known as ISO 646) character set. US-ASCII is known as a 7-bit character set, since it consists of only 128 characters and can be represented using just 7 bits (2^7). Of these 128 characters, 33 are special characters for controlling printing devices and communications lines. These characters are not printable and are indicated in the table by two- or three-letter character sequences that are mnemonically designated to represent their function. For example, NUL is a null character, BEL is the bell character (rings a bell), CR is carriage return, BS is the backspace character, and so on. In addition, the table marks the space character (decimal 32) with the symbol SP, as, otherwise, this would be invisible.

There are 128 additional characters in the ISO Latin-1 character set. The first 32 are nonprintable control characters: These are marked in Table A.1 by a double dash (—). The remaining characters are printable and consist of many of the accented and other special characters commonly used in western European languages.

URL CHARACTER ENCODINGS

As discussed in Chapter 2, any ISO Latin-1 character can be represented in a URL by indirect references or encodings. In a URL, any ISO Latin-1 character can be represented by the special character sequence:

`%xx`

Where xx is the *hexadecimal* or *hex* code corresponding to the character. Table A.1 shows both the regular decimal and hexadecimal codes for all the ISO Latin-1 characters. As an example, the URL *encoding* for the percent character itself would be:

`%25`

since the percent character is the thirty-seventh (hexadecimal 25) character in the character set.

HTML CHARACTER AND ENTITY REFERENCES

In HTML, any ISO Latin-1 character can be represented by either a *character reference* or an *entity reference*. A character reference represents each character through its decimal code. Thus, the character reference for a capital U with an umlaut (Ü) is:

`&#220;`

since this is the 220th character in the ISO Latin-1 character set. Numerical references are awkward and difficult to remember, so HTML also allows entity references for some of these characters. For example, the entity reference for a capital U with an umlaut (Ü) is

`&Uuml;`

In HTML, the four ASCII characters (>), (<), ("), and (&) are interpreted to have special meanings. Therefore, to display them in text as ordinary characters, you must use character or entity references. The special entity names for these characters are given in Table A.1. For example, the entity reference for the less-than sign is `&lt;`. Figures A.1 and A.2 show the use of entity references in an HTML document.

Not all computers use the ISO Latin-1 character set. UNIX computers and PCs running Windows use the ISO Latin-1 character set by default, while Macintoshes and PCs running DOS do not, although the first 128 characters of the Macintosh and DOS character sets are the same as the US-ASCII characters, as with ISO Latin-1. You therefore must take care on these platforms when preparing documents for use on the World Wide Web—it is always safe to use the character or entity references mechanisms for non-ASCII characters.

Table A.1 ISO Latin-1 Characters, Showing Decimal Codes, Hexadecimal Codes, and HTML Entity References

Character	Decimal	Hex	Entity Reference	Character	Decimal	Hex	Entity Reference
NUL	0	0		SOH	1	1	
STX	2	2		ETX	3	3	
EOT	4	4		ENQ	5	5	
ACK	6	6		BEL	7	7	
BS	8	8		HT	9	9	
NL	10	a		VT	11	b	
NP	12	c		CR	13	d	
SO	14	e		SI	15	f	
DLE	16	10		DC1	17	11	
DC2	18	12		DC3	19	13	
DC4	20	14		NAK	21	15	
SYN	22	16		ETB	23	17	
CAN	24	18		EM	25	19	
SUB	26	1a		ESC	27	1b	
FS	28	1c		GS	29	1d	
RS	30	1e		US	31	1f	
SP	32	20		!	33	21	
"	34	22	&quot;	#	35	23	
$	36	24		%	37	25	
&	38	26	&amp;	'	39	27	
(	40	28		)	41	29	
*	42	2a		+	43	2b	
,	44	2c		-	45	2d	
.	46	2e		/	47	2f	
0	48	30		1	49	31	
2	50	32		3	51	33	
4	52	34		5	53	35	
6	54	36		7	55	37	
8	56	38		9	57	39	
:	58	3a		;	59	3b	
<	60	3c	&gt;	=	61	3d	
>	62	3e	&lt;	?	63	3f	
@	64	40		A	65	41	
B	66	42		C	67	43	
D	68	44		E	69	45	
F	70	46		G	71	47	
H	72	48		I	73	49	

Character	Decimal	Hex	Entity Reference	Character	Decimal	Hex	Entity Reference
J	74	4a		K	75	4b	
L	76	4c		M	77	4d	
N	78	4e		O	79	4f	
P	80	50		Q	81	51	
R	82	52		S	83	53	
T	84	54		U	85	55	
V	86	56		W	87	57	
X	88	58		Y	89	59	
Z	90	5a		[	91	5b	
\	92	5c		]	93	5d	
^	94	5e		_	95	5f	
`	96	60		a	97	61	
b	98	62		c	99	63	
d	100	64		e	101	65	
f	102	66		g	103	67	
h	104	68		i	105	69	
j	106	6a		k	107	6b	
l	108	6c		m	109	6d	
n	110	6e		o	111	6f	
p	112	70		q	113	71	
r	114	72		s	115	73	
t	116	74		u	117	75	
v	118	76		w	119	77	
x	120	78		y	121	79	
z	122	7a		{	123	7b	
|	124	7c		}	125	7d	
~	126	7e		DEL	127	7f	
—	128	80		—	129	81	
—	130	82		—	131	83	
—	132	84		—	133	85	
—	134	86		—	135	87	
—	136	88		—	137	89	
—	138	8a		—	139	8b	
—	140	8c		—	141	8d	
—	142	8e		—	143	8f	
—	144	90		—	145	91	
—	146	92		—	147	93	
—	148	94		—	149	95	
—	150	96		—	151	97	
—	152	98		—	153	99	
—	154	9a		—	155	9b	
—	156	9c		—	157	9d	
—	158	9e		—	159	9f	
	160	a0		¡	161	a1	
¢	162	a2		£	163	a3	
¤	164	a4		¥	165	a5	
¦	166	a6		§	167	a7	
¨	168	a8		©	169	a9	
ª	170	aa		«	171	ab	
¬	172	ac		-	173	ad	
®	174	ae		¯	175	af	

Character	Decimal	Hex	Entity Reference	Character	Decimal	Hex	Entity Reference
°	176	b0		±	177	b1	
²	178	b2		³	179	b3	
´	180	b4		µ	181	b5	
¶	182	b6		·	183	b7	
¸	184	b8		¹	185	b9	
º	186	ba		»	187	bb	
¼	188	bc		½	189	bd	
¾	190	be		¿	191	bf	
À	192	c0	&Agrave;	Á	193	c1	&Aacute;
Â	194	c2	&Acirc;	Ã	195	c3	&Atilde;
Ä	196	c4	&Auml;	Å	197	c5	&Aring;
Æ	198	c6	&AElig;	Ç	199	c7	&Ccedil;
È	200	c8	&Egrave;	É	201	c9	&Eacute;
Ê	202	ca	&Ecirc;	Ë	203	cb	&Euml;
Ì	204	cc	&Igrave;	Í	205	cd	&Iacute;
Î	206	ce	&Icirc;	Ï	207	cf	&Iuml;
Ð	208	d0		Ñ	209	d1	&Ntilde;
Ò	210	d2	&Ograve;	Ó	211	d3	&Oacute;
Ô	212	d4	&Ocirc;	Õ	213	d5	&Otilde;
Ö	214	d6	&Ouml;	×	215	d7	
Ø	216	d8	&Oslash;	Ù	217	d9	&Ugrave;
Ú	218	da	&Uacute;	Û	219	db	&Ucirc;
Ü	220	dc	&Uuml;	Y	221	dd	&Yacute;
Þ	222	de	&THORN;	ß	223	df	&szlig;
à	224	e0	&agrave;	á	225	e1	&aacute;
â	226	e2	&acirc;	ã	227	e3	&atilde;
ä	228	e4	&auml;	å	229	e5	&aring;
æ	230	e6	&aelig;	ç	231	e7	&ccedil;
è	232	e8	&egrave;	é	233	e9	&eacute;
ê	234	ea	&ecirc;	ë	235	eb	&euml;
ì	236	ec	&igrave;	í	237	ed	&iacute;
î	238	ee	&icirc;	ï	239	ef	&iuml;
∂	240	f0	&eth;	ñ	241	f1	&ntilde;
ò	242	f2	&ograve;	ó	243	f3	&oacute;
ô	244	f4	&ocirc;	õ	245	f5	&otilde;
ö	246	f6	&ouml;	÷	247	f7	
ø	248	f8	&oslash;	ù	249	f9	&ugrave;
ú	250	fa	&uacute;	û	251	fb	&ucirc;
ü	252	fc	&uuml;	y	253	fd	&yacute;
þ	254	fe	&thorn;	ÿ	255	ff	&yuml;

```
<html>
<head>
<title> Entity References </title>
</head>
<body>
<h1> Example 12 - Entity References </h1>
<PRE>                    (
<B>"Special" Character References</B>

&amp;lt;      -  &lt;        &amp;gt;       -    &gt;
```

```
&amp;amp;       -   &amp;          &amp;quot;      -    &quot;

<B>ISO Latin-1 Entity References </B>

&amp;AElig;     -   &AElig;        &amp;Aacute;   -   &Aacute;      &amp;Acirc;    -   &Acirc;
&amp;Agrave;    -   &Agrave;       &amp;Aring;    -   &Aring;       &amp;Atilde;   -   &Atilde;
&amp;Auml;      -   &Auml;         &amp;Ccedil;   -   &Ccedil;      &amp;ETH;      -   &ETH;
&amp;Eacute;    -   &Eacute;       &amp;Ecirc;    -   &Ecirc;       &amp;Egrave;   -   &Egrave;
&amp;Euml;      -   &Euml;         &amp;Iacute;   -   &Iacute;      &amp;Icirc;    -   &Icirc;
&amp;Igrave;    -   &Igrave;       &amp;Iuml;     -   &Iuml;        &amp;Ntilde;   -   &Ntilde;
&amp;Oacute;    -   &Oacute;       &amp;Ocirc;    -   &Ocirc;       &amp;Ograve;   -   &Ograve;
&amp;Oslash;    -   &Oslash;       &amp;Otilde;   -   &Otilde;      &amp;Ouml;     -   &Ouml;
&amp;THORN;     -   &THORN;        &amp;Uacute;   -   &Uacute;      &amp;Ucirc;    -   &Ucirc;
&amp;Ugrave;    -   &Ugrave;       &amp;Uuml;     -   &Uuml;        &amp;Yacute;   -   &Yacute;
&amp;aacute;    -   &aacute;       &amp;acirc;    -   &acirc;       &amp;aelig;    -   &aelig;
&amp;agrave;    -   &agrave;       &amp;aring;    -   &aring;       &amp;atilde;   -   &atilde;
&amp;auml;      -   &auml;         &amp;ccedil;   -   &ccedil;      &amp;eacute;   -   &eacute;
&amp;ecirc;     -   &ecirc;        &amp;egrave;   -   &egrave;      &amp;eth;      -   &eth;
&amp;euml;      -   &euml;         &amp;iacute;   -   &iacute;      &amp;icirc;    -   &icirc;
&amp;igrave;    -   &igrave;       &amp;iuml;     -   &iuml;        &amp;ntilde;   -   &ntilde;
&amp;oacute;    -   &oacute;       &amp;ocirc;    -   &ocirc;       &amp;ograve;   -   &ograve;
&amp;oslash;    -   &oslash;       &amp;otilde;   -   &otilde;      &amp;ouml;     -   &ouml;
&amp;szlig;     -   &szlig;        &amp;thorn;    -   &thorn;       &amp;uacute;   -   &uacute;
&amp;ucirc;     -   &ucirc;        &amp;ugrave;   -   &ugrave;      &amp;uuml;     -   &uuml;
&amp;yacute;    -   &yacute;       &amp;yuml;     -   &yuml;

</PRE>
</body>
</html>
```

Figure A.1 An HTML document showing the use of HTML entity references.

Figure A.2 Mosaic for X-Windows rendering of the HTML document listed in Figure A.1.

MULTIPURPOSE INTERNET MAIL EXTENSIONS (MIME)

MIME, for Multipurpose Internet Mail Extensions, is an extension to the traditional Internet mail protocol to allow for multimedia electronic mail. The original Internet mail protocol, defined in the document RFC822, was designed with simple text messages in mind—it defined a number of message headers defining routing information about the message, but said little about the message content. At the time (which was not that long ago!), most electronic mail messages were plain text files, so concerns about other formats were unwarranted.

Today, however, there is enormous demand for more sophisticated messages. For example, today's electronic mail often contains many parts, such as a Rich Text or HTML document, encoded image files, and sometimes sound files. Such messages can be easily communicated only if all mail programs share a standard for constructing and transporting such multipart multimedia messages.

The MIME protocol is designed to allow this type of mail message by providing an open protocol for multimedia/multipart mail messages. MIME defines several new mail document headers that specify if a message consists of multiple parts and how those parts are separated, and includes additional headers within each subpart of the message to specify what each part contains. Thus, a message might look like:

```
MIME-Version: 1.0 Content-type: multipart/mixed; boundary=23
--23 Content-type: text/html
.... html document ....
--23
Content-type: audio/aiff
..... audio file ....
--23--
```

This simple example leaves a great deal out, but gives the general idea of the approach. The message contains two parts, a text file in HTML format and an audio file in AIFF format, with the MIME *multipart* message surrounding it, indicating that there is more than one component to the message and specifying the string used to divide the message parts.

THE MIME CONTENT-TYPE

The preceding was, of course, an overly simplified description of the MIME protocol; for further details, you are referred to the relevant documentation (RFC 1521). Of primary interest to us is the MIME content-type header. This should be already familiar to you, since this is the header used to indicate the contents of files being transferred using the HTTP protocol. Whenever you request a document from an HTTP server, the server must first determine the type of the document and send the appropriate content-type header ahead of it. Similarly, when a client uses the POST method to send data to the server, the data is preceded by a content-type header that tells the server the format of the data arriving, namely:

```
Content-type: application/x-www-form-urlencoded
```

(see Chapter 4); and when a CGI program generates data to be sent to the client, it must send the appropriate content-type header ahead of the data it returns to the client.

How do content-type headers work? Each header has a minimum of two parts giving the data *type* and *subtype*, using the format:

```
Content-type: type/subtype
```

Type can be any of image, audio, text, video, application, multipart, message, and extension-token (these names, like the string "content-type", are case-insensitive). The meanings of the first four are obvious and indicate the overall type of the data. The application type is for other data (perhaps binary) that needs to be processed in a special way. This could be a program to run, or maybe a PostScript document to be executed by a PostScript previewer. `Multipart` indicates a message containing more than one part, while `message` refers to an old-fashioned RFC822 message body. `Extension-token` is any name beginning with `X-`, and refers to experimental data types.

Subtype gives the specifics of the contents. Thus, `text/html` means a text file that is an HTML document, `application/postscript` means a PostScript file to be run through a PostScript interpreter, and so on. There are lots of content-types: Table B.1 lists the ones most important in WWW applications. Subtypes can also be experimental extension types, such as the `x-www-form-urlencoded` subtype shown previously.

Because of the flexibility of the HTTP client-server interaction, there are many content-types used by WWW applications that are not commonly used in electronic mail messages. Therefore, you should not see the list in Table B.1 as appropriate for electronic mail messages.

HOW DOES THE SERVER DETERMINE CONTENT-TYPE?

For the server to be able to send a content-type header, it must somehow know what a document contains. The convention is to use the filename extension or suffix to indicate the content type. Thus, files with the extension *.mpeg* are assumed to be MPEG movies, files with the *.html* extension are assumed to be HTML documents, and so on. With PC servers, these names have to be shortened to three letters; for example, *.mpg* for MPEG movies or *.htm* for HTML documents. You can specify more than one extension for each type if that is more convenient. When you place a document on a server, you must be sure to give it the filename extension matching the contents of your file. At the same time, you must be sure to update your server's extension-to-MIME-type database if you add a previously unknown type.

If the server does not know the type of a file, it assumes a default content-type—often, `text/plain`.

HOW DOES THE CLIENT DETERMINE
CONTENT-TYPE?

If a client receives a file from a Gopher or HTTP server, these servers themselves indicated the contents of the data: HTTP servers send a content-type header, while Gopher servers have another mechanism for indicating the data contents. With FTP or local file access, this support is not available, and the client must itself be able to determine the file content. Again, this is done by the filename extensions so that the client must *also* have a database matching filename extensions to data types. The location of this database varies from client to client, but, in all cases, it involves matching a filename extension to a file type/subtype. For example, with **Mosaic for X-Windows**, the database is found in a file called *mime.types*; with **WinMosaic**, the database is part of the *MOSAIC.INI* file; and with **MacWeb**, the database is part of the program resource fork and can be edited from the browser using a pull-down menu.

■■■■■ **Table B.1** MIME-Types Commonly Used in the World Wide Web, Showing Corresponding Filename Extensions and Data Types

MIME-Type/Subtype	Typical Filename Extensions	Description of Data Contents
message/rfc822	mime	MIME message
application/postscript	ai eps ps	PostScript
application/rtf	rtf	MS Rich Text Format
application/x-tex	tex	Tex/LateX
application/x-texinfo	texinfo texi	TexInfo format
application/x-troff	t tr roff	troff document
application/x-troff-man	man	troff with MAN macros
application/x-troff-me	me	troff with ME macros
application/x-troff-ms	ms	troff with MS macros
application/x-gtar	gtar	gnu tar format
application/x-tar	tar	4.3BSD tar format
application/x-ustar	ustar	POSIX tar format
application/x-bcpio	bcpio	Old CPIO format
application/x-cpio	cpio	POSIX CPIO format
application/x-shar	shar	UNIX sh shell archive
application/x-pdf	pdf	Adobe Acrobat pdf format
application/zip	zip	Pkzipped files
application/mac-binhex40	hqx	Macintosh Binhexed archives
appication/x-stuffit	sit sea	Macintosh Stuffit Archive
application/macwriteii	??	MacWrite file
application/msword	??	MS word document
application/octet-stream	tar dump readme	tar, binary dump, trick extension to force a save to disk
application/octet-stream	bin uu	Binary, UUencoded
application/octet-stream	exe	PC executable

MIME-Type/Subtype	Typical Filename Extensions	Description of Data Contents
application/x-dvi	dvi	TeX dvi format file
application/x-wais-source	src wsrc	WAIS "sources"
application/hdf	hdf	NCSA HDF data format
audio/basic	au snd	"Basic" SUN audio 8-bit u-law PCM encoding
audio/x-aiff	aif aiff aifc	Macintosh audio format
audio/x-wav	wav	Microsoft audio format
image/gif	gif	GIF format
image/xbm	xbm	X-Bitmaps
image/xpm	xpm	X-Pixelmaps
image/ief	ief	Image Exchange Format
image/jpeg	jpeg jpg jpe	JPEG images
image/tiff	tiff tif	TIFF images
image/rgb	rgb	RGB images
image/x-xwindowdump	xwd	X-Windowdump image
image/x-pict	pict	Macintosh PICT images
text/html	html htm	HTML document
text/plain	txt	Plain text
text/plain	c c++ pl cc h	Program listings
text/x-setext	etx	Structure enchanced text
text/richtext		
video/mpeg	mpeg mpg mpe	MPEG Movie
video/quicktime	qt mov	Macintosh QuickTime
video/x-msvideo	avi	Microsoft Video Format
video/x-sgi-movie	movie	SGI Movie Format
Special HTTP/WWW types		
application/x-www-form-urlencoded		See Chapter 4
application/x-www-pgp-request		See Chapter 4
application/x-www-pgp-reply		See Chapter 4
application/x-www-local-exec		See Chapter 5

REFERENCES

The Internet Mail Protocol is defined in RFC822, available at:

    ftp://ds.internic.net/rfc/rfc822.txt

(this is an archive site for all Internet RFC documents).

MIME is defined in RFC1521, available at:

    http://www.ncsa.uiuc.edu/SDG/Software/Mosaic/Docs/rfc1521.txt
    http://www.oac.uci.edu/indiv/ehood/MIME/MIME.html
    ftp://thumper.bellcore.com/pub/nsb

Introductory documentation, in PostScript, is also available:

```
ftp://ftp.uu.net/networking/mail/mime/mime.ps
```

while a definitive list of registered MIME-types is found at:

```
ftp://gum.isi.edu/share/in-notes/media-types/
```

Note that this list of electronic mail MIME-types is much shorter than the list used by WWW applications.

FINDING SOFTWARE

USING ARCHIE

Most of the software mentioned in this book is freely available on the Internet, and we have included URLs pointing to typical sites archiving the executable versions or source codes for these programs. However, you may find that a program has moved and is no longer available at the indicated location. In this case, you should not panic, but should use **archie** to locate an alternative archive site.

STANDARD ARCHIE

Archie clients (the software you run on your own PC or workstation) are available for almost all computer platforms. DOS, UNIX NeXT, and VMS versions can be found at:

```
ftp://ftp.cs.widener.edu/pub/archie/
```

Versions compiled for particular operating systems are indicated by the filename; for example: *archie-dos.zip* for PCs running DOS, and *archie-vms.com* for VAX/VMS computers, while the source code itself is found in the file *archie-1.4.1.tar.Z*. The source code compiles simply and easily on most UNIX workstations. Other sites containing **archie** are:

```
ftp://ftp.unipg.it/pub/unix/infosys/archie/
ftp://unix.hensa.ac.uk/pub/uunet/networking/info-service/archie/clients/
ftp://ftp.mr.net/pub/Info/archie/clients/
```

This command-line **archie** client works identically on DOS, UNIX, or VAX/VMS computers: You control the program through a series of command-line options you type after the name of the program, and **archie** prints the results of the search to the screen. Most often, you will want to make a *case-insensitive substring* search for filenames that contain the substring of characters that you type in. In this case, you give **archie** a character substring that is contained in the name of the package or program you are looking for: Giving a case-insensitive substring and not the entire name makes allowances for changing version numbers, for possible changes in capitalization, and for site-to-site variations in the name. For example, if you are looking for the program WinWeb, you would type at the command line prompt:

```
archie -s WinWeb
```

The string `-s` indicates a case-insensitive substring search, so **archie** will return all file or directory names containing the pattern `WinWeb` anywhere in the name, and with any combination of upper- and lowercase letters. For example, here is just part of the output from the preceding search:

```
Host ftp.einet.net
        Location: /einet/pc/winweb
                FILE -rw-rw-rw-    424263  Aug 10 10:21  winweb.zip
```

This gives the Internet domain name where the package was located (*ftp.einet.net*), the directory on this server that contains the file (*/einet/pc/winweb*), and the name of the file found (*winweb.zip*). You can then use anonymous FTP to access this site, or just use your WWW browser, pointing it to the URL:

```
ftp://ftp.einet.net/einet/pc/winweb/winweb.zip
```

Your **archie** client gets the information about file locations from an archie *server*. Each **archie** client has a built-in server name that it uses by default. Sometimes, this server is busy and does not return a prompt response. You can select another server using the command-line option `-h`. For example:

```
archie -h archie.sura.net -s winweb
```

means to search for the substring winweb on the alternate server *archie.sura.net*. Typing the command:

```
archie -L
```

gives a short list of **archie** servers. Here is a typical list:

```
archie.ans.net (USA [NY])
archie.rutgers.edu (USA [NJ])
archie.sura.net (USA [MD])
```

```
        archie.unl.edu (USA [NE])
        archie.mcgill.ca (Canada)
        archie.funet.fi (Finland/Mainland Europe)
        archie.au (Australia)
        archie.doc.ic.ac.uk (Great Britain/Ireland)
    * archie.rutgers.edu is the default Archie server.
    * For the most up-to-date list, write to an Archie server and give it the command
      'servers'.
```

Archie servers generate their own databases of files so that they do not all contain the same information. Therefore, if one machine does not give you a useful response, it is a good idea to try another.

ARCHIE FOR MACINTOSHES

Macintosh users have access to an elegant shareware program called **Anarchie**, which combines archie searches with an FTP retrieval package for retrieving files from amongst the returned list. To do an archie search with **Anarchie,** you select Archie... from the pull-down File... menu. You then select the archie server you want, type the search string into the Find: box, select the type of search to use, and press the Find button to start the search. **Anarchie** then displays a small window telling you it is working, and even gives an estimate of the time required to complete the search. You can even start up multiple parallel archie searches if you wish. When finished, **Anarchie** produces a window containing the list of successful results. Double-clicking on an item in this list starts up an FTP connection to the relevant site, and automatically downloads the file to your computer.

Anarchie is available at many sites. Some examples are:

```
    ftp://ftp.cac.psu.edu/pub/mac/comm/anarchie/Anarchie-121.hqx
    ftp://sumex-aim.stanford.edu/info-mac/comm/net/anarchie-110.hqx
    ftp://sics.se/pub/info-mac/comm/net/anarchie-110.hqx
```

DOWNLOADING FILES USING FTP

If you have a WWW browser, you can just type in the URLs to access files: Browsers come with the FTP protocol built in. Thus, to access the file *winweb.zip* from the server *ftp.einet.net* in the directory */einet/pc/winweb*, you would type in the URL:

```
    ftp://ftp.einet.net/einet/pc/winweb/winweb.zip
```

If you leave out the filename, that is:

```
    ftp://ftp.einet.net/einet/pc/winweb/
```

you get a content listing for the directory */einet/pc/winweb/*. You can then click on the file you want to download.

Sometimes, the preceding procedure doesn't work, and you get a terse message stating that that the browser was "unable to connect to the URL." This often means that the server you are trying to connect to already has too many people making FTP connections, and that it has refused you access. To test this, you can make the FTP access the old-fashioned way by running the standard FTP program. Here is an example FTP session (the string green:~> is the command-line prompt). Recall that, after making the FTP connection, you log in as user *anonymous* and give your *e-mail address* as a password. At this point, the FTP server may refuse your connection: Most FTP servers put a limit on the number of people who can access the server, and if the server is already full, your connection will be refused. But, at least now you know what is going on.

Here is an example FTP session to the site *ftp.einet.net*. I am trying to get the *winweb.zip* program I found with the earlier **archie** search. The user's input is boldfaced, while the computer response is in regular font; *commentary is added in italics.*

```
green:~> ftp ftp.einet.net      (start ftp, pointing to the desired Domain name)
Connected to ftp.einet.net.
220 ftp.einet.net FTP server (Version 6.42 Wed Jul 6 12:37:10 CDT 1994) ready.
Name (ftp.einet.net:igraham): anonymous
331 Send e-mail address as password (for example: joe@green.utirc.utoronto.ca).
Password:  (type in your e-mail address—it will not be visible)
230-
230- Welcome to the EINet public FTP server.  For information about
230- EINet, send e-mail to einet-info@einet.net.
230-
230- If you encounter any unusual problems, please report them via e-mail
230- to ftp@ftp.einet.net.  If your client hangs on multi-line responses,
230- please try using a dash (-) as the first character of your user name.
230- This will turn off the continuation messages that may be confusing
230- your client.
230-
230- All connections and transfers are logged.
230-
230-
230 Anonymous login ok; access restrictions apply.
Remote system type is UNIX.
Using binary mode to transfer files.
ftp> cd /einet/pc/winweb   (change into the directory containing what we want)
250 CWD command successful.
ftp> ls   (list the directory contents, just to see what's there)
total 1888
```

```
drwxr-xr-x   2 6522    2000           512 Aug  1 19:43 debug
drwxr-xr-x   2 6522    2000           512 Aug 19 15:36 parts
 rw-r--r--   1 6522    2000         22022 Jul 27 14:39 pkunzip.exe
 rw-r--r--   1 6522    2000        245756 Jul 27 14:40 vbrun300.zip
 rw-r--r--   1 6522    2000          7680 Aug  2 15:26 winvoke.wri
 rw-r--r--   1 6522    2000        596336 Sep 28 19:15 winweb.zip
 rw-r--r--   1 6522    2000        596336 Sep 28 19:15 winweb1.00A2.1.zip
 rw-r--r--   1 6522    2000        424263 Jul 26 19:50 winweb1.00A2.zip
226 Transfer complete.
ftp> bin    (set FTP session to binary mode to transfer zip files or programs)
200 Type set to I.
ftp>
get winweb.zip           (get the file from the server)
200 PORT command successful.
150 Opening BINARY mode data connection for winweb.zip (596336 bytes).
596336 bytes received in 122.55 seconds (4.75 Kbytes/s)
ftp> quit                (we're finished, so quit)
221 Goodbye.
green:~>
```

In the preceding session, the command bin was used to set *binary transfer* mode. This is needed for transferring binary data (such as images, movies, or sound files) and compressed program or archive files. If you are transferring plain text files, such as **README** files, or plain PostScript files (with the extension *.ps*), you should type the letter a to select *ASCII mode*.

VIRUS PROTECTION

Anytime you download programs from the Internet onto PCs, Macintoshes, or Amigas, you run the risk of importing a computer virus. You must be very cautious about this. Make sure that you have virus-detection software on your computer, and that you keep it up to date; computer viruses are evolving almost as fast as the World Wide Web. To date, there have been few cases where WWW software has been contaminated by a virus, but this is no reason to relax. Computer viruses are a major problem, and you should always be on guard.

LISTENING AT A TCP/IP PORT

This appendix contains the source code for the program **listen**, which is a simple program that *listens* at a TCP/IP port and prints to the screen (or terminal) any characters received at the port (Figure D.1). This program was used to observe the data that WWW client browsers send to HTTP servers.

Listen was written for UNIX machines, particularly for DECstations running the operating system Ultrix 4.3A, and some work may be needed to port this program to System V-based machines. Porting to PCs or Macintoshes may require a bit more work.

To run the program, simply type the program name at the shell prompt. Listen then prints the port number it is listening at, and then goes silent. Here is typical output:

```
% listen
listening on 2055
```

At this point, any data sent to port 2055 on this computer will be printed on the screen just below the string `listening on 2055`. You terminate the program by typing **CTRL-C.**

Listen was written by Norman Wilson of the Instructional and Research Computing Group at the University of Toronto.

```
#include <stdio.h>
#include <sys/socket.h>
#include <netinet/in.h>
main(argc, argv)
int argc;
char **argv;
{
        int verbose;
        int lfd, sfd;
        struct sockaddr_in myaddr, claddr;
        struct in_addr ia;
        int inane;
        int pid;
        verbose = 0;
        if (argc > 1 && strcmp(argv[1], "-v") == 0) {
                verbose = 1;
                argc--;
                argv++;
        }
        if ((lfd = socket(AF_INET, SOCK_STREAM, 0)) < 0) {
                perror("socket");
                exit(1);
        }
        myaddr.sin_family = AF_INET;
        myaddr.sin_port = 0;
        myaddr.sin_addr.s_addr = INADDR_ANY;
        if (bind(lfd, &myaddr, sizeof(myaddr)) < 0) {
                perror("bind");
                exit(1);
        }
        inane = sizeof(myaddr);
        if (getsockname(lfd, &myaddr, &inane) < 0) {
                perror("getsockname");
                exit(1);
        }
        if (listen(lfd, 5) < 0) {
                perror("listen");
                exit(1);
        }
        fprintf(stderr, "listening on %d\n", ntohs(myaddr.sin_port));
        fflush(stdout);
        while (inane = sizeof(claddr), (sfd = accept(lfd, &claddr, &inane)) >= 0) {
                if ((pid = fork()) < 0)
                        perror("fork");
                else if (pid == 0)
                        copydata(sfd, verbose);
                /* else parent */
                close(sfd);
                if (verbose)
                        fprintf(stderr, "accept %s:%d, pid %d\n",
                                inet_ntoa(claddr.sin_addr), ntohs(claddr.sin_port),
                                pid);
        }
        exit(0);
}
copydata(fd, verbose)
int fd;
int verbose;
{
        char buf[200];
        int mypid;
        FILE *fp;
        mypid = getpid();
        if ((fp = fdopen(fd, "r")) == NULL) {
                fprintf(stderr, "%d: can't fdopen\n", mypid);
                exit(1);
        }
        while (fgets(buf, sizeof(buf), fp)) {
                if (verbose)
                        printf("%d: ", mypid);
                fputs(buf, stdout);
                fflush(stdout);
        }
        exit(0);
}
```

■■■■■ **Figure D.1** Program listing for Listen.c

anchor The location of a hypertext link in a document. An anchor can be either the start of a hypertext link, or the destination of a hypertext link.

archie Archie is a system that automatically generates and maintains a contents database for anonymous FTP servers. An **archie** server accesses information from FTP servers and archives the directory listings. An **archie** client can access these databases and search for programs or files matching a particular name.

archive file An archive is a single file that contains a collection of different files and/or directories. Archive files are often used to transport collections of files across the Internet, since you can tranport a large collection in a single archive file. UNIX archives have the extension *.tar* (for **T**ape **AR**chive). **PKZIP** if often used to create archives on DOS computers (suffix *.zip*), while **StuffIt** is often used to create Macintosh archives (suffixes *.sea* or *.sit*). **PKZIP** and **StuffIt** archives are also *compressed*.

ASCII ASCII stands for the American Standard Code for Information Interchange. This is a 7-bit character code capable of representing 128 characters. Many of these characters are special control characters used in communications control, and are not printable.

attribute An attribute is a quantity that defines a special property of an HTML element. Attributes are specified within the start tag. For example, `<IMG SRC="image.gif">` means that the element **IMG** has an attribute **SRC**, which is assigned the indicated value.

browser A browser is any program used to view material prepared for the World Wide Web. **Mosaic, MacWeb,** and **lynx** are examples of browsers. Browsers are able to interpret URLs and HTML markup, and also understand several Internet protocols, such as HTTP, FTP, and Gopher.

CERN *Centre Européen pour la Récherche Nucleaire.* CERN is a large physics particle-accelerator laboratory located in Geneva on the French-Swiss border. The World Wide Web originated here, largely due to the efforts of Tim Berners-Lee.

CGI Common Gateway Interface. This is the specification for how an HTTP server should communicate with server gateway programs. Most servers support the CGI specification.

client   A client is a program used to extract information from a server. For example, a browser, such as **MacWeb,** is a client that can access data from HTTP (and other) servers.

compressed   Many files on the Internet are compressed—this reduces the space taken up by the files and makes transmitting them over the Internet faster. The user must then have a program to decompress the files.

CRLF   The combination of a carriage-return (CR) and a linefeed (LF) character. This combination is used by several Internet protocols to denote the end of a line.

domain name   Computers on the Internet can have *domain names* that are mapped onto the computer's formal numeric Internet (IP) address. Domain names allow you to reference Internet sites without having to know the numerical address.

download   You are *downloading* a file whenever you transfer it from a remote computer to your computer.

DTD   Document Type Definition. An SGML document type definition is a specific description of a markup language. This description is written as a plain text file, often with the filename extension *.dtd*. The HyperText Markup Language, HTML, has its own Document Type Definition file, often called *html.dtd*.

element   An element is a basic unit of an HTML document. HTML documents use start and stop *tags* to define structural elements in the document. The name of the element is given in the name of the tag, and specifies the meaning associated with the block. Some elements are *empty*, since they don't affect a block. Elements that have contents are also often called *containers*.

firewall   A *firewall* is used to separate a local network from the outside world. In general, a local network is connected to the outside world by a *gateway* computer. This gateway machine can be converted into a firewall by installing special software that does not let unauthorized TCP/IP packets pass from inside to outside, and vice versa. You can give users on the local network, and *inside* the firewall, access to the outside world by using the **SOCKS** package or by installing the CERN HTTP *proxy server* on the firewall machine.

FTP   File Transfer Protocol, or FTP, is an Internet client-server protocol for transferring files between computers.

GIF   GIF, for Graphics Interchange Format, is a format for storing image files. It is one of only three formats that can appear inline in an HTML document, the other two being X-Bitmaps and X-Pixelmaps.

Gopher Gopher is a protocol for distributed information delivery commonly used in distributed information systems. Gopher clients give you access to this information. Gopher is a menu-based delivery system and does not have hypertext capabilities.

helper A helper application is a program launched or used by a browser (such as **Mosaic** or **MacWeb**) to process files that the browser cannot handle internally. Thus, you have helpers to view JPEG images or play sound files, and also to decompress compressed files, or to unstuff archives.

home page The home page is the introductory page for a World Wide Web site. A home page usually provides an introduction to the site, along with hypertext links to local resources.

HTML Abbreviation for HyperText Markup Language. HTML is a markup language defined by an SGML Document Type Definition (DTD). To a document writer, HTML is simply a collection of tags used to mark blocks of text and assign them special meanings.

hypertext A hypertext document is any document that contains *hypertext links* to other documents. HTML documents are almost always hypertext documents.

inline image An inline image is merged with the displayed text. This is often described as *inlining* the image.

Internet provider An Internet provider is the company from which you purchase your Internet connectivity. This could either be a dedicated connection (for example, a telephone connection that stays open 24 hours a day) or a dial-up connection. Usually, you run software, such as PPP or SLIP, to allow Internet connectivity across the line.

Internet resources The collection of data, documents, and databases available on the Internet.

ISO International Standards Organization. An international organization responsible for setting international standards, such as the ISO Latin-1 character set.

ISO Latin-1 This is an 8-bit character code developed by the International Standards Organization. An 8-bit code contains 256 different characters. In the ISO Latin-1 code, the first 128 characters are equivalent to the 128 characters of the US-ASCII character set (also called the ISO 646 character set). The remaining 128 characters consist of control characters plus a large collection of accented and other characters commonly used in European languages.

JPEG From Joint Photographic Experts Group, JPEG is another image format. In general, JPEG allows for higher-quality images than GIF. Browsers cannot display JPEG images inline and, instead, must display them using *helper* programs.

LAN LAN is an acronym for Local Area Network.

link A *link*, or *hypertext link*, is the connection between one hypertext document and another. Links are associated with hypertext anchors.

linux **Linux** is a freeware clone of UNIX for 386-based PC computers. **Linux** consists of the linux kernel (core operating system), originally written by Linus Torvalds, along with utility programs developed by the Free Software Foundation and by others. Since PC hardware is inexpensive and **linux** is essentially free, the combination of the two is a practical way of developing inexpensive and reliable HTTP service.

Lynx **Lynx** is a very popular character-mode World Wide Web browser.

MIME MIME, or Multipurpose Internet Mail Extensions, is a scheme for allowing electronic mail messages to contain mixed media (sound, video, image, and text). The World Wide Web uses the MIME content-type to specify the the type of data contained in a file or being sent from an HTTP server to a client.

Mosaic **Mosaic** is a graphical browser for the World Wide Web, developed at NCSA. There are also several commercial versions of **Mosaic**.

MPEG MPEG stands for Motion Picture Experts Group, and is an acronym for a common video file compression method.

NCSA National Center for Supercomputing Applications. The NCSA is situated at the Urbana-Champaign campus of the University of Illinois. The NCSA software development team developed the programs **Mosaic** and the NCSA HTTPD server.

packet A packet is a small package of data. The TCP/IP Internet protocol breaks messages up into packets, and sends each packet independently to the message destination. The protocol ensures that there is no error in transmission and that the entire message arrives.

perl Practical Extraction and Reporting Language. A scripting language written by Larry Wall. Because powerful data and text manipulation programs can be written quickly and easily using perl, it has become a popular language for writing CGI applications.

port number Any Internet application communicates at a particular port number specific to the application. For example, FTP, HTTP, Gopher, and telnet are all assigned unique port numbers so that the computer knows what to do when contacted at a particular port. There are accepted standard numbers for these ports so that computers know which port to connect to for a particular service. For example, Gopher servers generally *talk* at port 70, while HTTP servers generally *talk* at port 80. These default values can be overridden in a URL.

PPP Point-to-Point Protocol. Software that allows you to turn a dial-up telephone connection into a point-to-point Internet connection. This is commonly used to run WWW browsers over a phone line.

provider See *Internet provider*.

protocol A protocol is simply an agreed convention for intercomputer communication. Thus, the TCP/IP protocol defines how messages are passed on the Internet, while the FTP protocol, which is built using the TCP/IP protocol, defines how FTP messages should be sent and received.

proxy server A *proxy* server acts as an intermediary between your computer and the computer you want to access. Thus, if you make a request for a resource from computer *A*, this request is directed to a proxy server, which makes the request, gets the response from computer *A*, and then forwards the response to you. Proxy servers are useful for accessing World Wide Web resources from inside a *firewall*.

RFC An RFC, or Request for Comments, is a document, written by groups or individuals involved in Internet development, that describes agreed-upon standards or proposes new standards for Internet protocols. For example, the rules for electronic mail message composition are specified in the document RFC822.

server A server is a program, running on a networked computer, that responds to requests from client programs running on other networked computers. The server and client communicate using a client-server *protocol*.

SGML Standard Generalized Markup Language. This is a standard for describing markup languages. HTML is defined as an instance of SGML.

shell The UNIX *shell* is the program that interprets the commands typed at the terminal. A shell can also be used to run simple script programs called *shell scripts*. There are several different shells, with slightly different commands and syntax. The most common are the Bourne shell (sh), the C shell (csh), and the Korn shell (ksh).

SLIP Serial Line Internet Protocol. Software that allows you to turn a dial-up telephone connection into an Internet connection. This can be to run WWW browsers over a phone line, but is less stable than a PPP connection.

SOCKS SOCKS is a package that allows hosts inside a firewall to communicate with the outside world. To allow access to the outside world, a secure network must run a SOCKS server on its gateway/firewall machine and must configure all its networking software to talk to the SOCKS server. SOCKS is a proxy server without the special caching capabilities of the CERN HTTP server.

tag (HTML) HTML marks documents using *tags*. A tag is simply typed text surrounded by the less-than and greater-than signs, for example: <TAG>. An end tag is similar but has a slash in front of the tag name, such as </TAG>.

TCP/IP Transmission Control Protocol/Internet Protocol. TCP/IP is the basic communication protocol that is the foundation of the Internet. All the other protocols, such as HTTP, FTP, and Gopher, are built on top of TCP/IP.

telnet Telnet is a terminal emulation protocol that allows you to make a terminal connection to other computers on the Internet. This requires that you run a telnet client on your computer and connect to a telnet server on the other machine.

TIA TIA stands for The Internet Adapter. This is a program that you can run on a dial-in UNIX account and that allows you to create a SLIP-like connection between your home computer and the dial-in site. TIA is useful if you have a UNIX account with a company that does not provide PPP or SLIP service.

TIFF TIFF, for Tag Image File Format, is a graphic file format developed by Aldus Corporation. TIFF is the standard format of many graphics and desktop publishing programs.

URL URL stands for Uniform Resource Locator, and is the scheme used to address Internet resources on the World Wide Web.

USENET USENET is the Internet's worldwide bulletin-board system, consisting of over 5,000 topical discussion groups, called newsgroups. The newsgroups related to the World Wide Web are: *comp.infosystems.www.misc*; *comp.infosystems.www.providers*; *comp.infosystems.www.users*; and *bionet.software.www* (for biological applications only).

viewer A viewer is a program launched by a browser (such as **Mosaic** or **MacWeb**) to view files that the browser cannot handle internally. Thus, you have viewers for JPEG images, sound files, and MPEG movies. Viewers are also often called *helpers* or *helper applications*.

visit When you access a World Wide Web document, you are said to be *visiting* the site.

whitespace A *whitespace* refers to any combination of space or tab characters that separate two character strings.

WWW The World Wide Web. Also called the Web or W[3].